The Chess of
BOBBY FISCHER

The Chess of
BOBBY FISCHER

ROBERT E. BURGER

Foreword by
FRANK BRADY

Epilogue by
ISAAC KASHDAN

CHILTON BOOK COMPANY
Radnor, Pennsylvania

Copyright © 1975 by Robert E. Burger

First Edition   *All Rights Reserved*

Published in Radnor, Pa., by Chilton Book Company
and simultaneously in Don Mills, Ontario, Canada,
by Thomas Nelson & Sons, Ltd.

Designed by Anne Churchman

Manufactured in the United States of America

LIBRARY OF CONGRESS CATALOGING IN PUBLICATION DATA

Burger, Robert E.
  The chess of Bobby Fischer.

    1. Fischer, Bobby, 1943–   2. Chess — Collections
of games. I. Title.
GV1439.F5B87   794.1′092′4   74–32125
ISBN 0–8019–5949–7

When you are lonely, when you feel
yourself an alien in the world, play chess.

ARISTOTLE

Foreword
The Mind of Bobby Fischer

by FRANK BRADY

There is probably no other topic that intrigues chessplayers as much as the inner machinations of the mind of Bobby Fischer. Among world chess champions of the past, there has always been a strong equation between their demonstrable talents in other intellectual areas and their supreme proficiency in chess—despite attempts by the general press to depict them as bizarre, egotistical, single-minded renegades from society. Emanuel Lasker was a noted mathematician, philosopher, and friend of Albert Einstein. Alexander Alekhine paused in the middle of his pursuit of the championship to take a law degree at the Sorbonne and was a prolific writer in several languages. Mikhail Botvinnik has been highly decorated by the Soviet Union for his work as an engineer and has done pioneer work in the field of computer chess. Capablanca was a diplomat—honorary, it is true, but effective nevertheless. Euwe has been a professor of mathematics and is currently the president of FIDE, the world chess organization. And I could go on down the list of other great players.

At first glance, however, it seems that Bobby Fischer has few other skills than his ability to play chess. Since he is possessed of the most significant chess talent of this era, Fischer therefore represents a break with the pattern of the past. We are faced with a paradox. How can he play so consistently with such brilliance? Is his intelligence really as high as it has been reported to be? Is his memory as gigantic as it appears? How many moves can he see ahead? Do his mental processes function in a way that is somehow unique to the ability to play chess?

The speculation seems endless, and replete with contradictions. Chessplayers feel that if they can discern specifically how Fischer's mind operates, they can apply what they learn to their own approach to the game, and improve by emulation and application. Yet in his interviews and books, Fischer exhibits nothing more unusual in his thinking than the tendency to be down-to-earth to the point of being untactful, and precise to the point of being paranoid about mistakes.

Until such improbable time as Fischer subjects himself to further interviews, examinations, and extensive testing by psychologists and educational experts, we are left with only fragments as the key to his mental faculties. What really goes on inside the mind of Bobby Fischer—or anybody's mind, for that matter—when he studies the thirty-two not-so-inanimate pieces for hours at a time probably can never be properly documented and analyzed. Let's examine, however, the evidence we do have.

In previous writings I have cited Fischer's I.Q. as in the range of 180, a very high genius. My source of information is impeccable: a highly regarded political scientist who coincidentally happened to be working in the grade adviser's office at Erasmus Hall—Bobby Fischer's high school in Brooklyn—at the time Fischer was a student there. He had the opportunity to study Fischer's personal records and there is no reason to believe his figure is inaccurate. Some critics have claimed that other teachers at Erasmus Hall at that time remember the figure to be much lower; but who the teachers are and what figures they remember have never been made clear.

It is probably a reflection of the "chess-champion paradox" that the 180 figure is considered unrealistic. Fischer's apparent lack of intellectual attainments, in contrast to the champions of the past, would seem to make a high I.Q. unbelievable. He is considered by many to be almost an *idiot savant*. Perhaps some of the following anecdotes will dispel the doubts of the unbelieving.

Before playing the match with Spassky in Reykjavik, in 1972, Fischer toured Iceland for a few days to get the feel of the land. One morning he telephoned his old friend Frederick Olaffson, Iceland's only grandmaster. Both Olaffson and his wife were out of the house, and a little girl answered the phone. Fischer said, "Mr. Olaffson, please." Olaffson's daughter explained, in her native Icelandic, that both her mother and father were out of the house and would return in the early evening for dinner. Fischer does not know a word of Icelandic and had to hang up with an apology. Later that day, talking to another Icelandic chessplayer (who did speak English), Fischer remarked that he had tried to reach Olaffson. "It sounded like a little girl on the phone," he said. He then repeated every Icelandic word he had heard over the telephone, imitating the sounds with perfect inflection, so well, as a matter of fact, that the Icelander translated the message word for word.

In 1963 Fischer played in and won the New York State Open Championship at Poughkeepsie, New York. During the last round I was involved in a complicated ending with Frank S. Meyer, the late senior editor of *National Review*. Fischer, on his way to the washroom, briefly paused at my board—for perhaps five seconds—and then walked on. A few months later, he visited me at my office, then located at the Marshall Chess Club. "How did that last round game turn out?" he inquired. I told him I had won, but with difficulty. "Did you play Q-B5?" he asked. I told him quite frankly I couldn't remember what I had played. He immediately set up the exact position to "help" me remember, and then demonstrated the variation I should have played to have secured a much more economical win. The main point is that he did not simply remember the position, then analyze it in front of me; he remembered not only the position but also his fleeting analysis as he had passed my board months previously.

Anecdotes like this lead to speculation of how many moves Fischer sees ahead, and in what period of time. Masters who have traded Pawns with him in speed chess (usually five minutes for the entire game for each player) claim that postmortem analysis shows Fischer sees three or four moves ahead in any position, with a glance of a second or two. If he studies the position for all of five seconds, he can see five or six moves ahead, sometimes more. Occasionally for fun, against strong players, Fischer will place the hands at one minute on his clock and give his opponent ten minutes. Invariably he will win with time to spare.

Even more remarkable is the fact that Fischer can remember most of his speed games. At the conclusion of the unofficial Speed Championship of the World at Hercegnovi, Yugoslavia, in 1970, Fischer rattled off the scores of all his twenty-two games, involving more than 1,000 moves, from memory! And just prior to his historic match with Taimanov, in Vancouver, British Columbia, Fischer met the Russian player Vasiukov and showed him a speed game that the two had played in Moscow fifteen years before. Fischer recalled the game move by move.

Whatever his degree of intelligence or memory facility may be, it is an unimportant question in appraising Fischer's contribution to chess. We do know that he has an eidetic memory when it comes to remembering positions and moves; we do know that he can move with rapid-fire precision that is phenomenally superior to his contemporaries' ability. Since chess is Bobby Fischer's profession, his business, and his art, is it really germane to try to evaluate his prowess in other fields? Or can we finally begin to take his acknowledged chess ability as evidence enough of his remarkable intelligence?

The discussion of Fischer's mental qualities is an embarrassment to him personally. He claims not to know what his I.Q. is. It is a wise policy of school boards, indeed, not to reveal actual figures to the student. In the spring of 1974, Fischer castigated his friend Bernard Zuckerman for reporting to a Soviet chess weekly that Fischer's I.Q. was "astronomical."

Fischer believes that his statement, as an artist and as a man, lies in his chess. That is what this volume is all about; accordingly, *The Chess of Bobby Fischer* is a ground-floor approach to the workings of Fischer's brain. Though the speculation about his intelligence and memory is fascinating, it will be by his games that he will be remembered. They are the true testament, perhaps the only one possible, to his mind.

Contents

Introduction

On the following pages I have used the chess of Bobby Fischer as a touchstone for a general presentation of chess itself. Fischer's games are so full of ideas, from opening adventures to the themes of composed endings, that they are in themselves the best introduction to the pleasures of the game. In the arduous path to chess mastery, enjoyment is the surest driving force. In the words of Bobby Fischer, "You can get good only if you love the game."

So much has been written about Fischer as a personality that the general public, including the chess fraternity, has been blinded to his chess. His games have been analyzed over and over in the chess journals. He has published three books himself, with varying degrees of help from other authors. Yet his winning methods, his unique contributions to the larger body of chess knowledge, and his rightful place in the history of the game have been overshadowed by all the publicity.

A study of Fischer's 750 known clock games shows that he has no "chess secrets." He is alert and accurate. He takes each game seriously, even when the outcome may not have any effect on his tournament standing. He is persistent and not easily discouraged. Such qualities are more a matter of character than of talent. In this sense his real strength is as a man, not as a player. How different is the image which the press has seized upon in its search for the "angle" on the man!

Fischer must be considered the most successful player the game has ever known. He has lost about 10 percent of his games and drawn about 30 percent, for a batting average of .750. It is true that

Capablanca lost only thirty-five games out of the seven hundred he played in a thirty-year career. But Fischer has never been willing to concede the restful draw, or to play to the score. And his competition over the twenty-year career he has now enjoyed has been intense.

Among the Russians, several still hold a plus score against him as a result of his early games. On the other hand, he has lopsided margins against many fine players: Reshevsky 9–4, Petrosian 8–4, Taimanov 7–0, Saidy 6–0, Sherwin 7–0, Bisguier 13–1, and Larsen 10–2.

In trying to give an adequate account of the massive body of Fischer's "works," I have carefully combed all of his published games for what might be interesting to the *complete* player. I have chosen the key positions in his games that illustrate or relate to a wide variety of chess stratagems, combinations, endgame subtleties, even chess problems and studies. In this sense, this book is a horizontal rather than a vertical view of the game. It is not merely about a player's games, or about the middle game, or about combinations, but about chess.

The reader may start almost anywhere without missing part of the plot. He can browse without having to set up the pieces; but he is not surfeited with diagrams at every other move. A basic skill the player must learn is to analyze without "tickling the pieces," to visualize the topography of future positions without having to see them anywhere but in his mind's eye.

Mindful of the principle that you can never offend someone by telling him something he already knows, I have kept the text simple and basic. This book has not been written for the chess specialist, but for the general reader who has some knowledge of the game. At the same time, I have carried the analysis out to its full limits. In many cases, such as in the analysis of key positions from the 1971–1972 world championship series, I have offered new material and annotations which even the specialist can appreciate.

I have asked two friends, Frank Brady and grandmaster Isaac Kashdan, to help place Bobby Fischer in historical perspective as only they can. This much is certain: the chess of Bobby Fischer, like the art of Pablo Picasso or the music of Artur Rubinstein, deserves a wide audience.

Robert E. Burger
Berkeley, Calif., 1975

Acknowledgments

I wish to acknowledge the help of several chess enthusiasts of various levels of expertise: Edmond G. Addeo and Guthrie McClain, both of whom I sensed looking over my shoulder when I was tempted to take shortcuts; David Forthoffer, for his insights into computer chess; Ted Johnson, for his editorial acumen; and Theresa Burger, for looking the other way.

I *Notation*
The Language of Chess

When Bobby Fischer lost his historic Olympics game to Spassky (Siegen, 1970), the score sheet recorded the event in more ways than one. As his game became shaky, and finally deteriorated, Fischer's rough penmanship collapsed into a drunken scrawl. At the "Resigns" line one could not determine what move it was. Yet here again was Fischer uniqueness: What other score sheet in all of chess history has merited any attention at all?

The ability to replay a game, move by move, nowadays often with clock recordings, has no parallel in any other "spectator" sport. We have films of great athletic events, instant replays of television presentations, and excellent reportage of the local football or soccer matches. But no aficionado can as easily dip into the history of his avocation as the chess player.

When Fischer summed up the contribution of America's finest player up to his time, Paul Morphy, he startled the traditionalists. He called Morphy the most *accurate* player of all time, although everyone had heard from the analysts that Morphy either was the most brilliant (Sergeant), or the best equipped in modern strategic ideas (Fine), or simply the first man to understand the virtues of rapid development. This was not an argument over whether a Joe Louis could beat a Jack Dempsey; the scores were there for all to examine. Perhaps Morphy's opposition was not as strong as twentieth-century opposition. But when it was, it was not a matter of conjecture: the game could be replayed at will.

The content recorded on score sheets is so complete, so irrefutable, that it seems trivial when an argument erupts over the algebraic versus the descriptive notation. There is a certain parallel here between the metric versus the "English" system of measurement. Symbolism can be refined for efficiency, for ease of conversion, for space. Descriptive notation is used in this book for the simple reason that it is currently the most widely understood system in English publishing.

3

(There are excellent reasons why algebraic notation works better for problems and studies, where reference points to the starting positions of the pieces seem particularly out of place. There are also good reasons for resisting uniformity in this as in many other enterprises.)

Styles change, too, with the times. Fifteenth-century manuscripts are cryptic and virtually modern in their notation. In a more leisurely age, the early nineteenth century, a score sheet was almost a scenario. A correspondence game played in 1828 in England was recorded as follows:

No. 1   Commences by advancing King's Pawn to King's 4th square.

No. 1   The same.

As detailed as the notation was, however, the first player succeeded in making a mistake in the score on his fifth move. As the game went on into 1829, the first player began to let his feelings about the course of the game creep into the score. In retaking after just losing the exchange, he records:

No. 31   King murders Queen's Knight.

Four moves later, he is reduced to an abject Pawn move:

No. 35   Queen's Bishop's Pawn crawls one square forward.

Fischer has been most precise about keeping score, no matter what his handwriting at the time. Contrary to popular opinion — which is generally synonymous with newspaper accounts — Bobby is not litigious. He knows the rules about repetitions of positions (which most players, even grandmasters, often confuse with repetitions of *moves*). And he doesn't argue about them, he uses them. He saved a crucial game against Petrosian in the final Candidates match in 1971, and probably two games in the World Championship match with Spassky, 1972, by alert reference to this rule. He was apologetic, even embarrassed, with Petrosian in an improper offer of a draw at Curaçao, 1962. He has never been involved in a dispute over score sheets and time control — probably because he is seldom in time trouble.

As traditional as it may seem, the English-speaking world has generally made one giant concession to simplification, which this writer abhors. This is the prevalent practice of abbreviating "Knight" with "N" — on the presumption that "Kt" is either too long or too easily confused with "K." No other language makes such a gauche assumption. In this book we hold out for the last little purism.

II The Endgame

1 King Position

King position is an aspect of endings which is so universal a theme that it underlies virtually every other type of endgame. The greatest prophet of the "fighting King" was Wilhelm Steinitz, unofficial but generally recognized World Champion from 1866 to 1894. To make his point he even practiced King walks in the openings. In spite of this legacy, chess players today seem as hesitant about advancing their Kings as those who marveled at the "eccentricities" of Steinitz.

Bobby Fischer has excelled in willingness to sacrifice Pawns or pieces to advance his own King or to restrict the opposing King. In one of his earliest tournaments he showed how an apparently even ending is easily won by the commanding position of the King. The player of the White pieces was Arpad Elo, the statistician who orchestrated a rating system eventually adopted by the entire chess fraternity.

FISCHER

After 43 K-Kt4

ELO

Milwaukee 1957

The Black King has infiltrated the enemy camp, and in one move the Black Bishop not only denies entry of the White King but also initiates the dissolution of the White central stronghold.

43 ...	B-Kt3
44 K-B3	B-R4+
45 K-B2	B-Q8!

Now either the King or the Bishop must desert the White Pawns, but the Black King is so strong that he has nothing to fear in 46 ... B-Kt6 47 P-B5, BxB.

46 K-Kt3	B-K7
47 P-B5	KxP
48 B-K6	K-Q5
49 B-B5	K-K6
Resigns	

Two years later, Fischer embarked on a South American tour and found that his technique needed sharpening. Among his reverses during this period was the following game in which his two-Pawn advantage was easily overcome by his opponent's King position:

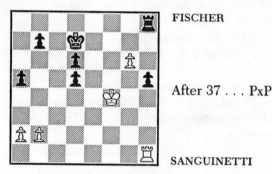

FISCHER

After 37 ... PxP

SANGUINETTI

Santiago 1959

| 38 RxP! | RxR |

. . not liking R-KKt1 39 K-Kt5, Fischer tries to hold out against a Queen. The White King suddenly swarms all over the Kingside.

| 39 P-Kt7 | R-K4 |
| 40 P-Kt8 (Q) | ... |

... and White easily eroded the Black defense with pressure against the Queenside Pawns.

In his important and aborted match with Reshevsky, Fischer missed two opportunities to capitalize on a King-position situation, once by commission and once by omission:

FISCHER

After 53 K-B3

RESHEVSKY

Match, Los Angeles 1961

	53 ...	R-QKt2?

Hoping to win through complications, Fischer overlooks the simple 53 ... RxR+ 54 BxR P-R4 when Black's King will seize the fourth rank (55 K-B4 R-R5+). Now it is White who gains the fourth rank:

54	R-K6+	K-B4
55	R-K5+	K-B3
56	R-Q5!	...

The necessity of defending the RP ends Black's winning chances:

56	...	R-Kt6+
57	K-Kt4	Draw

In the following position, Fischer failed to notice a hidden resource in White's more active King. White can afford to take the time to guard his QKtP because — even after the threatened exchange of Rooks — his King plays a far more active role than Black's:

FISCHER

After 35 ... RxP

RESHEVSKY

Match, New York 1961

36 P-QR4!   ...

... and Fischer was forced to give up his BP, eventually losing the game, since the following sequence would have also been hopeless:

36 ...	R-QB4
37 RxR	KtPxR
38 K-Kt3	P-Q4
39 K-B4	P-Q5
40 K-K4	K-Kt4
41 P-QKt4	...

The centralized King makes this coup possible: If now 41 ... PxP 42 KxP! and the King remains in control of the Black Pawn. But another precaution must be taken before P-QKt4, for now the *Black* King gains a commanding position with 42 ... K-B5 or K-R5, when White will lose the Kingside Pawns. Instead of 41 P-QKt4, White can afford to protect the Kingside with P-KKt3, since Black cannot improve his King or Pawn position.

Fischer has yet to produce *classic* examples of forceful King play comparable to those of Lasker and Capablanca in their prime, no doubt because Fischer usually reaches a decision earlier! Golombek has remarked that endgame virtuosity is still not Fischer's strong suit. This may have been true in his early days. In his pursuit of the World Championship he missed only one or two endgame opportunities against the likes of Taimanov, Larsen, Petrosian, and Spassky. The following two positions will have to stand as models of King play until Fischer is required to outdo them. The first position illustrates the sheer force that an active King exerts on a position. The second shows how subtle this force can often be.

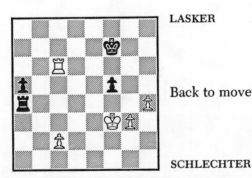

LASKER

Back to move

SCHLECHTER

Match, 1910

Lasker, already down a point in a ten-game match for the World Championship, was looking down the barrel of a gun here. His King is cut off on the second rank; White has an extra Pawn, protected and outside. Worse yet, White threatens to move his King into the battle with P-B4 and K-B4. In this depressing situation the champion gives up a second Pawn just to get his King into action first:

1 ...	**R-K5!**

This has been hailed as a move designed to cut off the White King, but actually R-KKt5 would work equally well. The point is that the Rook threatens to get *behind* his RP, and in preventing this White must allow the Black King to come forward.

2 R-B5	K-B3
3 RxP	R-B5!
4 R-R2	R-B6+
5 K-Kt2	K-K4

In five moves the positions have been reversed—at the cost of a Pawn. It's worth it.

6 R-Kt2	K-B3
7 K-R3	R-B3

Not falling for the diabolical trap 7 ... P-B5 8 R-Kt3! RxP 9 R-KB3! winning the final Pawn more favorably, since 9 PxP results in the infamous BP and RP ending, which can be drawn by Black.

8 R-Kt8	RxP

... and the draw is assured because the White King cannot assume an active role.

Finally, the lightness of touch that is required in advancing the King is well illustrated in the following barebones position of more recent vintage:

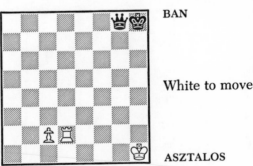

BAN

White to move

ASZTALOS

Match, Vienna 1956

The first move is expected:

1 R-R2+   Q-R2!

Black tries to avoid the loss of a move: 1 ... K-Kt2 2 R-Kt2+, K-B2 3 RxQ KxR 4 K-Kt2! and White will reach the fourth rank first. This may also be analyzed as "having the distant opposition," which is incidentally true. But even without the opposition—*the state of being on the same colored square as the enemy King, with no further advance possible by the enemy King with best moves on both sides°* the White King need only get to the fourth rank to win the King and Pawn ending.

2 K-Kt2!   Resigns

2 ... QxR+ is forced, giving White that extra move forward. It's all a matter of King position!

° Many examples of the opposition appear separately in other chapters.

2 The Rook Distance

The two most evenly matched pieces on the board may be the Knight and Bishop—but it often seems that King and Rook fight more subtle duels.

Their respective powers are quite dissimilar. But what the Rook has in long-range scope the King makes up for in short-range voracity. Endgame books generally refer to "Rook and Pawn" endings; but the battle hinges less on the fight between Rooks or between Rooks and Pawns than between Rook and King. This simple fact explains a lot about "mysterious" R-and-P endings. I emphasize this feature in the title of this chapter because it has occurred repeatedly in Bobby Fischer's games, and he has spent some time analyzing it.

When the stronger side is trying to promote a Pawn, the chief defensive resource is harassment of the King by the defending Rook. If the King can find shelter from checks—by hiding behind his Rook or the enemy King, by sacrificing Pawns, or by failing to capture enemy Pawns—he can generally have his way. More often, the King escapes from repeated checks by approaching the Rook. With multiple Pawns on the board, of course, the attacking side is the one with superior King position or more advanced Pawns.

The mystical quality that surrounds basic R-and-P endings can often be reduced to more rational analysis by noting the simple fact that the King can find shelter or he can't. The position below is dramatic evidence:

DURAS (1908)

White to play and win

13

The second White Pawn is obviously the only difference between this and standard (drawn) endings. It blocks the Black Rook from guarding the Knight file, and, as we shall see, it guards a critical square on Black's second rank. The problem, however, is to find shelter for the White King, since he is driven back by checks whenever he moves:

1 R-Q6!   . . .

A spectacular coup, yet why? True, in the main lines of play below, the White King escapes checks. But does Black *have* to capture the Rook or play any other particular move? Yes! Because the threat is 2 K-B7, when the Rook can interpose at B6. 2 R-B6 at once is not a threat, since K-Q2 answers everything.

1 . . .	**KxR**
2 K-B8	**R-B8+**
3 K-Q8	. . .

. . . and the Pawn will queen with check. The threat of 2 K-B7 can also be prevented another way:

1 . . .	**R-QB8**
2 R-QB6!	**RxR**
3 K-R7	. . .

. . . and the Pawn will queen because it cannot be pinned along the second rank.

Capablanca carried this motif to extremes in a sensational endgame against one of the great philosophers of the game:

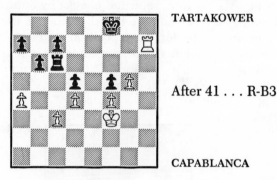

TARTAKOWER

After 41 . . . R-B3

CAPABLANCA

New York 1924

It is one thing to look at such a position half a century later and try to find the known win. It is another thing to have *foreseen* the win, over the board, when White allowed this position to occur. White gives up two Pawns to break through with his King to an unassailable position:

42 K-Kt3!	RxP+
43 K-R4	R-KB6
44 P-Kt6!	RxP+
45 K-Kt5	R-K5

The third Pawn would be too much, in view of the back-rank threats. But now White maintains all his threats and leaves the Black BP as a shelter from checks on the file:

46 K-B6

And White won in a few moves.

Fischer combined elements of both of the above studies in a remarkable endgame early in his career:

BISGUIER

After 67 . . . K-B4

FISCHER

New York 1958–59

68 K-Q5	R-Q6+
69 K-B6	P-Q4
70 P-Kt4	P-Q5
71 K-Q5!	. . .

The King now uses the Black Pawn to improve his defensive position, first by driving the Black King away another file, then by neutralizing the effect of the enemy Pawn.

71 . . .	R-Q8

BISGUIER

After 71 . . . R-Q8

FISCHER

72 R-B2+	K-Kt5
73 K-B4	. . .

White cannot enter a simple Pawn race here, since Black will trade Pawns with R-QKt8 when his Pawn reaches the seventh. Now the White King overpowers the Rook and Pawn:

73 . . .	P-Q6
74 K-B3	R-QKt8
75 R-Q2 and wins.	

Hiding behind other pieces (including the enemy's) is the obvious way to find shelter from checks by the Rook. Nullifying the distance advantage of the Rook is another. Perhaps the most famous endgame ever published (with a single, forced line of play—this rules out the Lucena position) demonstrates a standard King-versus-Rook tactic with a few "goodies" thrown in for good measure:

SAAVEDRA (1895)

*White to play
and win*

1 P-B7	. . .

No trouble finding this; but now the Rook checks begin.

1 . . .	R-Q3+
2 K-Kt5	. . .

The King must avoid Kt7, because then the Rook will pin the Pawn. Thematically, he must avoid the Rook file (because this gives up the Bishop file to the Rook); and he must avoid the Bishop file (because this allows a "skewer" check with R-Q8 and R-B8+).

2 . . .	R-Q4+
3 K-Kt4	R-Q5+
4 K-Kt3	R-Q6+
5 K-B2	. . .

Now it seems that the Rook is out of checks or counterthreats. He has one last arrow:

5 . . .	R-Q5!

Now if White queens the Pawn, R-B5+ forces stalemate or loss of the Queen. But the King now shows that he is a great infighter.

6 P-B8(R)!	R-QR5
7 K-Kt3	...

In one move the King attacks the Rook and again unleashes a mate threat. There is no answer to this final double threat.

By a curious twist of fortune, nature imitates art in the following position that could have arisen in a critical game of Fischer's. The same theme recurs: In defending against Rook checks, the King must retreat to his second rank. But why and what happens next gives a new dimension to this classic idea:

FISCHER

After 55 R-Kt4+
(Analysis)

BOTVINNIK

Varna 1962

55 ...	K-B4!

The King can't go to B6 because White would queen with check in the pawn race that would follow. And the Knight file is taboo because 56 R-Kt8 would threaten an eventual "skewer" on the Knight file. But where is the King going?

56 R-Kt5+	K-B3
57 R-Kt6+	K-Kt2
58 R-Kt7+	K-R3!

Just to save a critical move, the King makes an end run around the Knight file to get to R6, where he will be sheltered from checks.

59 R-Kt6+	K-R4 etc.

Sounds simple? The player of the White pieces missed this basic idea in three separate published analyses. He was World Champion at the time.

The apparent scope of the Rook is diminished by the placement of the pieces, but the King is even more limited by the edge of the board. In the following study, which repeats a main line of the Saavedra study, the win is simple enough:

EM. LASKER (1890)

*White to play
and win*

1 P-B7   RxKt+

One small embellishment is that 1 . . . R-B1 is answered by 2 Kt-B7+ and 3 Kt-K8. Now after another King walk in which the King keeps just the proper distance (2 K-Kt5 R-K4+ 3 K-Kt4 etc.) the Rook runs out of checks. But if the position were moved one file to the right, the King would be severely hampered.

(Visualize the KR file missing.) Now after 1 P-B7 RxKt+ 2 K-Kt5 R-K8! Black will check on Kt8 and on B8, winning the Queen, when and if the Pawn queens.

If the Rook has sufficient distance not to be troubled by the King, it can often severely restrict the King's movement. As in the Fischer-Bisguier ending above, the King can team up with the Rook to drive the opposing monarch back to a losing position. Emanuel Lasker demonstrated this possibility in one of his earliest compositions (and, as we shall see, he continued publishing studies into the 1930s). We may as well point out here that there is often a good deal of confusion between Edward Lasker, the American master, and Emanuel Lasker, World Champion from 1894 to 1921. They were distantly related, if at all; they were close friends in Germany and in New York over a long time span. They are alike in their humanism and delightful writing abilities. Edward Lasker perhaps lacked that element of struggle which Emanuel considered the essence of the game; nevertheless, he was a dominant figure in American chess for several decades.

By a see-saw action, Lasker shows how the Rook exerts great power at a distance:

EM. LASKER (1890)

*White to play
and win*

White's first move (and subsequent moves) is dictated by the fact that Black threatens RxP unless the King protects it. Surprisingly, White can protect it while driving the Black King all the way to R7!

1 K-Kt7	R-Kt7+
2 K-R7	R-QB7
3 R-R5+	K-R5
4 K-Kt6	. . .

Encroachment begins. Each time the White King defends the Pawn, he forces the Rook to check (otherwise, White plays RxP) and thus gains space at the expense of his opposite number.

4 . . .	R-Kt7+
5 K-R6	R-QB7
6 R-R4+	K-R6
7 K-Kt6	R-Kt7+
8 K-R5	R-QB7
9 R-R3+	K-R7
10 RxP!	. . .

. . . and now the Pawn must queen.

The King likes nothing better than to be able to get an enemy Rook at close quarters. This is the reason why some Rook and Pawn endings are won (when the defending Rook is on the "short" side of an advanced Pawn). For example, with an advanced White Pawn on the Queen file, the Black Rook would be on the "short" side on the Queen Rook file. The difference is that the White King can fend off further checks by playing to the Queen Knight file, without giving up the Queen Pawn. It's a matter of distance.

Fischer has played two critical endings in which he saw demonstrated the importance of the Rook having two squares between itself and the opposing King in any attempt at continued check-ing. Both occurred early in his career:

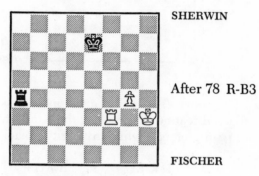

SHERWIN

After 78 R-B3

FISCHER

Portoroz 1958

Fischer has just made a last try at winning, by cutting off the Black King on the Bishop file. And Sherwin obliges:

78 ...	K-K3?
79 K-R4!	R-R1
80 P-Kt5!	...

How subtle but how basic! Once the Pawn gets to Kt5, the King can try to advance around it, since the Rook checks at "too short a distance": the King can advance to R5, then Kt6, and on checks go to R6 and Kt7. Black could have drawn with:

78 ...	R-R1!

And now notice the difference. If the King tries to advance ahead of the Pawn, he is checked back all along the line. And if he plays 79 P-Kt5, R-R5! cuts him off from ever advancing. Typical in such endings is 80 P-Kt6 (the Pawn outrunning its support), R-R3 and White is stymied.

Just about a year later, Fischer ran up against a similar position — on the Queenside instead of the Kingside, and on the other end of the barrel. Again his opponent blew it!

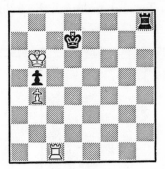

FISCHER

After 52 . . . R-R1

GLIGORIC

Bled 1959

Gligoric fell into the identical drawing position that Sherwin could have forced. With 53 KxP? R-Kt1+ 54 K-R4 R-R1+ 55 K-Kt3 the King was driven back to a position from which he could no longer advance his Pawn. Fischer claimed the draw elegantly with 55 . . . R-QB1! 56 RxR KxR 57 K-B4 K-Kt1! and now wherever the King goes, the Black King grabs the "opposition."

But Gligo could have kept the Black Rook out of the Queenside and avoided the troublesome checks with:

53 R-B7+!	K-Q1
54 R-B5	

or

53 ...	K-Q3
54 R-B6+	

. . . followed by KxP. In either case, Black does not get an effective check in on the back rank. It's interesting that Fischer fails to give the exact reason why 53 R-B7+ works, in his extensive analysis of this game. The slight variation from one position to another in Rook and Pawn endings masks the rationale behind each move.

No less than hallucinations can occur when the Rooks and Pawns are so placed that one can hardly tell who is moving up the board! At the important Interzonal Tournament that vaulted Fischer into the World Championship matches, he faced Geller in a critical round when the lead was very much in doubt. The Russian had been his nemesis (and still holds a plus score against Fischer). Here Fischer's sitzfleisch paid off. After a bitter up-and-down struggle, with a draw offer and a refusal, the following ending was reached:

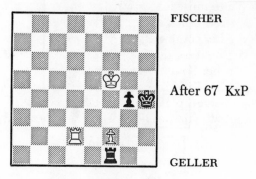

FISCHER

After 67 KxP

GELLER

Palma 1970

67 ...   P-Kt6

Fischer's move, and the upside-down character of the position, confused Geller. After the game, he said he thought that he could play (for White) 68 PxP+ followed by KxR (as if his King were a Rook!).

68 P-B4   K-R6

Missing a winning chance. Again, the Rooks in this type of ending belong where they can check the opposing King, which in this case was at QR8. The King move could wait.

69 R-Q3   ...

Now the Black King will have no shelter from checks after the plausible 69 ... K-R7 70 K-Kt4 P-Kt7 71 R-R3+ K-Kt8 72 P-B5 K-B7 73 R-R2! and the Rook will sacrifice himself for the Pawn, since his own Pawn will require the same of the Black Rook. So the King must retreat.

69 ...   K-R5
70 R-Q2   ...

The blind leading the blind. White repeats moves, not realizing that his opponent has not made the best moves. White should have (again!) established his "Rook distance" with R-Q7, allowing for checks on both rank and file.

70 ...   R-QR8
71 K-K5   ...

A second mistake now loses the game. 71 R-Q8 would just hold. For example, 72 P-Kt7 R-R8+ K-Kt6 73 R-Kt8+ K-B6 74 K-K6, again willing to sacrifice the Rook and promote his own Pawn.

> 71 . . .   K-Kt5!
> 72 R-B5   R-R4+

Now White must lose his Pawn, so he resigns.

We will see other examples of Fischer's use of the "Rook distance" in other combinations in this book. But we cannot leave this subject without some indication of how subtle the King-Rook enmity can be. Sometimes the Rook can check at the wrong time; sometimes the King can advance too hastily. In the following position, the average player would assume that the White King need only get into the battle some way, any way, and it would be all over:

KASPARIAN (1946)

*White to play
and win*

To have two connected passed Pawns, so far advanced, so well protected, with the enemy King confined to the back rank, seems overwhelming. Yet whenever the White Rook moves away, the Black Rook attacks the Rook Pawn. Incredible though it may seem, the only move to win for White is:

> 1 K-R2!!   . . .

In order to see why this diffident advance is a winner, we have to look at what happens when the King moves directly to the Kingside. If 1 K-Kt2 R-KR6 2 K-B2 R-KKt6 3 K-Q2 R-KR6 4 K-K2 R-KRt6 5 K-B2 R-KR6 and now we have a *Zugzwang* position:

KASPARIAN (1946)

(Analysis)

After 5 . . . R-R6

The main point is that if the White King approaches the Rook with 6 K-Kt2, he now sets up a defensive combination based on the fact that he is on the Knight file. Black answers 6 . . . R-R6, and now the White Rook cannot leave the Rook file (as he would ordinarily be allowed to do) because after 6 R-Kt7 R-R4! the White Rook must return to defend the Rook Pawn. It cannot advance because Black forks the King and the Knight Pawn with R-Kt4+.

Even more interesting is the fact that the White King cannot "triangulate" or otherwise gain a move. In the above position, 6-K-B1 is answered by R-B6+ and 6 K-K1 is answered by R-K6+! The King must now move to either a black or a white square. The Rook answers by moving either to KR6 or KKt6 respectively.

This same procedure can be applied to the initial position. After 1 K-Kt1, for example, Black plays R-Kt6+ and then retires to a square the opposite color of the square chosen by the King. By playing 1 K-R2 initially, White guarantees arriving at the above position with Black on the move, when he must relinquish the direct attack on the RP and the *potential* attack on the KtP (because the check at KKt4 no longer exists).

The King and the Rook are indeed natural enemies.

3 Lust to Expand

Pawns are generally considered the unit of value in chess. With a Pawn measured at 1, Knights and Bishops are worth about 3, Rooks 4–5, and the Queen 9. These numerical values (which differ slightly from theorist to theorist) are obviously subject to great change depending on the position of the pieces. And certain pieces seem to work better with each other. The famous "two Bishops," idolized by Janowski and dear to the heart of Fischer, are fearsome on an open board for the simple reason that, together, they can create a wide variety of threats. Paradoxically, this is true to a lesser extent of two Knights working together (see the chapters on combinations). Pawns share in this idiosyncrasy, with a crucial difference. Nimzovitch has described it poetically as "the lust to expand."

Pawns increase in value, one might say, as they move up the board. There is one important proviso: Their value is meaningless if they are subject to easy attack. Nevertheless, a Pawn on the sixth rank is "worth" about 2 and a Pawn on the seventh 3 or 4, not only because such a Pawn *will* queen, but merely because it *threatens* to queen and thus ties up enemy forces. Inexperienced players typically underestimate the increased value of "lustful" Pawns. They often continue to search for combinations and threats against the King when the straightforward advance to the queening square would rapidly force the game to a decision.

Fischer has given us a wealth of examples of this precept: Passed Pawns are to be pushed. More to the point, he has achieved scores of Pawn-promotion combinations by foreseeing his Pawn potential well before the critical endgame stage is reached.

First, some examples of how defending pieces are cleared from the path of advanced pawns:

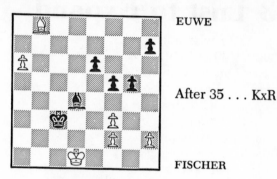

EUWE

After 35 . . . KxR

FISCHER

Leipzig 1960

The Black Bishop and King are lined up for a skewer:

36 B-K5!   Resigns

There is no stopping the QRP. The inattentive player would have prolonged the agony with 36 P-R7 BxP 37 BxB K-Q6. This game, incidentally, fits that marvelous characterization of Emanuel Lasker: "Most well-played games last less than forty moves. Its story is soon told, for such a game has no redundancies. A slight mistake is committed; the opponent, subtly yet energetically, drives the advantage home; the efforts of the defender are at first auspicious, then desperate, and finally futile."

Like all great players, Fischer exhibited a firm grasp of Pawn-promotion technique at an early age. This phase of the game seems to appeal to the developing player as much as Kingside attacks. In the "match of the teenagers," Bobby had to end the game cleanly because his opponent had Pawn-advancing ideas of his own:

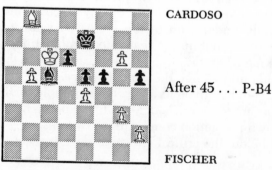

CARDOSO

After 45 . . . P-B4

FISCHER

Match 1957

With advanced Pawns on both sides of the board, the theme is to overburden the defense, even at the expense of a sacrifice, and then count to see who queens first!

46 BxP+!   **Resigns**

It is White who queens first after 46 ... BxB 47 P-Kt7 K-B2 48 KxB PxP 49 P-Kt6 P-K6 50 P-Kt7 P-K7 because White can either have two queens with a rapid mate, or a queen alone after the standard time-gaining combination 51 P-KKt8(Q)+ KxQ 52 P-Kt8(Q), again with check.

This rather direct combination is reminiscent of what is perhaps the most dramatic promotion combination ever played. Harry Nelson Pillsbury, the second in a triumvirate of native American prodigies from Morphy to Fischer, entered the last round of the powerful Hastings 1895 tournament a half-point ahead of his nearest rival. With Pawns equal and only two minor pieces on the board, a draw appeared imminent. But the American, just out of his teens and in his first international event, had seen more deeply into the position than anyone else:

GUNSBERG

After 26 . . . Kt-Kt1

PILLSBURY

Hastings 1895

If the Black Knight succeeds in blocking the passed Pawn at B3, Black's position is solid. "The only piece which is not harmed by watching a Pawn is the Knight"—Reuben Fine. So White first creates a diversion, threatening to force holes in the Kingside:

27 P-B5!   **P-Kt4**

It turns out that Black's QP is the weakling. After 27 ... KPxP 28 PxP P-Kt4 it will be lost to Kt-Kt4. And after 27 ... KtPxP 28 PxP Kt-B3 it will be lost to Kt-B4.

28 Kt-Kt4   **P-QR4**

The idea of supporting the advance of the QBP is not so remarkable as how White intends to *continue* to support it after this undermining.

29 P-B6!   . . .

First, this standard advance against the "blind side" of the Knight: 29 . . . PxKt allows the Pawn to queen after 30 P-B7.

29 . . .	K-Q3
30 PxP!	. . .

GUNSBERG

After 30 PxP

PILLSBURY

Now the White Knight is again "protected" because 30 . . . PxKt would force the same "fork" of two queening squares after 31 P-K7 KxP 32 P-B7.

30 . . .	KtxP
31 KtxKt	KxKt
32 P-K4!	. . .

The final point. White will get connected passed Pawns, impregnable against the enemy King, allowing the White King to roam the board. Black will finally force a passed Pawn of his own, but only at the cost of freeing the KKtP because Black's Pawns on that wing are backward ("one unit holds two").

32 . . .	PxP
33 P-Q5+	K-Q3
34 K-K3	P-Kt5
35 KxP	P-R5
36 K-Q4	P-R4

Desperation, but the White King is just in time to stop—and win—the Queenside Pawns.

37 PxP	P-R6
38 K-B4	P-B4
39 P-R6	P-B5
40 P-R7	Resigns

Just in time to merit Lasker's maxim about the length of a good game, and dramatic enough to earn for the winner the sobriquet "hero of Hastings."

Now a few examples of Fischer's foresight in pushing Pawns in the middle game to set up later Pawn-promotion possibilities. In one of his earliest tournaments, when he was still learning that "won" games had to be *won*, Fischer forced a thematic advance in the certain knowledge that the advanced QP would win in spite of the reduction of forces:

CAMILLO

After 27 . . . RxR

FISHER

Washington, D.C. 1956

28	P-K5	BxB
29	QxB	PxP
30	BxP	Q-Q1
31	P-Q6!	. . .

. . . and White soon won with a dramatic coup (see the chapter "One-liners"). The advanced Pawn is indirectly protected by the possible pin on the Queen file with R-Q1.

Often it is worthwhile to sacrifice heavy material to get a Pawn on the seventh rank. In the following position Fischer actually was willing to give up four Pawns in some variations to achieve P-Q7:

DONNER

After 27 . . . P-KKt4

FISHER

Havana 1965

With his Pawns under attack on both sides of the board, Fischer gains time for a central advance with a neat Rook maneuver.

28 R-K5	B-Q6

Apparently the Bishop has only been driven to a better square.

29 P-QB5!	RxP
30 P-Q6!	RxP

The point is that Black cannot afford to take the time to exchange Rooks, giving White *connected* passed Pawns.

31 P-Q7	PxP
32 QR-K1	B-Kt2

. . . and Black lost quickly. The full extent of Fischer's sacrifice could be seen in the somewhat better line 32 . . . PxP 33 R-K8 PxP + 34 K-R1 and after B-Kt4 White must get a Rook to the KKt file to force matters.

Connected passed Pawns are extremely dangerous when they reach the fifth or sixth ranks. It is a well-known maxim that two connected passed Pawns on the sixth rank cannot be stopped by a Rook on the move, unless, of course, one of them is *en prise.* But they tend to be helpless when not far advanced and carefully watched by a Rook. Fischer himself grossly overestimated his connected passed Pawns in the following position, and eventually lost a very winnable game:

KORCHNOI

After 28 . . . B-B4

FISCHER

Curaçao 1962

29 P-B5?   . . .

Fischer avoids the prosaic 29 R-R2 in search of a sharp winning line. The point then is that 29 . . . BxP 30 RxB RxB 31 P-B5 leaves Black defenseless against the connected Pawns. Fischer could even have tried the exotic 29 B-Kt6! P-R4 (to prevent mate) 30 P-B5,

BxP 31 P-QKt4 B-Q6 32 R-Q1 B-Kt4 33 R-Q6, forcing the Pawn advance.

29 ...	BxP
30 P-B6	RxP!

Simple enough. The queening square can now be watched by the Black Bishop.

31 P-Kt4?	...

A further hallucination in an attempt to deprive the Bishop of the square KB4. Perhaps he was hoping Korchnoi would fall for 31 ... R-QB6 (the standard defense — getting behind the advanced Pawn) 32 B-B5! and the back-rank mate threat wins the Rook.

31 ...	R-Kt6+

... and Black won the KKtP and had a Pawn avalanche of his own!

The Rook obviously belongs *behind* advancing connected or even solitary passed pawns. Fischer produced two striking examples of this tactic in his 1972 Championship match with Boris Spassky. In both cases he managed to win, but only with the co-operation of his opponent: the final game of the match and the position below:

SPASSKY

After 40 ... K-B2

FISCHER

Match, 1972

Threatening though they may seem, the connected Black Pawns are fixed by the White Rooks. Nevertheless, it is difficult to see how White can make any progress. Black's last move, a retreat by the King from the pin at B3, opened the door for some Kingside action, which would have been hampered by 40 ... P-Kt4 (advance the Pawns!). Miscalculations have a way of happening at the last move of the time control.

41 K-K2!	R-Q4
42 P-B4!	P-Kt3
43 P-Kt4	...

The winning idea now began to jell. The Black Rook is on a potential line of pin at Q4, and with the King reduced to a defensive stance by the White Pawns, White will simply play R-QKt5 followed by KRxP. That accomplished, the win was a matter of time.

Fischer's games sparkle with subtle twists which enable him to wring the last drop of poison out of an advanced Pawn. In apparently peaceful positions with adequate defenders watching the queening square, he has been able to break through with a bold stroke.

TAIMANOV

After 41 . . . R-Q5

FISCHER

Palma 1970

White's KRP is attacked, but it appears that 42 P-KKt3 or even 43 P-R5 would leave White with an advantage. Fischer, however, takes immediate advantage of the fact that Black has temporarily deserted his back rank with one of the Rooks:

42 P-B5!	RxP+
43 K-Kt1	R-QKt5

He would not be able to digest a second Pawn because after 43 . . . RxP 44 PxP R-QKt5 45 P-Kt7! RxR 46 R-B8+ K-Kt2 47 RxR Kt-Q2 48 R-Q8 the Pawn will cost a piece.

44 RxR!	...

One way or another, White will get his passed Pawn, even if it requires some clumsy maneuvering by the other Rook.

44 ...	PxR
45 R-B4	PxP
46 RxBP	K-Kt2
47 P-R5	R-K1
48 R-B1!	...

Making sure that it's *his* Rook which gets behind the Pawn. In a few more moves the advanced Pawn forced resignation.

Fischer has even been known to sacrifice his Queen to take advantage of a Pawn on the seventh:

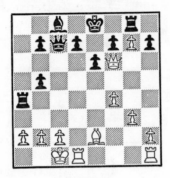

TAL

After 19 O-O-O

FISCHER

Bled 1961

To bring the attack along quickly, Fischer has offered the QRP in return for the centralization of the Rooks.

19 ...	RxRP
20 K-Kt1	R-R3

An attack by 20 ... Q-R4 is shortlived: 21 P-Kt3 guards the mate threat and leaves the Rook bottled up.

21 BxP	...

Fischer keeps his attention focused on the winning of the King Rook with B-Q3 and BxRP, but pauses along the way to regain a Pawn. He could have forced a middle-game decision with 21 B-R5 P-Q3 22 KR-K1 when the threat of P-B5 or Q-R6 is unanswerable.

21 ...	R-Kt3
22 B-Q3	P-K4
23 PxP!	...

Giving up his Queen to avoid general exchanges and to anchor the Pawn at Kt7.

23 ...	RxQ
24 PxQ	Q-B4
25 BxP	...

. . . and White's material advantage won in another twenty moves.

Fischer has been on the receiving end of some advanced pawn combinations, naturally enough. He and other grandmasters fail to solve the intricacies of queening complications far more often than other types of situations. A slight shift in emphasis and an advanced Pawn can change from a sword of Damocles into a butter knife, and vice-versa.

FISCHER

After 39 . . . R-K7

JANOSEVIC

Skopje 1967

40 KtxB	KtxKt
41 P-R5!	. . .

Fischer wriggled for another dozen moves, but was eventually forced to give up a piece for the advanced Pawn.

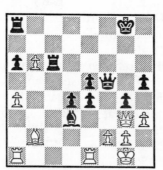

FISCHER

After 27 . . . RxP

IVKOV

Zagreb 1970

Bobby has worked up what looks like an overpowering position, and has just snatched one of the advanced Pawn "weaklings." But

there is unexpected sting in his neighbor, and it is Black's Pawns
which turn out to be overextended:

| 28 BxP! | P-R5 |

Black chooses to force a simplification at the cost of another
Pawn, since the Bishop would control everything at K3. The small
point of the Bishop offer is that 28 . . . PxB would allow the Pawn
to expand to his full girth with 29 P-Kt7, since the Queen would
now control the queening square.

| 29 QxKP | QxQ |
| 30 BxQ | RxP |

Fischer managed to save this miserable position, as we shall see
in a later chapter.

With advanced Pawns on both sides of the board and Queens
supporting them instead of Rooks, it can be expected that things
get even more complicated. Fischer in fact made four endgame
mistakes in fewer than twenty moves, to his opponent's one, and
still managed to draw this position from his first U.S. Championship:

FISCHER

After 39 KtxP

BERLINER

New York 1957–58

| 39 . . . | P-R7+? |

Fischer goes for the jugular instead of contenting himself with
the simple Pawn grab 39 . . . PxP 40 KxP Q-Q5+ and QxP. Later
he was to proclaim as an item of his faith that complicated moves
likely to produce quicker wins are too dangerous over the board:
Play the simple but sure way, even if it takes longer.

| 40 K-R1 | Kt-B4 |

The threat of QxKt followed by Kt-Kt6+ seems overwhelming,
especially since the Knight can't move without allowing mate. But
there is a way out—an improbable Pawn advance!

41	P-QKt4!	Kt-Kt6+
42	KtxKt	QxKt
43	Q-K4	. . .

This happy square for the Queen guards three Pawns, defends against mate, and threatens a Pawn advance. This is called centralization. . . .

43	. . .	K-Kt1
44	P-Kt6	. . .

As we have remarked elsewhere, moves which are forced always seem to have greater impact because they appear to be merely defensive to the other player. White cannot wait, since after P-Kt4 he would be out of moves. Black hopes to achieve a Zugzwang position by bypassing the Pawn, but its arrival on the sixth rank enlarges its ego enormously.

44	. . .	P-R3
45	Q-B5!	QxQP?

The point of Black's play was a mistake all along. He had to give up his QRP with 45 . . . Q-Q8+ 46 KxP QxP+ followed by K-Kt2 to maintain the safety of his King.

46	Q-Q7!	. . .

FISCHER

After 46 Q-Q7

BERLINER

White threatens Q-R7+ followed by P-Kt7+, queening. Black again must give up his advanced Pawn to dispose of White's, with 46 . . . Q-Q8+ and Q-B7+. In that case Black's King Pawn will be just as fast as White's Knight Pawn, since the White King will have to seek shelter from checks *ahead* of that Pawn. Yet Fischer still has illusions of winning.

46	. . .	K-B1?
47	P-Kt5	Q-Q8+
48	KxP	Q-R5+

The one wasted move, 46 ... K-B1, now gives White an extra jump in the race of the Pawns which would occur after 48 ... Q-B7+ followed by QxKtP6.

49	K-Kt2	Q-Kt5+
50	K-B2	Q-B4+
51	K-Kt3	Q-Q4+
52	K-R3	P-K5
53	Q-KR7!	Q-Q6+
54	K-R4	Q-Q5+
55	K-R5	Q-R8+
56	K-Kt6	. . .

FISCHER

After 56 K-Kt6

BERLINER

56 ...	Q-B3??

The fourth mistake should have been immediately fatal. He has the luck of being able to find the right move one turn later. It's not often one can afford to squander tempi in the ending.

57 K-B7??	. . .

Returning the favor, and practically forcing Black to make the right move. By simply winning the KP with 57 P-Kt7+, White would quickly either transpose into a won King and Pawn ending by exchanging Queens, or advance the QKtP.

57 ...	Q-Kt2+!

Now both sides queen and there is nothing left to argue over.

In one of Fischer's finest efforts, a typical Ruy Lopez theme with White attacking on the Kingside and Black on the opposite wing, the following crucial position was reached:

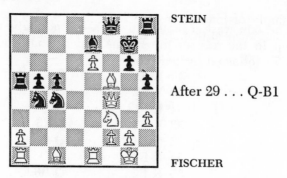

STEIN

After 29 ... Q-B1

FISCHER

Sousse 1967

Fischer now chose to transpose to a favorable ending with the safe retreat 30 B-K4 QxQ 31 BxQ, when RxP would have given Black excellent drawing chances. Fischer won against Stein's cautious play, but he could have made full use of his advanced Pawn by luring away its blockader:

30 Kt-R4!	BxKt

Otherwise Black's Kingside deteriorates rapidly. White is not inconvenienced at all by 30 . . . P-Kt4 31 Q-Kt3 since the King has nowhere to hide.

31 QxB	QxB
32 Q-K7+	

And after two further checks bringing the Queen to QB7 and the Black King to Kt1, the Pawn makes his triumphal march to K7 — especially fitting in a King Pawn opening.

Finally we come to the epitome of advanced Pawn positions — the infamous thirteenth game from the 1972 Fischer-Spassky World Championship match. This is only the final stage of that fascinating struggle. If an endgame composer had concocted this position, he would have been told by all his chess-playing friends that it is interesting, but too far-fetched to occur in actual play.

There are two or three lessons even in this short section of a very full game. First, every analyst to date has concluded that it's a draw with best play on both sides; and from this the conclusion is drawn that Spassky's earlier missing of a forced draw was not critical to the logical outcome of the game. (We discuss this aspect of annotating games under the part title "The Logic of Chess.") As we will see, Fischer still has a forced win. Second, the position illustrates a standard maneuver used by minor pieces to interfere with a Rook's guard of the queening square. Third, it shows how vital King position is in advancing Pawns. Finally, it is the only

example of four Pawns reaching the seventh rank at one time —
Black Pawns at that, and in a World Championship!

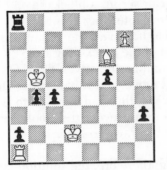

FISCHER

After 59 . . . P-R6

SPASSKY

Match, Reykjavik 1972

60 B-K7   R-KKt1

The Bishop threatened to interfere at KB8, and thus clear the
way for the Pawn to queen. In any ending of this kind, it is always
important to distinguish between a tactic which (1) forces the
Pawn to the queening square at the expense of an enemy piece, or
(2) forces the Pawn in without being captured at all. Bishop, Knight,
or Rook can perform this type of interference, but the Bishop has
the unique distinction of being able to imprison the Rook.

61 B-B8

FISCHER

After 61 B-B8

SPASSKY

Here Fischer played 61 . . . P-R7 and after 62 K-B2 White was
able to maintain a blockade on the Queen file. When Fischer had
to sacrifice the KRP to move his King across the Queen file, he was
just short of being able to force a win against accurate defense.
There is, however, a direct and logical winning line, whose elements can be summarized as follows:

1. If Black is to win, he has to cross the Queen and the King files with his King to support the queening of a Pawn.

2. The White Rook can set up a blockade on either the King or the Queen file once the White King gets to QB2.

3. After 61 . . . P-B6+, however, the White King must go to Q3 to prevent the intrusion of the Black King at B5. (Krogius, Spassky's psychologist and a grandmaster, gives 62 K-Q3 an exclamation point! Yet it is a forced move, and it blocks the Queen file as long as the Black King is at Kt4, threatening to go to B5.)

4. Given time, Black can prevent the Rook from staying on the King file by advancing his Pawn to KB7.

With a little counting, therefore, the solution falls into line:

61 . . .	P-B6+!
62 K-Q3	P-R7
63 R-KB1	P-B5

Just in time to avoid being taken with check. The White Rook cannot leave the back rank, so it is immaterial whether the White King shuttles between Q3 and Q4, or the Rook between R1, B1, and Q1. With best play, the Rook arrives at Q1 when Black must make his break for the Kingside.

64 R-Q1	P-B6
65 K-Q4	P-KB7
66 K-Q3	K-B3!
67 K-B2	. . .

Four Pawns reach the seventh after 67 K-B4 P-B7 68 R-QB1 K-Q2! (This is a very deep reverse in the backfield!) 69 KxP K-K3 70 K-B3 K-K4 71 K-Q3 K-B5 72 K-K2 K-Kt6 73 B-Q6+ K-Kt7 74 BxP R-K1+, etc.

67 . . .	P-QR8(Q)!

An interesting switch on the actual game, where Fischer gave up the KRP to draw the Rook off the Queen file.

68 RxQ	K-Q4
69 K-Q3	P-B7!
70 KxP	K-K5
71 K-Q2	K-B6
72 BxP	RxP and wins.

If Fischer could have won this way instead of because of a blunder by his opponent, the whole complexion of the game would have been different. Yet it will always remain a classic example of giving the Pawns a full head of steam.

4 Pawn Running

There is a separate branch or aspect of Pawn endings which differs from King position, from advanced Pawns, and from outside Pawns in the way in which it affects the calculations of the players. I have called it "Pawn running," for the reason that the usual case involves a race between Pawns on both sides, rather than a particular winning method by the stronger party. In short, the defender relies on pushing his own Pawns or Pawn to defend against his opponent's advance. And the calculation is fraught with danger.

The first position is a typical case. Long before White spent the time and trouble to shepherd his Pawn to QB7, he had to calculate whether it would be worth the candle. Here it happens to be, by a single move:

KALME

After 51 . . . K-B4

FISCHER

New York 1958–59

41

52	P-B8(Q)+	RxQ
53	RxR	P-Kt4
54	K-B6	P-Kt5
55	K-Q5	K-B5
56	K-Q4	K-B6
57	K-Q3	Resigns

After 57 ... P-Kt6 the White King "turns the corner" with 58 R-B8+ followed by K-K2. If the White King can be kept at a distance, the Black King need not be driven in front of his own Pawn by a Rook check:

BOGOLYUBOV

White to move

ALEKHINE

Match, 1929

The relative position of Pawns, Rooks, and Kings is the same as in the Fischer-Kalme endgame. Here, however, is where White and Black must calculate their respective races for the back rank.

1	R-QKt1	R-Q6+
2	K-B6	R-Q1
3	P-Kt6	K-Kt5?

As we will see, the King should go to the King file to inhibit the later return of the White King.

4	P-Kt7	P-B4
5	P-Kt8(Q)	RxQ
6	RxR	P-B5
7	K-Q5	

... and the White King overhauls the Pawn.

Let's suppose that instead of being at Kt5 the Black King is now at K5 (after 6 ... P-B5):

BOGOLYUBOV

(Analysis)

ALEKHINE

The position is nearly identical to the Fischer-Kalme game, except that the White King is one move behind:

7	K-B5	P-B6
8	R-KB8	. . .

Now a Rook check does not drive the King in front of the Pawn, but to Q6. And whenever the Rook returns to the KB file the Black King simply guards it at K7.

8	. . .	K-K6
9	K-B4	P-B7
10	K-B3	K-K7
11	R-K8+	K-Q8!

With not a move to spare! Draw.

The following miscalculation in another slippery Pawn race cost Fischer a first prize. He could have won the game earlier; he most certainly should not have lost it at this stage:

LETELIER

After 46 . . . K-K3

FISCHER

Mar del Plata 1959

47	P-R4	K-Q3
48	P-R5?	. . .

Not content with the obvious draw after 48 PxP PxP 49 P-KKt4, Fischer overextends himself. The subtle difference will be that the extra Pawns on the Rook file will give Black winning chances in one critical variation below.

48 ...	K-K3
49 P-Kt3	...

Realizing that Black can hold everything after 49 P-KKt4 P-B5 50 PxP PxP. If the Kingside Pawns are liquidated, Black will still have time to reach his QB1, all that is required to draw this ending.

49 ...	K-Q3
50 P-B5	PxP+
51 KxP	...

LETELIER

After 51 KxP

FISCHER

51 ...	K-Q4!

Suddenly it is White who is in danger of losing. This clever King advance keeps the White King out of the square of the Black Pawns, and since the Black QKtP will queen with check Black can afford to waste two moves in a winning attempt.

52 P-KKt4	K-Q5
53 P-Kt5	P-B5
54 PxP	P-Kt5!
55 P-B5?	...

Still hoping for complications. The Bishop Pawn often draws against the Queen because the defending King can be stalemated in the corner when the Pawn is captured. Here the other King is too close. Fischer did not like his chances in the Queen ending because Black could threaten to exchange Queens and win the Pawns. Now it is all over—all because of the threat latent in the Black Pawn at QR3.

55 . . .	P-Kt6
56 P-B6	P-Kt7
57 P-B7	P-Kt8(Q)+
58 K-K6	Q-Kt2
59 K-Q7	K-Q4
60 P-Kt6	Q-B3+
61 K-Q8	Q-Q3+
Resigns	

An aspect of Pawn running that always pleases the onlookers is the heroic efforts of minor pieces to overtake runaway Pawns. In Reti's famous studies (see "Combinations"), the King accomplished the impossible by choosing a diagonal instead of a vertical path. The other piece that gains time with double threats (usually checks) is the lowly Knight.

Fischer caused himself no end of trouble by missing a simple draw in the following position (and after plenty of time to study it— it had been adjourned!):

FISCHER

After 41 Kt-B8

ELISKASES

Buenos Aires 1960

41 . . .	B-B4?

True to his style, Fischer presses for more than the simple draw after 41 . . . BxRP! 42 KtxP BxP 43 KtxP B-B8. ("If you are one Pawn ahead, in 99 cases out of 100 the game is drawn if there are Pawns on only one side of the board"—Reuben Fine.)

42 P-QR4!	. . .

And now the game entered a new stage. Black penetrated with his King to the Queenside, sacrificed his Bishop, and in a dozen more moves seemed to have established an unstoppable Pawn:

FISCHER

After 55 . . . P-B6

ELISKASES

56 Kt-R5!   . . .

The Knight which apparently moves farther away from the threatening Pawn actually has chosen the only square from which he can overtake it! Now if 56 . . . P-B7 57 Kt-B4 and the Knight will fork Queen and King after either 57 . . . P-B8(Q) or 57 . . . K-B6 58 K-K4!, holding a square for the Knight at Q3. This is the reason why 56 Kt-Q7 won't work in the original position; the Knight must be able to get to both Q3 and K2.

56 . . .	KxP
57 Kt-B4	P-Kt4
58 Kt-K2!	P-B7
59 Kt-B1	Resigns

The King and Knight can successfully hold the KtP from causing trouble simply by letting it advance to Kt6; then, with the White King at B3, P-Kt7 is answered by KxBP. The Kingside Pawns decide the issue. In this instance the Knight was quite a long-range piece.

Studies involving Pawn races abound. To emphasize the treacherous nature of this territory, I conclude with an endgame which has had to have corrections at least three times since its first publication, and it involves but six men:

TROITZKY (1908)

*White to play
and win*

Troitzky's intention was to show the drawing idea inherent in the Bishop Pawn—but with the Pawn only at B6 with the White Queen on the move!

1 P-K6	P-B5
2 B-B3+	BxB
3 P-K7	. . .

The position seems hopeless. But Black, too, has a "clearance" move by his Bishop, which also happens to block a vital diagonal for a later Queen check:

3 . . .	B-B6+!
4 KxB	P-B6
5 P-K8(Q)+	K-Q7!
6 Q-Q8 or Q7+	K-B8!

. . . and there is no way to prevent the Pawn from reaching B7. Because of stalemate, Rook Pawns and Bishop Pawns draw against a Queen, unless the opposing King is close enough to support a mating attack, as in the Fischer-Letelier game above.

But the story isn't over. White still can win, as Selsnieff, Cheron, and Addison have pointed out over the years, each correcting minor errors.

1 B-K7!	B-R4
2 BxP	B-Q1+
3 K-Kt6	K-K7
4 P-K6	. . .

Here Cheron considered only 4 K-B7, when the Bishop has time to get to either diagonal.

4 . . .	K-Q6
5 B-B8!	. . .

The idea is to get the Bishop to B6 in two moves, and at the same time to have the B8 square available when Black chooses the defense B-K2. This possibility rules out 5 B-R3. The Black Bishop cannot be challenged successfully by B-K7 because the Bishop blocks its own Pawn, allowing the Black Bishop time to regroup.

5 . . .	K-K5
6 B-Kt7	B-K2
7 K-B7	B-Kt5
8 B-B8!	. . .

. . . and now the Bishop must abandon the blockade of the Pawn.

5 The Outside Pawn

Every textbook tells us the outside passed Pawn wins. What they do not tell us is that it has to be foreseen. Foreseen or not, Bent Larsen prolonged the following ending against Fischer in a way that was not worthy of a grandmaster.

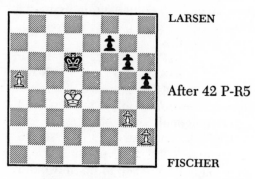

LARSEN

After 42 P-R5

FISCHER

Match, 1971

As long as the Black Pawns cannot advance or exchange themselves for *all* the adverse Pawns, there is no hope of a draw. The game continued:

42 . . .		P-B3
43	P-R6	K-B3
44	P-R7	K-Kt2
45	K-Q5	P-R5
46	K-K6	Resigns

48

White has to maintain a Pawn other than a Rook Pawn, but other than that his task is easy.

This elementary position is the basis of many calculations that must be made long before the endgame. Fischer showed how this theme works equally well when the outside Pawn is not so obvious — in a game almost fifteen years before the above:

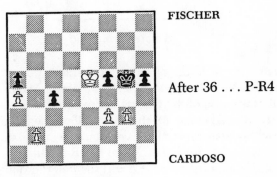

FISCHER

After 36 . . . P-R4

CARDOSO

Match, 1957

Superficially, White has excellent King position, and all Pawn advances are covered. Unfortunately, he has to make a move. A closer inspection reveals that the White King is trying to guard against Black's P-B5, and any King move gives up the defense of that crucial square. The alternative is a matter of counting:

37 P-B4+	K-Kt5
38 K-B6	KxP
39 KxP	P-R5
40 K-Kt5	P-R6
41 P-B5	P-R7
42 P-B6	P-R8(Q)
43 P-B7	Q-KR8

. . . and Black soon resigned — but again not as soon as he should have.

There are a few exceptions to the rule that the outside passed Pawn wins, especially when the defending Pawns can advance and threaten to trade off. The following case was thought to be an exception for many years:

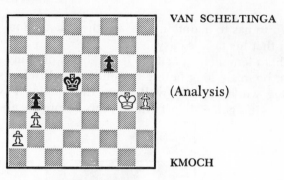

VAN SCHELTINGA

(Analysis)

KMOCH

Amsterdam 1936

Basic Chess Endings (Fine) considered 1 . . . K-K5 to be the equalizer. But after 2 P-R5 P-B4+, White makes a double threat! In this case, one of the threats is the *avoidance* of an enemy threat, namely the advance of the Black Pawn with check. The other "threat" is also the defensive idea of simply stopping the Black Pawn. If the reader will refer to the Reti studies shown under the part title "Combinations," he will see that the White King can guard his KB1 equally well from either Kt3 or R3. Since 3 K-R3! prevents a gain of a tempo (3 K-Kt3? K-K6! followed by a Pawn check), this move simultaneously keeps an eye on KB1 and defeats Black's threat. It took World Champion Mikhail Botvinnik to point out this idea.

The establishment of an "outside" passed Pawn is often so disconcerting that the weaker side makes a few moves just to reassure himself that he is indeed lost. In the following position Fischer could have won with Kt-Kt2, but simpler was:

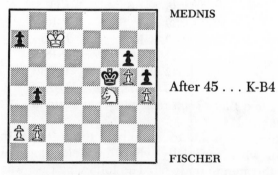

MEDNIS

After 45 . . . K-B4

FISCHER

Cleveland 1957

46 KtxKtP   . . .

Mednis should resign, of course. But he played a few more moves before realizing that with the King tied down to the passed Pawn the ending is lost even against a computer!

Ten years later Fischer encountered a more complex position, but treated it with the same simplicity that has characterized the body of his games:

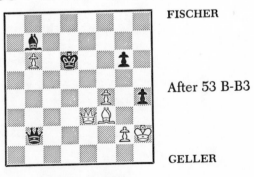

MATULOVIC

After 23 R-R1

FISCHER

Skopje 1967

With his last move Fischer has not only relieved the pressure on his advanced Pawn, because of the threat against the Black Bishop, but has also induced an exchange that will secure the passed Pawn in the ending:

23 . . .		BxB
24 RxR		RxR
25 PxB		

. . . and White won handily.

The apparent simplicity of these stratagems (after they occur!) gives instant hope to the novice. He feels that he could win such positions with ease, if only they came his way. But how would you win the following game position—against Fischer?

FISCHER

After 53 B-B3

GELLER

Havana 1965

Fischer may have thought that a general exchange of material would allow him to win the passed Pawn, but as in his game with Larsen (above) a single remaining Pawn is enough to score the point:

53 . . .	BxB
54 Q-K5+!	QxQ
55 PxQ+	. . .

Obviously an important check, an idea that recurs in many positions.

55 . . .	KxP
56 PxB	K-Q3

Now the Black King is in the square of the passed Pawn, but because it is *outside* White need only keep the Kingside Pawns from protecting themselves and he can win them:

57 P-B4!	Resigns

6 Reach

Much poetic nonsense has been written about the dogleg move
of the Knight and the strange fascination it holds for chess players.
Nabokov's chess-master hero in *The Defense* "sat there leaning on
his cane and thinking that with a Knight's move of this lime tree
standing on a sunlit slope one could take the telegraph pole over
there . . ." And his Humbert Humbert, in *Lolita,* describes the
position of a pane of glass as "a Knight's move from the top."
The Knight's tour—a series of moves by which a Knight touches
every square on the board only once—has intrigued mathemati-
cians since Euler devised several in 1759. We have seen how a
Knight can cover a lot of territory with the interpolation of checks
(in "Pawn Running"). Given all of this, the Knight remains only a
sentimental favorite in most middle games, and is definitely inferior to the Bishop in the endgame.

The reason is *reach.* The Bishop can keep an eye on both sides
of the board in most open positions. Like the Queen and Rook,
it can act as the battery piece in discoveries. It can pin. Except
when it is locked in by its own Pawns, it outruns the Knight handily
on the half of the board it is privileged to move on.

Fischer's games abound in the classic duel of Bishop against
Knight. Salo Flohr has remarked, "It is amazing that in games
with Taimanov, Larsen, Petrosian, and also Spassky Fischer's
Bishop is stronger than the Knight." Robert Byrne puts in bluntly:
"He wins a classic theme over and over again—the superior Bishop
versus the inferior Knight."

What is not well understood about this predilection is that

several other factors are usually present for Fischer to seek out such an ending (or simplified middle game, we should often call it). First, the Bishop needs plenty of squares. Accordingly, the Pawn position must be very loose or decimated. Second, the Knight must lack a secure position (the "Ewige" or eternal base where it cannot be ousted by a Pawn or minor piece). Third, the Bishop must have targets.

All three conditions coincided in the sixth game of the Fischer-Spassky 1972 match. This was to be the finest performance by either participant, perhaps the only time in chess history when the loser joined the spectators in applause after the game. In the following position, Fischer with White has just played 20 P-K4. There is a special irony in the fact that this game marked the first real break from Fischer's consistent advocacy of P-K4 on the first move. (On two or three occasions he had tried 1 P-QKt3 or 1 P-QB4, but never in a critical game. He has called 1 P-K4 "best by test" and has said that he never opens in any other way than 1 P-K4 "on principle.") But here P-K4 is a stunning positional break, designed to give his Bishop more scope and to weaken Black's center Pawns.

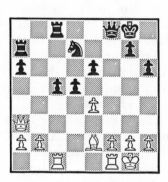

SPASSKY

After 20 P-K4

FISCHER

Match, Reykjavik 1972

20 ...   P-Q5?

That such a natural-looking move should be bad further under-lines the dominance of the Bishop. A protected passed Pawn is as little to be feared as the possible loss of a Pawn by 20 ... PxP. In both cases the Pawns lose their flexibility and so the Knight will have a hard time finding a firm location. Better was to make a

stand with 20 . . . Kt-B3. With his next two moves Fischer anchors
the Knight and prepares a typical Fischer breakthrough.

21	P-B4!	Q-K2
22	P-K5	R-QKt1
23	B-B4	K-R1
24	Q-R3!	. . .

A hard move to find, since Black had apparently tied the Queen
down to the defense of the KtP. The superiority of the Bishop
becomes obvious in a situation such as this. Black must worry
about the attack on his QRP; he must defend his KP; if he ever can
take White's QKtP he must consider whether B-Kt3 would trap the
Rook; and meanwhile his central Pawns are blocked. All of this,
because of the centralized Bishop. For the purposes of this chapter,
this is all there is to consider. Fischer went on to double Rooks
on the KB file and to finish with a Kingside attack in which he first
threatened mate because of his Bishop being at Q3, and finally
forced resignation because of his Bishop being at B4!

The "reach" of the Bishop is most evident in its ability to trap
the Knight at the side of the board. Two young players winning
their spurs at the U.S. Open arrived at the following basic position:

ADDISON

After 28 . . . KtxR

FISCHER

Cleveland 1957

29 B-K5!   . . .

Black is helpless. An exchange of minor pieces allows White's
Queenside Pawns to march through. Black's Kingside Pawns cannot advance effectively because the Bishop "watches" them.

Several years and much experience later, Fischer came upon a
similar situation—and flubbed it!

RESHEVSKY

After 44 Kt-Kt1

FISHER

Match, Los Angeles 1961

Fischer could now have forced a Rook exchange and trapped the Knight as in the above diagram:

45	R-B7+	R-B2
46	RxR+	KxR
47	B-Kt5	. . .

. . . when not only is the Knight vulnerable to attack by the King, but the advance of the Pawns would win quickly. Fischer had "seen" the move in analysis, but unaccountably played 45 B-K4? and only drew.

The Knight is a poor defender of advanced Pawns, even though he can cover both white and black squares. Again, it is a matter of "reach."

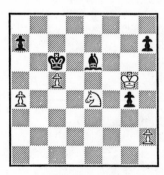

FISCHER

After 34 KtxP

UHLMANN

Leipzig 1960

Both Bishop and Knight are defending advanced Pawns. But the Bishop can prepare to switch from defense to attack—against the QRP. He is tactically justified in this because he can still defend his own KRP at long distance if White should try to set up his own passed Pawn. Meanwhile, his QRP becomes a winning threat:

34 ...   **P-QR4!**

White cannot prevent 35 ... B-Kt6 without losing both Queen-side Pawns.

When Rooks are also on the board, the side with the Bishop has more difficulty making an incursion with his King. Most masters would hesitate to exchange Rooks, however, in the following position:

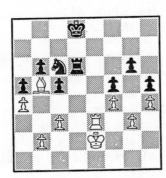

TAIMANOV

After 42 ... K-Q1

FISCHER

Match, Vancouver 1971

It would appear that Black has an impregnable fortress with his Knight at K2 and his King at QB2. Nevertheless, Fischer typically went for a simplification:

43 R-Q3!   **...**

... and after the exchange of Rooks and a King journey, the expected position was arrived at:

TAIMANOV

After 61 B-K8

FISCHER

Unfortunately, Black must now move and upset his defensive formation.

61 . . .	K-Q1
62 BxP!	KtxB
63 KxP	K-Q2
64 KxBP	. . .

White now has three Pawns for the Bishop, but the key consideration is that he can get his Pawns moving before Black can regroup.

| 64 . . . | Kt-K2 |

The poor Knight is hobbled to the end. It would take five moves just to attack the KKtP. Meanwhile, White pushes through:

65 P-QKt4!

. . . and won.

With Pawns on one side of the board only, the superior side generally can't win—even with Bishop against Knight and with a Pawn more. Therefore, Rooks here *favor* the better party (in contrast to the above example) just because of the complications they may conjure up. The following position is one of the more celebrated adjourned games in recent years. The Russian team had worked out a draw, but at the moment of truth Petrosian deserted his defensive posture and lost.

FISCHER

After 41 . . . K-Kt4

PETROSIAN

Match, Buenos Aires 1971

| 42 Kt-K2 | B-R4 |

The idea is to win the RP without exchanging Rooks. Black "masks" the Rook file, then the Knight file after winning the Pawn. Finally, when Petrosian made the mistake of playing his

Rook to the seventh, the Bishop was used to cut the Rook off from returning to the defense.

In the very next game of the match, Petrosian was treated to another classic use of the Bishop. Here, with a pair of Rooks on each side, the "reach" of the Bishop is intensified because of the greater number of threats that they can generate in concert.

PETROSIAN

After 25 R-K2

FISHER

Match, Buenos Aires 1971

Black is practically without a move. If the Knight leaves Q2, KR-K7 destroys the seventh rank.

25 ...	P-Kt3
26 K-B2	P-KR4
27 P-B4	...

At his leisure, White prepares to advance his King to Q4 without even allowing Kt-K4. To prevent this, Black will then become desperate and play P-Q5. Then to avoid the loss of this Pawn he will try for complications with Kt-Kt3. White doubled Rooks on the seventh and mate could not be avoided.

In all of these examples, the superiority of the Bishop had little to do with combinations: with forks, skewers, pins. The Bishop merely "observed" both sides of the board. The Knight's resources were purely combinational. The difference between theory and practice with Knights and Bishops is in *knowing* when the Knight's doglegged attempts at combinations can be quietly restrained. This is one of Fischer's fine gifts.

7 The Indelicate Queen

The beginner is typically fascinated by the power of the Queen. Indeed, when a player fails to progress to the finer points of the game he wearies of the usual cast of characters and is often lured to other inventions. And so his eye catches a game in which more powerful forces maraud across the board in some more literal parody of warfare.

Even experienced players "miss" the Queen in those openings which quickly involve the exchange of the major pieces. With Queens off the board, they feel a lot of the action is gone, too. They are surprised to see Fischer offer an early exchange of Queens in so many of his games.

There is a great deal of difference, of course, between the duffer who avoids a Queen trade-off at all cost (with the idea that he's not "chicken"), and the master who waits until he can use a Queen exchange to transpose into a favorable ending. It is the master who realizes that minor-piece play is usually more complex than Queen maneuvers, and that the strength of the Queen is a very "delicate" sort of power.

The Queen obviously has more options on an open board, and in a two- or three-move sequence those options multiply. In the endgame especially the precision of the first move in a series of Queen moves therefore becomes extremely important. Bobby Fischer has given us more than the normal master's share of examples of exactitude in handling the Queen.

Delicacy in positioning the Queen is called for in two general cases: when the Queen must guard or attack certain squares, and when the Queen must avoid stalemating the opposing King. In the latter case, the Queen is often indelicate to the point of overkill.

Perhaps the most famous example of Bobby's fine touch with the

Queen on an open board is a position that actually never occurred! The Chess Olympics at Varna, Bulgaria, in 1962, brought together Fischer and then World Champion Mikhail Botvinnik for the first time. Together with some offhand games with Reuben Fine, several encounters with Dr. Max Euwe (world champion from 1935 to 1937, and current president of FIDE), and perennial struggles with Keres and Reshevsky, this completed Fischer's first-hand experience with the great pre-World War II generation of masters. The game was an epic struggle. It has provided several examples of Fischer's technique for other chapters of this book. But the drama of the occasion culminated in a subtle trap which Botvinnik set for Fischer in the adjourned position, allowing the Russian to escape with a draw and dash the young American's hopes of "handling" the World Champion.

When the game appeared in the world's chess journals, most analysts followed Botvinnik in claiming that even if Fischer hadn't walked into the trap the ending was drawn. But Botvinnik's notes began to look suspiciously superficial. He corrected them twice in Soviet publications, finally arriving at the original conclusion that he could hold the ending against best play.

It was not until the appearance of Bobby's long-awaited *My 60 Memorable Games* that the other side was heard from. Fischer was obviously not ready to let his baby get thrown out with the bath water. Taking special pains to point out Botvinnik's inaccuracies in analysis, he systematically reduced the best lines on both sides down to an ending where Botvinnik queened one move after he did. Botvinnik had also reached this position in his notes, and had dismissed it as a draw. Fischer claimed it was a win. It all came down to this:

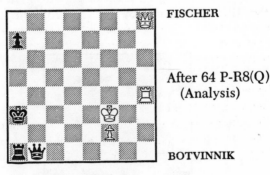

FISCHER

After 64 P-R8(Q)
(Analysis)

BOTVINNIK

Varna 1962

Obviously, with both Kings unsheltered, whoever gets in the first series of checks is likely to win material or checkmate in a hurry. Botvinnik obviously assumed that the Black Rook can be kept out of the fight, and the Black Queen will soon run out of checks. For example, 64 . . . Q-Q6+ 65 K-B4, Q-Q7+ 66 K-B3 is safe enough, and 64 . . . Q-B4+ 65 R-B4, Q-Q4+ 66 R-K4 might even be dangerous, as the White Rook gets into checking range. However, a check by the Queen which keeps several options open for the *second* check rousts the White King out of hiding:

> 64 . . .   Q-Kt6+!
> 65 K-K2   . . .

The King has to commit himself to this dangerous retreat, for after K-B4 or K-Kt2 he has lost the shield of the Rook, and he would be driven to a square where he could be checked by the Black Rook: 65 K-B4 Q-B2+, or 65 K-Kt2 Q-Q4+. So the point of 64 . . . Q-Kt6+ becomes clear: from that square Black can check as required on either the long diagonal or on the Bishop file.

> 65 . . .   Q-Q8+
> 66 K-K3   R-Kt8!

Now Black can afford the leisure of a developing move, since the Queen holds the QR5 square and the Rook or Queen can interpose at Kt6 — with check — on the only other available checks:

> 67 Q-B8+   K-R7

Fischer now concludes, ". . . and White's King will be without shelter from the coming avalanche of checks." Actually, it is not quite that easy, for now the Black Rook will be pinned:

> 68 Q-B7+   R-Kt6+
> 69 K-K4   . . .

Now what? 69 . . . Q-K7+ drives the King to a square which breaks the pin, but any check it takes will obviously be answered by a checking "discovery" by the King. And the White Rook cannot be forked.

FISCHER

After 69 K-K4
(Analysis)

BOTVINNIK

69 . . .	Q-Q6+
70 K-K5	K-Kt2!

A second "quiet" move now unleashes all Black's force.

71 R-K4!	. . .

Following the instinctive rule that the King in the center of the board should wrap himself in whatever pieces are at hand.

71 . . .	Q-B6+!

Precise to the end. The King must not be allowed to escape to B4, so Black must preserve the option of 72 . . . Q-B6+ in that event. The White Rook threatens to team up with the remaining Pawn to form a bastion for the King on KB3.

72 K-B5	. . .

After 72 R-Q4 Black wins the Queen in a way that is typical of this entire ending: 72 . . . R-Kt4+ 73 K-K4 Q-B7+ 74 K-K3 R-K5+ and the King is finally driven to the Bishop file for the fatal check either by Queen or Rook.

72 . . .	Q-B6+
73 R-B4	R-Kt4+

And now a Queen and Rook "ladder" forces the King back to the second rank, where he will be impaled with his Queen.

74 K-Kt6	Q-R4+
75 K-Kt7	R-Kt4+
76 K-B8	Q-R1+
77 K-K7	R-Kt2 winning.

It is interesting to note that even grandmasters have such a distrust for certainty in Queen and Rook endings that Fischer's winning line has never been wholeheartedly accepted as fact. Larry Evans prefaces this game by saying Fischer threw away "the win he *maintains* was still there." (Emphasis added.)

"Preserving options" is the watchword in handling the Queen, as shown here and as strikingly illustrated in the following studies.

Perhaps no other player in history has had so much fun with chess as Sam Loyd, America's legendary problem composer, puzzle maker, and minor master of the last century. Somewhat prophetically, his old friend Professor Daniel Willard Fiske had proposed to Loyd late in life that they combine to encourage the playing of chess in Reykjavik, Iceland. "He is going to print a book of my problems," said Loyd, "and we are going to write stories again as we did forty years ago—but think ot it, all in Icelandic, a language only one person in America can read, and that's himself."

One of Loyd's early masterpieces showed once and for all how the Queen has the uncanny ability to anticipate the possible defenses of the enemy:

SAM LOYD (1869)

Mate in three

The key move, 1 Q-KB1, disdains the immediate threat of mate in favor of waiting for Black to commit himself. Not even QxB is threatened, since there is then no conceivable way to mate in three. The Bishop would seem to have ample room to move, to answer the threat of 2 Q-QKt1 (forcing 2 . . . P-Kt3 3 QxB mate). Yet B-Kt7 is likewise met by Q-QKt1; B-B6 or B-B5 is answered by Q-Q3; and B-K4 or B-B3 is answered by Q-B5. The idea behind this simple yet stunning position is that the square KB1 is the only one on the board from which the Queen can reach QR1, QKt1, Q3, and B5 on the second move. It is incidental, but pretty, that 1 . . . P-Kt6 allows 2 Kt-Kt6+, since on PxKt the Queen can mate at R3.

In the case of a problem (by definition, where the stipulation of mate in a given number of moves is made), it is vitally important that play be precise. In many games, the exact order of moves will not change the outcome. A player can repeat moves, make an exploratory sortie to test his opponent's defenses, and generally waste time. If the Loyd position were a game, most players would simply play 1 Kt-Kt6+ and queen the Pawn. The Botvinnik-Fischer endgame is all the more extraordinary for requiring precise timing as well as choice of squares.

The Queen need not be as aggressive in multiplying its options as the above examples indicate. Consider:

A. KRAEMER (1950)

Mate in three

The logic of this position is clear-cut: The Queen would like to make an attack on Q7, providing for the two defenses possible against that attack at the same time. The defenses are (either) PxP. The Queen can make provision against QPxP by being in a position to check on the QR4 to K8 diagonal. It can provide against BPxP by being able to capture at KKt6. So the first move must be to QB2, the only square which fulfills both conditions, since the Queen cannot play to K4 on the first move. There is no threat, incredible though this may seem. Black is in Zugzwang, and must, in effect, weaken his defense to the point of allowing the Queen to threaten White's Q7 at the same time as the Queen maintains the above two provisions. If 1 . . . B-KR4, then 2 Q-Q1! If 1 . . . P-R4, then 2 Q-Q3!

The second major "indelicacy" of Queen moves is that they often tend to overwhelm the opposing King with unwanted force, leading to stalemate. Early in his career Fischer had several "Queen" experiences with Paul Keres, and learned a double lesson in the intricacies of stalemate possibilities.

FISCHER

After 68 . . . P-Kt7

KERES

Curaçao 1962

Here, a few months before the Olympic epic with Botvinnik, Fischer had started poorly. The Russian hegemony was, if we are to take Fischer at face value, as much a matter of connivance as of psychology. But if he was frustrated on the cross-table, he nevertheless produced memorable positions on the board. Paul Keres was a model of deportment and "class" that Bobby aspired to. Fischer's notes on the opening stages of this game reveal his respect for Keres' style. After move 12 by White, a necessary evil, Fischer writes: "Poker-faced, as always, Keres made this move as though it were the most natural one on the board. But it was the last thing he wanted to do. . . ." Fischer then let his advantage slip, but persisted in trying to win. With mistakes on both sides, the above position was reached, one that Bobby fully expected to win. He had calculated that his King could find a haven from checks at R2:

69 Q-Kt4+	K-B2
70 Q-Kt3+	K-Kt2
71 Q-Kt3+	K-R2

Now all that White seems to have left is to give up the Bishop for the advanced Pawn, with 72 B-B5+ QxB and 73 QxP. Fischer was ready to chalk up the full point after 73 . . . Q-B5+ 74 Q-Kt4 when the exchange of Queens leaves Black with the opposition and a won Pawn ending. But Keres has sensed something else:

72 Q-K5!   . . .

FISCHER

After 72 Q-K5!

KERES

Not only does Keres ignore the Pawn that is about to Queen; he places the Queen on a less "aggressive" square. But it soon becomes clear that Black must be deprived of a check on his K8, for after 72 Q-Kt5 Q-K8+ 73 K-R3 or R5 Q-R8+ allows the Pawn to queen with check. Yet what is White thinking about?

72 ...	**Q-B7+**

Fischer actually played 72 ... Q-R8+ 73 B-R3 QxB+ followed by P-Kt8(Q), drawing, because 73 ... P-Kt8(Q) allows a stalemate after 74 Q-R5+ and Q-Kt6+.

73 K-R3	**P-Kt8(Q)**

Brilliant but just short of the mark is 73 ... P-Kt8(Kt)+ 74 K-Kt4 Q-R5+! 75 KxQ (otherwise Black wins the Bishop) Kt-B6+ 76 K-R5 KtxQ 77 B-K8 and the Black King cannot penetrate to attack the Queenside.

74 B-B5+	K-R3
75 Q-B6+	K-R4
76 B-Kt6+!	QxB
77 Q-Kt5+!	KxQ

Stalemate

The "desperado" nature of the defending Queen when her King is in a stalemate position is typical of this type of ending. The Queen seems to be able to offer herself up almost anywhere, but as the above sequence shows the exact square for the self-immolation is critical.

Keres might well have put this ending into the form of a study for publication, except that it is just about perfect as it stands! Both Keres and Lasker have published significant studies as a result of analysis of their own games. Perhaps less well known in our own time is a study which epitomizes the delicacy and precise logic of Queen vs. Queen endings.

In the summer of 1903, a position unfolded at the chessrooms of the Mechanics' Institute in San Francisco that resisted the efforts of the best analysts in the club:

J. DOLAN (1904)

*White to play
and win*

First it seemed that the White forces had an easy win. Though material was equal, the base of the Black Pawn chain was subject to attack, and Black could never afford to exchange Queens. Yet the buried character of the Black King was his strongest defensive weapon: he could easily be stalemated, with Queens on the board, much as in the Keres-Fischer finale.

One of the players, James Dolan, finally mastered the intricacies of the position and published it as a study. The legendary San Francisco master Dr. W. R. Lovegrove, who had just defeated the touring Harry Nelson Pillsbury in an exhibition match, was the first to produce a complete solution. The *Literary Digest* picked it up in 1904 as a promotional competition; only one correct solution was entered. The notoriety of the study was such that around the world it was familiarly referred to as "The San Francisco End-game."

The complete solution involves several Zugzwangs, several stalemate possibilities, and tempo moves by both sides. A simple runthrough of the main line leaves even experienced players somewhat mystified. The correct approach in this, as in every evenly balanced position, is to lay out some guidelines:

1. The Black Queen cannot be captured by her opposite number on the back rank when the Black King is at R2. This is obviously stalemate. Not so obvious is the corollary that when the White Queen goes to the eighth rank the Black Queen can become a "desperado" and offer herself to the opposing King anywhere on the board. Thus a first stab at a solution is often the illusory:

1 K-Q7	Q-Kt1
2 Q-Q8	Q-B1
3 Q-K8?	Q-Q3+! forcing stalemate

Other facts about the position start to become clear from the above try:

2. If Queens are exchanged, the White King has two moves for every one of Black, and so easily forces him into the corner, winning the Bishop Pawn.

3. The only way White can make progress is for the King to approach the Bishop Pawn via K7. An apparent start in this direction is:

1 K-Q7	Q-Kt1
2 Q-K8	Q-B1
3 Q-Q8	Q-Q3+
4 K-K8	. . .

The Bishop Pawn and the Queen are both threatened, but Black can wiggle for quite a while:

4 ...	Q-K3+
5 K-B8	...

A theme that will recur from now on is that White makes no headway after 5 Q-K7 Q-B1+ because 6 KxP would allow Q-Kt1 mate! This should be generalized for other positions:

4. The King cannot capture the Pawn with the White Queen on either K7 or on the diagonal leading to the Pawn, since mate or loss of the Queen would follow when Black can play Q-KKt1+.

5 ...	K-R1
6 Q-B7!	...

Equally good is 6 Q-K8. But Black must not be allowed to defend the Pawn with the Queen on his second rank, as would happen after 6 Q-K7 Q-B1+ 7 Q-K8 Q-B2 8 QxP Q-K2+ stalemate! From this variation we can generalize that:

5. If the Black Queen can defend the Pawn from B2, with the Black King at R1, it cannot be captured without stalemate.

The final variation will show that it is only because the Black Queen can reach only Kt2, rather than B2, that the defense fails. Returning to the main line:

6 ...	Q-Q4
7 QxP	Q-Q1+
8 Q-K8	Q-Q2!

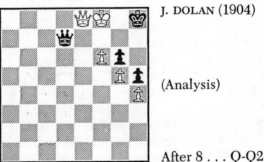

J. DOLAN (1904)

(Analysis)

After 8 ... Q-Q2

How can White free his King? 9 Q-R8 is met by Q-Kt2! But White need only avoid a few traps and he's out.

9 Q-K5	Q-Q1+
10 K-B7	Q-Q2+
11 Q-K7	...

But not 11 KxP Q-R2 mate. Now the Pawns fall. So we see that
Black falls on his face after 3 . . . Q-Q3+ in the above line. He's a
hero with the subtle

3 ...	Q-B4!
4 K-K8	K-Kt1!

His Queen no longer being *en prise*, as it was above, he can
afford the luxury of defending the Pawn with his King. We can lay
down another rule from this:

6. As long as the Black King is allowed to go to Kt1 without being
checked, he can defend the Pawn.

Therefore, the idea of invading the back rank at once with either
2 Q-K8 or 2 Q-Q8 is a false start. Let's go back to the original task
after 1 K-Q7 Q-KKt1:

J. DOLAN (1904)

(Analysis)

After 1 . . . Q-KKt1

The problem now is to free the square for the White King. Whenever the White Queen leaves it, the Black Queen plays to KB1,
guarding it. But there is a way:

2 Q-Q6!	...

The beginning of a neat "triangulation" which puts Black on the
spot. The Queen is headed for K5, where she will have the option
(that word again) of going to K7 or to Q6, depending on where the
Black King is. Now there are many ways to get to K5, including
on the move! But two things dictate the exact choice above. First,
the immediate 2 Q-K5 is answered by Q-Kt1! 3 Q-Q6 Q-Kt2+, setting progress back several moves. Second, any move which does
not allow for the interposition of the White Queen at Q8 gives
Black the defense 2 . . . Q-QR1 3 K-K7 K-Kt1.

2 ...	Q-KB1
3 Q-Q5!	...

From now on almost every White move deserves an exclamation
point, because it must be exact. Here 3 Q-Q4 won't do, for example,

because the Black Queen can run to R6, not being tied down to the defense of the Bishop Pawn. So the Black monarch must make a move.

3 ...   **K-Kt1**

There is no reason why K-R1 is any worse. It looks as if Black can perform a little triangulation of his own in the corner, but it is illusory. White is interested only in whether the Black King is on the second or the first rank. Another general observation suggests itself from this fact:

7. Capturing the Bishop Pawn with check is the chief threat White has. This can happen directly, with the King on R2 and the White Queen capturing; or indirectly, with the King on R1 and the King capturing with a *discovered* check.

The significance of this observation will become clear as the solution progresses.

4 Q-K5   ...

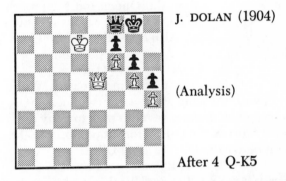

J. DOLAN (1904)

(Analysis)

After 4 Q-K5

A little reflection will reveal that the White Queen will choose either K7 or Q6, depending on where the Black King goes, up or across. What surprises most chess players is that this little folderol by the White Queen forces Black to yield the K7 square to the White King.

4 ...   **K-R1**
5 Q-K7   ...

Alternatively, 4 ... K-R2 is answered by 5 Q-Q6 immediately.

5 ...   **K-R2**
6 Q-Q6!   ...

Round and round we go, but now it is Black's turn to get off the merry-go-round. The King can't move, so the Queen must be off.

6 . . .	**Q-QR1**
7 K-K7	**Q-QKt1**

J. DOLAN (1904)

After 7 . . . Q-QKt1

Black's indirect defense of the BP puts White to the real test. Instead, 7 . . . Q-KKt1 allows the exchange of Queens: 8 Q-Q8 Q-B1+ 9 KxQ (of course).

8 Q-Q8   . . .

One way or another, the Queen must approach the BP via Q8. The direct approach, 8 Q-Q5, only wastes several moves after 8 . . . Q-B2+ 9 Q-Q7 Q-B1! Also 8 Q-B6 Q-QR1 9 Q-K8 Q-Kt2+ 10 K-B8 K-R1 11 Q-Q8 arrives at the same position.

8 . . .   Q-Kt2+

Q-R1 or Q-B1 loses a little more easily. White is aiming for a position with his King at K8 and his Queen at Q7, in effect "building a bridge" along the seventh rank to deny that rank to the Black Queen. After 8 . . . Q-R1, for example, 9 K-K8 and Black has nothing better than Q-Kt2 10 Q-Q7.

9 K-B8   . . .

But not 9 K-K8 K-Kt1 and Black can claim a draw!

9 . . .   K-R1 (or Q-R2)
10 Q-Q6!   . . .

Returning to Q6 a third time, now in order to prevent Black's only defense to K-K8, namely, K-Kt1. There is no other way to get at the BP!

10 . . .   K-R2 (or Q-Kt2)
11 K-K8

. . . and there is no answer to 12 Q-Q7.

The Queen on an open board has another unique capability: "staircasing." With a series of checks made appropriately first on a diagonal and then on a horizontal, the Queen can "walk" herself to a desired destination. In the Keres-Fischer position referred to in the first part of this chapter, Fischer employed an "anti-staircase" effect, which is quite a bit more common than this elaborate name might imply:

FISCHER

After 68 . . . P-Kt7

KERES

Curaçao 1962

On 69 Q-Kt4+ Fischer carefully selects K-B2, instead of the immediate K-Kt2, which would invite endless checks commencing with Q-Kt4+. Now, after 70 Q-Kt3+, his only unguarded checking square (he would naturally prefer QB4 if it were not guarded by the White Queen), the Black King finds a haven: 70 . . . K-Kt2 71 Q-Kt3+ K-R2. As we have seen, however, Keres had one more trick up his sleeve.

The Queen often keeps a perpetual check in hand by checking on the correct "focal point" of a diagonal and horizontal. In the same tournament, eleven days before the above encounter, Fischer grabbed a Pawn against Pal Benko with an apparently overwhelming position:

BENKO

After 19 KtxKP

FISCHER

Curaçao 1962

Benko replied 19 . . . BxKt and eventually lost. If he wished it
(or saw it), he could have had a perpetual with:

19 . . .	BxP+
20 KxB	Q-Kt5+
21 K-B1	Q-R6+
22 K-Q2	. . .

So far, White seems to be escaping. On 22 . . . Q-Kt5+ 23 P-B3
Q-Kt7+ 24 B-B2 R-K1 there are certainly adequate complications
for Black, but he can say QED with:

22 . . .	Q-R4+

. . . since 23 P-B3 now allows the check at R7 (QxRP+), immediately winning the Knight.

"Staircasing" in exaggerated form is seen in many classic endings. The following position is surprising because of its stark
simplicity:

R. BURGER (1969)

*White to play
and win*

The win would be obviously possible if the White Queen could
"close in" with checks at K4 and R4. But how to get to K4 without
loss of time (i.e., by a series of checks)?

1 Q-Q5+	K-R7

The King is held to R7 and Kt7 for one of three reasons: to avoid
loss of the Queen by QxQ, to avoid the fork Kt-Kt3, and to avoid the
mate Q-Kt3—depending on the check.

2 Q-Q6+	K-Kt7
3 Q-B6+!	. . .

Heading for QKt7! Black is safe enough after 3 Q-Kt3+ K-B8, just
as the discovered checks in the initial position are empty.

3 . . .	K-R7
4 Q-B7+	K-Kt7
5 Q-Kt7+	K-R7
6 Q-R7+	. . .

The only route to a check on K4.

6 ...	K-Kt7
7 Q-K4+	K-R7
8 Q-R4+	K-Kt7
9 Kt-B4+	K-Kt8
10 Q-K1+	K-R7
11 Q-B2+	

... and mate next move.

It's obvious that the Queen has to have an open field to show her full powers. This fact dictates the amazing first move of the following gamelike study:

B. KOZDON (1959)

Mate in four

Black is afflicted with a weak back rank, which he must defend with his Queen. At the same time, he has reason to fear a "staircase" series of checks on the diagonal, then on the Rook file. But where is White's threat? The answer is ... Black is in Zugzwang!

    1 R-K1! ...

The reason why the Rook must avoid every other square on the King file becomes apparent in the following variations:

1 ...	P-R7
2 Q-R2+!	K-R1
3 QxP+	K-Kt1 (QxQ 4 R-K8 mate)
4 QxQ mate	

... or:

1 ...	Q-QB1
2 Q-Kt3+!	K-R1
3 QxP+	

... or:

| 1 ... | Q-Q1 |
| 2 Q-B4+! | |

The Queen must avoid other moves on the back rank for more prosaic reasons.

Who gets the greater pleasure from such feats of the Queen—the composer of such a study, or a player such as Fischer? In the examples shown in this chapter, the Queen maneuvers from "actual games" actually never occurred. In another sense of the word, studies and post-mortems "occur" as much as moves written on a score sheet. And the ultimate pleasure is experienced by the millions of players whose luck it is to replay these little classics, and perhaps discover again that the most powerful chess piece can often be the most sensitive and delicate.

8 Mate in the Afternoon

One of the delightful little surprises of chess is the occasional checkmate that occurs with only a few pieces left on the board — late in the afternoon of the game. The result can be comic or tragicomic, breathtaking or exasperating. What the reader will find instructive about this chapter is not so much the technique of weaving mating nets as the realization that it is so easy to fall into one.

In the endgame one's attention is usually riveted to advanced Pawns or to other materialistic considerations. In the following position Fischer had established a Pawn on the seventh and another threat against the KRP:

SANCHEZ

After 52 . . . BxP

FISCHER

Santiago 1959

But Black's last move gave him the opportunity to end the agony quickly:

53 B-Q2!   Resigns

After 53 . . . BxB 54 R-K7 is mate. This same team of Rook and Knight collaborate in several other alignments in which the enemy King is easily led to the slaughter:

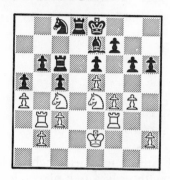

DURAO

After 31 . . . R-Q1

FISCHER

Havana 1966

32 R-R3!   B-B1

This innocent defense of the RP, quite necessary, leaves the square KB3 unguarded, so:

33 KtxRP!   . . .

And now Black saw the danger and retreated with R-B2. He would have been mated after:

33 . . .   PxKt
34 Kt-B6+   K-K2
35 R-Kt7+

. . . and the death of both Rooks cannot save their King.

The complexity of a position often masks a simple version of the Knight-Rook mate. The simplest occurs in the corner, and even Taimanov underestimated its seriousness in the first game of his match with Fischer:

FISCHER

After 35 . . . Q-Q2

TAIMANOV

Match, Vancouver 1971

36 Kt-Q4   . . .

As Larsen has pointed out, White should stay in the middle game
with 36 Q-Kt5. He erroneously feels the two Bishops and the imminent win of a Pawn give him good endgame chances. He reckons
without the Knights.

        36 . . .   **Q-Q3+**

        37 P-Kt3   . . .

The first clue that something is amiss—a hole appears at KB3.

        37 . . .   **Q-Kt5**

        38 Kt-B6   **Q-Kt3**

There is great psychological force in this retreat. White believes
he thwarted Black's threat of Q-K8 because of the threat of 39
QxP+, with mate to follow. He also feels quite happy about the
following "see-through" combination. But he misses the main
point: The White King will be in a mating net.

        39 KtxP   **QxQ**

        40 BxQ   **R-K8!**

It all seems so innocent, but the Bishop cannot find a square to
guard KB3. In fact, he sealed:

        41 B-Kt4

        And resigned

After 41 . . . Kt-K4, Black will knock off the Bishop, play Kt-B6,
and advance the QP. The typical corner mate would occur if White
had played the Bishop to the other diagonal. Then there is no
defense against mate by Kt-K4 and Kt-B6, except by opening Kt4
to the other Knight with P-KR4.

The limited force involved in some positions is typical of a
composed setting:

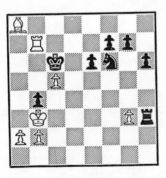

PETROSIAN

After 35 . . . K-B3

FISCHER

Bled 1961

        36 K-B4!   **Resigns**

There is no defense against 37 R-R7 mate. In the old days, White would have "announced" mate in two after his thirty-sixth move, since Black's only other move was the futile R-R5+. Modern players don't announce mates; they are happy enough taking them. The Rook and Bishop team shown here is typical, but if this were a composed problem many players would complain that the Bishop could never have gotten to QR8!

A composer could hardly get more basic than in the following Fischer position — which opened his first tournament on the way to the World Championship.

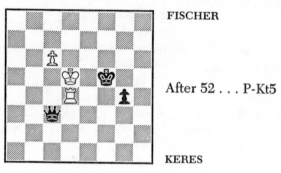

FISCHER

After 52 . . . P-Kt5

KERES

Bled 1959

> ### 53 R-B4   . . .

In all fairness, White has nothing better. The optimism of chess players is limitless.

> ### 53 . . .   Q-K4 mate

Whenever the Queen checks at pointblank range, the King has only two possible "flight" squares. Here, both are blocked by his last remaining pieces. The geometry of the Queen vis-a-vis the King is one of those little pieces of shorthand which the practical player should have at his fingertips.

The Queen can also be very neat at a distance of a square. Here Fischer has just threatened 38 Q-R8 mate:

FISCHER

After 37 . . . Q-Kt8

MEDNIS

New York 1958–59

It should be noted that without this mate threat, White is not too badly off. But he must resign, because:

38 P-KKt4   PxP mate

In problem terms, this is a "model" mate: the guarding of the King field is efficient down to the last square.

The Queen is not the only piece which can mate single handed, provided the enemy King is suitably cushioned by his own men:

AVERKIN

After 69 RxP

TAL

USSR Championship,
1973

The only question here is, who is going to be mated? Tal is obviously up against the wall. This was the last round of the tournament, and a draw meant missing the "cut" for the 1974 USSR Championship—surely a crushing thought for an ex-World Champion. But Caissa has a poetic sense of justice.

69 . . .   R-B5??
70 Kt-Q5!   Resigns

Black must lose his Rook, or allow Kt-K7 mate! Tal lives!

Mating possibilities occur when least expected, when all other types of combinations seem more likely. The following position occurred in (also) one of the less likely *events*, the North-South match in California in 1969, the last year of this institution, which has faded away along with other traditional matches throughout the United States. The good-fellowship and college-effort chess that characterized these events often led to effervescent positions. An informal preliminary to the main match at the North-South was the "Insultation," the rules of which are best conveyed by the quoted description from *The California Chess Reporter:*

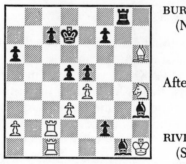

BURGER-GROSS
(North)

After 31 R-B1

RIVISE-ALMGREN
(South)

Pismo Beach 1969

"Dropping the Rook on the floor as he successfully prevented it from coming to rest at Kt5, the North player now went into a deep study as his opponents, the audience, and even his partner laughed loud and long. While another round of Slivowitz was served, and now carrying the Rook in his hand, the North player announced that there *must* be a Rook move that would win and he was going to find it! There was 100% disbelief at this, and more scoffing. Then the North player found a strange and rare checkmate, and disbelief changed to belief, and scoffing to applause:

31 ...	R-Kt6!!
32 RxP+	K-Q1
33 Resigns	

"... for ... B-Kt7+ 34 KtxB R-R6 mate cannot be prevented."

I don't think the problemists have yet been able to duplicate the humor and contrariness that are part of the game of chess. Sam Loyd did perhaps in his more outrageous tricks. A contemporary of his, concert pianist Willmers, produced a little study which is the fitting conclusion to this inquiry into mating nets. The point of the study, to me, is not that it is precise, or illustrates model mates, or is economical, or is difficult to solve. The very funny point is that White says, "I am going to construct a mating net around you, my friend, whether you like it or not."

R. WILLMERS (1859)

Mate in four

The first move is indeed hard to find, and pretty:

    1 R-R7!   **P-R7**

The curious thing is that White will play the following moves no matter what Black does—advance the Pawn or move his King to and fro.

    2 Kt-R5(+)   —
    3 R-Kt7(+)   —
    4 P-Kt4 mate

The key to setting up the net is getting the Rook to the seventh rank, so that it guards R7 and B7 in the event of the King trying to flee in that direction of move 1. The lesson for the practical player, I think, is that singlemindedness in purpose goes a long way, especially when your purpose is to net the King.

III The Name of the Game

9 The King's the Thing

The direct attack on the King is, strangely enough, not as common with the general run of chess players as it should be. Too many players reach a level of sophistication in which the accumulation of small advantages numbs them to the stark realities of checkmate. Reshevsky once overlooked a mate on the move, two moves running, in a game in a Candidates tournament. There are no examples of a similar chess blindness on Fischer's part, probably because he has seldom been in time trouble. Even more striking is the regularity with which Fischer pursues a direct attack on the King, even at the expense of his own King's safety. In this he is like Spassky, and unlike Botvinnik, Alekhine, and Capablanca.

The popularity of the Sicilian Defense may be either the cause or the effect of modern Kingside aggressiveness. Since Fischer seems to like either side of this imbalanced opening, it is natural that he gets his share of attacks. Early in his career, Fischer established something of a reputation as a "Dragon killer," by rolling up Black's fianchettoed King position typical of this variation of the Sicilian.

LARSEN

After 21 Kt-R4

FISCHER

Portoroz 1958

87

22 RxKt!   . . .

The characteristic follow-up to P-KR4, P-KR5, PxP.

22 . . .   **PxR**

23 P-Kt6   . . .

. . . and the strength of the King Bishop gave White a winning attack.

Where the line of the King Bishop is blocked, the simple threat of ganging up on the KR file is often decisive:

GLIGORIC

After 25 . . . Kt-R4

FISCHER

Bled 1959

26 RxKt!   **PxR**

27 QxP   **B-K1**

28 Q-R6!   . . .

A typical stratagem: the King is kept from running away before the attack by R-R1 or P-Kt6. White won quickly.

The fianchettoed Bishop can be a difficult man to unseat, but there are ways:

PUREVZHAV

After 17 . . . P-K4

FISCHER

Varna 1962

18 Kt-B5!   . . .

Since 18 . . . PxKt is answered simply by BxB and Q-Kt3+, Black
was forced to exchange the Bishop or allow the Pawns to enter the
attack after 18 . . . BxKt.

It is often a case of Who Gets There First? Fischer has occasionally perished by the sword he has taken up, but only against
the finest talents:

GELLER

After 19 . . . KtxP

FISCHER

Skopje 1967

20 P-QR3?   . . .

The general rule in defending the King is never to touch one of
the protecting Pawns unless forced to. It was difficult to see, but
this move weakens QKt3.

20 . . .   **Q-Kt2**

21 Q-KB4   . . .

This move a move earlier would have won, according to Fischer's
ingenious analysis. The threat is R-R5, with all kinds of mating
possibilities (21 . . . P-Q4 22 Q-K5 and now Black cannot interpose
at B3 because two captures and it's mate).

21 . . .   **B-R5!**

The difference is that White's threat can be met by knocking out
the King Bishop, since the Black King can flee to B2: 22 R-R5 BxB
23 BxP+ KxB 24 Q-R6+ KxP. And because White has weakened the
support of the Bishop, 23 PxB is met by the ominous QxP.

22 Q-Kt4   **B-KB3**

23 RxB   **BxB!**

Resigns!

Black's threat of B-R7+ followed by mate cannot be met.

As the positions become increasingly complex, the player who
can make the more accurate countdown of threats and defenses has

a tremendous advantage. The following position finds Fischer defending against the typical Sicilian Pawn storm, but he has correctly calculated that a piece attack gets there first:

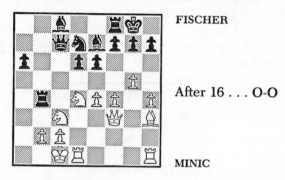

FISCHER

After 16 . . . O-O

MINIC

Zagreb 1970

17 Kt-B5   . . .

The alternative 17 KtxP PxKt 18 BxP+ K-R1 19 Kt-Q5 Q-B5 is advantageous to Black. The theme of Black's defense is (1) to attack and win the KP, thereby (2) exchanging one of the King's defenders, and then (3) to bring both Rooks to bear on the Queenside. The following sequence of moves becomes quite understandable in this light, since White can't afford to slow his own attack:

17 . . .	Kt-B4
18 KtxB+	QxKt
19 P-R5	B-Kt2
20 P-R6	BxP
21 KtxB	KtxKt
22 PxP	R-B1!

. . . and Black's attack soon broke through.

In these examples from the beginning of Fischer's career to recent games, the attack on the King is deliberate and direct. Far deadlier is often the attack that seems to spring out of nowhere, or that comes as an apostrophe to some other objective. This is where the world's great attacking players shine—in sensing a flaw in the King's armor in an otherwise calm situation. In the following chapters are choice examples of how Fischer never takes his eye off the central figure in the game. For in Russian, at least, checkmate *is* the name of the game.

10 Exposure

More Kings die from exposure than from any other cause. In the basic sense of exposure, the condition exists when the King has to leave his normal habitat and seek shelter abroad. Bobby Fischer, like Alekhine, does not like to be mated. But more than any other World Champion he has been willing to endanger his King for purely positional considerations.

First, a classic example with Fischer on the winning end:

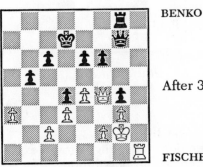

BENKO

After 32 . . . . R-Kt1

FISCHER

Bled 1959

The Black King is rather naked. All White has to do is find a way to get to him, and he does:

       33 P-R4!   **PxP**
       34 R-QKt1   **P-K4**

This attempt to batten down the hatches is just a move too late.

35 R-Kt7+   K-Q3
36 RxQ   PxQ
37 RxR   ...

A case where one wishes his Queen were *not* defended!

37 ...   P-B6+
38 K-Kt1   K-B4
39 R-Kt8!   Resigns

A nice example of the "Rook distance" and Zugzwang. Either the King or the Pawn must desert the other.

Fischer's King in the following position has no real home. In time trouble, his opponent fails to find the simple threat that could have clinched matters:

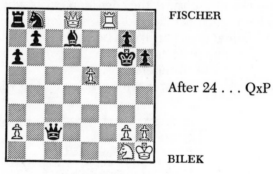

FISCHER

After 24 ... QxP

BILEK

Stockholm 1962

25 R-Kt8?   ...

A key consideration in dealing with an exposed King is how to increase one's checking possibilities. For this reason alone, 25 Q-K7 recommends itself. To avoid the disastrous check at B7, Black must play 25 ... Q-B5, when 26 R-B3! carries the deadly threat of R-Kt3+. Now the threats are over:

25 ...   Q-B7 winning

Fischer has not always been so lucky. At a special match arranged to exhibit the *Wunderkind,* former World Champion Dr. Max Euwe showed that it can be dangerous indeed to invite an enemy into the camp:

FISCHER

After 13 Kt-B4

EUWE

Match, New York 1957

13 ...	Q-Kt3
14 BxKt	BxB
15 Q-Q3	KR-Q1

Black must now run with his King, since P-Kt3 invites KtxP, etc.

16 QR-K1!	Kt-Kt5

... falling into a subtle trap. White has carefully blocked the escape at K2, as we shall see.

17 Q-R7+	K-B1

FISCHER

After 17 ... K-B1

EUWE

18 P-QR3!	KtxB

A curious twist is that White forces Black to make the move he played to Kt5 for.

19 Kt3xP!	RxKt
20 KtxR	Resigns

In the King's Indian Defense, Black typically launches a King-side attack to balance White's action on the other wing. But here

White quickly turned his attention back to the Kingside upon inspecting the windy Black King position:

FISCHER

After 18 . . . KtPxP

TAL

Bled 1959

	19 P-B4	. . .

If it can be tactically justified, this is the way to nullify a connected Pawn phalanx. Here, the tactical justification is that 19 . . . P-K5 ends any Black threats and leaves Black with a Bishop hemmed in by his own Pawns.

19 . . .	KPxP
20 QxP!	. . .

. . . going after the denuded King.

20 . . .	PxP
21 B-Q3!	PxP
22 QR-K1	Q-B3
23 R-K6!	. . .

Avoiding the specious 23 BxP+, because he still has a piece *en prise* at B3, so Black could afford to trade off. Now White won in a few moves:

23 . . .	QxKt
24 BxP+	RxB
25 QxR+	K-R1
26 R-B3!	. . .

. . . and White wins.

There is nothing essentially wrong with Black's position here, since both sides are equally developed. Yet there is a subtle weakness in Black's King position: K2 and KR3 are open to enemy invasion.

FISCHER

After 20 . . . KtxP

BENKO

Buenos Aires 1960

21 Kt-Q5!   Q-B2

The troublesome Knight cannot be taken because of the King-Knight fork on the diagonal.

22 B-R6!   . . .

And now White will simply trade off at Kt7 and win with a fork at either B7, or, in the case of R-B1, at K7.

Fischer's only losses in the World Championship preliminaries were the result of risky King positions. The chess world was stunned at the news of this early defeat at the hands of an unknown:

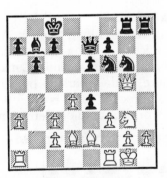

KOVACEVIC

After 18 P-B3

FISCHER

Zagreb 1970

Fischer is flirting with danger. Black's heavy artillery is lined up on the Kingside and his Queen is trying to hold back the tide with gimmicks.

18 . . .   P-K6!

This ends the gimmicks. The Queen cannot play QxP because Kt-Q4 is too fast. But if:

19 BxP   Kt-B1!

And the Queen must now desert the Kingside, allowing Kt-Q4.
Fischer soon resigned.

Pawn advances on the Kingside left Fischer with a difficult
defensive task in his first match leading to the World Championship.

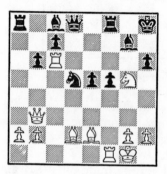

FISCHER

After 19 . . . K-R1

TAIMANOV

Match, Vancouver 1971

Taimanov flinched at this decisive moment, and played the safe
20 Kt-B3. Fischer then drove the attack off with 20 . . . B-Kt2
21 R-Kt6 Kt-B5. Instead, the Russian concert pianist could have
played *con moto:*

20 Q-KR3   . . .

. . . when the threat of RxP+ is hard to meet. After 20 . . . Kt-B3
21 B-QKt4 all White's pieces are in on the attack.

It seems that Fischer has been sensing Capablanca's "smell"
of danger more and more as the years go by. The closest he has
come to a King debâcle in recent years is the following game from
his match with former World Champion Petrosian:

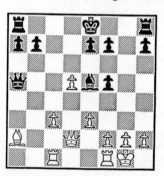

FISCHER

After 17 . . . Q-R4

PETROSIAN

Match, Buenos Aires 1971

Fischer has postponed the settlement of his King for some time. Now it is getting desperate, since the Pawn at B4 is a goner. Yet it takes *élan* on the part of the White forces to drive home the point.

18 Q-B2	P-B5
19 P-B4	PxP
20 P-B5!	...

One of those unique positions where a Pawn advance is not for the sake of queening, nor for a storming of the Kingside. It's just to loosen up the position, and shake out the enemy King.

20 ...	Q-Q7
21 Q-R4+	K-B1
22 QR-Q1	Q-K7

There's no hope in 22 ... P-K7 23 RxQ BxP+ 24 KxB PxR(Q) because White's Pawns are too fast, beginning with 25 P-Q6.

| 23 P-Q6! | Q-R4 |

So Fischer completes his famous "Queen around" maneuver to bring his Queen to the defense of the King. Here it is not enough.

| 24 P-B4 | P-K7? |

But now 24 ... B-B3 would have kept the game alive. White demonstrates it is the King he is after, the King who must now run for his life.

25 PxB	PxR(Q)
26 RxQ	QxKP
27 R-KB1!	P-B3
28 Q-Kt3	K-Kt2
29 Q-B7+	K-R3
30 PxP	P-B4
31 RxP	Q-Q5+
32 K-R1	Resigns

One had the feeling in watching this game that Fischer played the role of the matador, and prodded the reluctant bull until he had to be gored.

11 Breaking and Entering

The logic of chess dictates that a concentration of superior force decides most issues. So the *modus operandi* of the attacker is either to reduce the defenders or to marshal more pieces for the attack. In many cases, it is simply a matter of going after the King on any available open line:

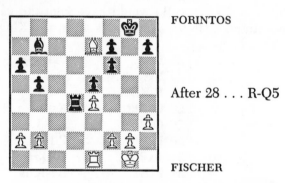

FORINTOS

After 28 ... R-Q5

FISCHER

Monaco 1967

29 R-K3! ...

This little possibility, threatening mate by R-Kt3+ and BxP+, forces Black to capture the King Pawn with his Bishop, so as to interpose at Kt3. Not a great concession, but sufficient to win the ending, whereas if Black could play 29 ... RxP the opposite-colored Bishops would ensure a draw.

The most popular attacking move in the game is Q-KR5, and it is incredible how often *masters* underestimate its force:

UNZICKER

After 46 . . . Q-Kt1

FISCHER

Leipzig 1960

47 Q-R5   **. . .**

. . . and since the RP can't be defended, all White had to calculate
was whether the advance of the Pawn to Kt6 (after QxP+, Q-R8+,
QxP) was worth the loss of the Bishop. It was.

Opening up lines of attack often requires X-ray vision: one
must be able to see through the obstructing Knights and Pawns,
and visualize what might happen if the obstructions could be
forcibly removed. The can opener in the following case happens
to be a Knight at the very focal point of the Bishop and King Rook.
Yet it seems impossible that in only four moves both Bishop and
Rook will have threatened the White King:

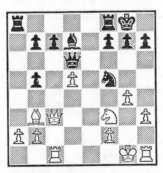

FISCHER

After 21 P-Kt4

TAL

Curaçao 1962

21 . . .   **Kt-Kt6!**

In every "sacrifice," it is always important to ask if the proffered
piece *must* be taken. Here there's no question: The Rook is attacked and the "family check" at K7 is threatened.

| 22 PxKt | QxP+ |
| 23 K-B1 | P-B4 |

Meaning to open the Bishop file for the Rook.

| 24 P-Kt5 | P-B5! |

Opening the diagonal for the Bishop. With this maneuver
Fischer was able to draw a difficult game.

When the opening of lines must be prepared by an anticipation
of the defensive reaction, the result is usually a stunning move.
Here it is obvious that P-K5 is the door opener for the attack. The
reply is equally clear, since there is only one: P-KB4. Putting two
and two together, Fischer produces a classic "defense anticipation." Not given to theoretical shop talk, Fischer would call it
simply a "shot" — and it is all of that:

BENKO

After 18 . . . PxB

FISCHER

New York 1963–64

19 R-B6!	K-Kt1
20 P-K5	P-KR3
21 Kt-K2!	. . .

Pausing in the middle of an assault on the King to attack a
piece, the Knight. The point is that if the Knight moves, Q-B5
mates. Black resigned. Coming as it did in the penultimate round
of a U.S. Championship which Fischer was to sweep 11–0, this
piquant game must have been especially sweet.

The effect of sheer concentration of force is well illustrated in
the following standard position. White's advantage consists solely
in the fact that he has been able to bring his King Rook to bear on
the enemy King:

KUPPER

After 19 . . . B-B3

FISCHER

Zurich 1959

20 BxP!	PxB
21 Q-K3	B-Kt2
22 P-B6	R-KR1
23 R-KB1!	. . .

There is no hurry to win the Bishop, since B-B1 blocks the King's escape, allowing Q-K4+. Mate soon followed.

The Black King is left to his own devices, too, in this position. All Black's major pieces are lined up for the attack that isn't there; meanwhile, White crashes through the back door:

MEDNIS

After 31 . . . PxKt

FISCHER

New York 1957–58

32 RxP!	BxP

Black tries to vacate the K2 square so that the White Rook won't join in the action with check (32 . . . KxR 33 Q-Kt4+ K-B2 etc.).

33 KtxB	KxR
34 Q-Kt4+	K-K2
35 R-KB2	R-K1

Black tries to wrap himself in his Rook, but the lineup of Queen and Rook on the seventh proves fatal (see the next chapter, "Doubling").

36 Q-Kt5+	K-Q2
37 R-B7+	K-B1
38 Q-B5+	K-Kt1
39 Q-Q7	Resigns

Again, White's forces are unable to return to their King's defense:

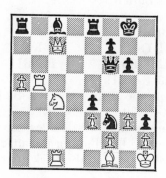

FISCHER

After 34 QxP

BISGUIER

Western Open 1963

| 34 ... | KtxP! |
| 35 KxKt | ... |

After this, Black's Queen and Bishop will swarm all over the King. A more tenacious player would have tried 35 Q-B4 QxQ 36 KtPxQ KtxB 37 RxKt B-R3 38 KR-QKt1. As Alekhine said, "I really do not like to be mated."

35 ...	QxP+
36 K-R1	B-Kt5
Resigns	

No less instructive is the following well-balanced position, where both sides have mating ideas. Fischer gets the all-important preponderance of forces, even if it is only a Pawn:

CARDOSO

After 22 . . . P-Kt5

FISCHER

Match, New York 1957

23 BxP+	. . .

It has been suggested that 23 Q-R5, threatening P-Kt6, is better, since 23 . . . P-B3 24 P-Kt6 P-R3 25 B-K3 leaves nothing in doubt.

23 . . .	KxP
24 Q-R6+	K-R1
25 P-Kt6	BPxP
26 PxP	Q-B4+

The attack lives even after 26 . . . R-B2! 27 PxR R-KB1 28 Q-K6, but it is an interesting attempt to reduce the attacking force.

27 R1-B2	Q-Kt4+
28 QxQ	BxQ
29 RxR+	RxR
30 RxR+	K-Kt2
31 PxP!	Resigns

A final grace note to a heavy-handed assault, and necessary, too, since the Knight can now finally find the time to get out of take.

Early in his career, Fischer had a special liking for a slow build-up of the attack involving a Pawn at K5 (to force the defending Knight from KB3), a fianchettoed King Bishop which later joined the attack, and a Queen at R5 or R6. The following two positions show how successful he was with this awkward-looking way to beard the King. The positions typically grow out of a French or Sicilian Defense, or even a "King's Indian with White."

IVKOV

After 16 . . . Kt-R4
P-KKt4

FISCHER

Santa Monica 1966

17 P-KKt4!　　　. . .

Alekhine once said of a similar Pawn advance of his own, "This little Pawn threatens by its further advance to set fire to the King's residence, and from that dark design it cannot be stopped."

17 . . .	**BxKt**
18 BxB	**P-Kt3**
19 Q-R6	**Kt-Q4**
20 P-B5!	. . .

Here it comes. Now, after 20 . . . R-K1, Black had no defense against PxKtP and KtxP.

One would hardly suspect the King Bishop would fly in the face of the Black Pawn phalanx and reduce it to rubble in a matter of four moves:

PANNO

After 26 . . . Q-Q1

FISCHER

Buenos Aires 1970

27 Kt-Kt5	**Kt-B1**
28 B-K4!	. . .

. . . and now there is no stopping KtxRP followed by PxP and BxKtP. The Bishop is immune because its capture would allow the Knight to find a path to KB6. Dr. Siegbert Tarrasch would have loved this performance. Partly in jest, but not without reference to positions like this, he said, "Just as Rousseau could not compose without having his cat beside him, so I cannot really play chess well without my King Bishop. Without it the game seems lifeless and empty, and I cannot devise any plan of attack."

The massing of forces against the King can result in a simple win of material—it need not be mate. A glance at the position below shows White's heavy pieces again out of action. The Rook at QKt1 is in fact nothing but a target (it is the reason why 28 P-Kt3 PxP 29 BPxP Kt-B6+ won't work, because the Knight forks Rook and Bishop with Kt-Q7).

FISCHER

After 27 . . . Kt-R5

LARSEN

Match, Denver 1971

| 28 Q-Q3 | B-B4 |

White tries to bring his troops home; Black whittles them down.

| 29 K-R1 | P-B6! |

Opening lines for the Rooks, breaking communications between the defenders, opening up squares (B6 and R6), this move is a chess player's dream.

30 Kt-Kt3	PxP+
31 K-Kt1	BxB
32 QxB	Kt-B6+
33 KxP	Kt-Q7

Resigns

The fork again—but also Black will win the KBP.

The rapidity with which Fischer (or any other good attacking player) can bring mating threats out of nowhere is one of the mysteries of chess—not just for beginners, but for masters. The Fischer-Spassky match in 1972 produced several sparkling examples, but this one has defied even two years of post-mortems.

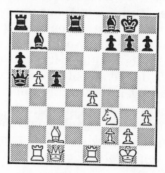

SPASSKY

After 25 . . . QxP

FISCHER

Match, Reykjavik 1972

Korchnoi and Botvinnik have both roundly criticized Black's last move (from QB6). They still believe, perhaps, that 25 . . . P-B5 would have saved the game. But 26 P-K5! would have forced QxP anyway (even after 26 . . . P-Kt3 27 R-K3), because of the threat of BxP+ winning the Queen. Then 27 Kt-Kt5 P-R3 28 KtxP KxKt 29 P-K6+ is better for White than the actual game:

> **26 B-Kt3!**   . . .

Again the King Bishop finds his niche. White's pieces converge on KB7, the traditional soft spot in the Kingside.

> **26 . . .**   PxP
> **27 Q-B4**   R-Q2
> **28 Kt-K5**   Q-B2

It would seem that Black has defended against each new attacking piece brought into action. But now a mating idea wins the exchange:

> **29 QR-Q1!**   R-K2

At this level of play mates occur only in the footnotes. The Rook is overburdened, for 29 . . . RxR allows the typical mate 30 BxP+ K-R1 31 Kt-Kt6+ PxKt 32 Q-R4 mate. Now Fischer was forced to try to win a long endgame, which he did with Black's help. Yet it is incredible that in six moves from the diagrammed position White had mating possibilities.

Considering the risks Fischer has been willing to take with his own King—and we shall see that this is a chink in his armor—it is noteworthy that he rarely succumbs to an attack on his King without at least being one move away from mate himself. In his youth, however, he learned a few lessons in the danger of allowing the King to fend for himself:

FISCHER

After 32 . . . R-KB1

OTTESON

Milwaukee 1957

33 RxB!	PxR
34 QxP+	K-Kt2
35 Q-K5+	K-B2
36 P-B4!	. . .

. . . shutting the enemy Queen out from the King's defense. Now White simply takes everything in sight.

36 . . .	R-B1
37 Kt-R6+	K-B1
38 Q-R8+	K-K2
39 QxP+	K-Q3
40 QxP+	. . .

. . . and White wins.

Fischer got a rude awakening in the following position: All White had to do was remove the Queen from the defense of the KKtP and the game was won. But how?

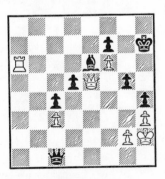

FISCHER

After 36 . . . K-R2

OLAFSSON

Bled 1959

37 R-R1!   Q-B5+

Black had to exchange Queens, and go into a lost ending, because 37 . . . QxQ 38 QxKtP forces mate in one! Also after 37 . . . Q-Q7 38 R-Q1! pursues the same idea one step further.

It was said of Capablanca that he could "smell" a dangerous position and safeguard his King before his opponent was aware of the danger. But it is less a matter of instinct or "smell" than the balance of forces. As these examples demonstrate, forced entry into the King's camp is generally a matter of having one extra piece — or Pawn — to throw into the battle.

12 Doubling

The attack on the King is aided by certain geometries of the board. When lines are opened, the horizontal force of the Rooks and Queen is able to create many mating nets. And they have a distinctive feature: The nets are easy to find, difficult to answer.

When Queen and Rook get lined up on the Knight file, for example, mate is threatened not only on that file, but on the Rook file (all other Pawns and pieces not considered). Fischer "learned" it the hard way:

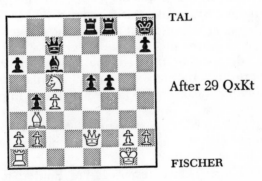

TAL

After 29 QxKt

FISCHER

Bled 1959

| 29 ... | BxP! |
| 30 KtxP | Q-R2+ |

Black forces the King to take, opening the Knight file.

109

31 KxB	R-Kt1+
32 K-R3	Q-KKt2
33 B-Q1	R-K3!
Resigns	

A third attacker is too much.

The power of doubled "linear" pieces (Rooks) is well illustrated in this spare position:

G. J. BOUMA (1966)

Mate in three

The composer of this study made a discovery as basic as the discovery of a new move in the opening. Both creative efforts have this in common: they represent a certain truth which the tides of fashion can never overcome. Middle-game combinations recur, but a position like this is unique.

The wonder of such studies is that greater strategy is often shown with fewer pieces. The sheer lack of force requires elemental ideas rather than ad hoc tactics. In order for White to mate here, in three moves, against best play, and only one way, the following ideas have to be demonstrated in practice:

1. The Black King must be restricted to a "back rank" on the first move. Hence 1 R-B7, K7, QKt3, or QKt4 must be the first move—but which one?

2. Black's defensive resources are limited to guarding either the mating square, or interposing on one of the Black squares next to the King.

3. The above defenses immediately rule out:
   a. 1 R-K7, B-R3! (guarding the mating square)
   b. 1 R-B7 B-B5! (threatening to interpose at Kt1). It is an irony of logic that the Bishop must go to that square which is *doubly* guarded. It amounts to a "time interference." The

Rook at K4 can't capture because it cannot then get to the back rank for a mate. The Rook at B7 would only lose a move (fatal in problems) by taking the time to capture.

    c. 1 R-QKt3 B-K6! The logic is the same as above, and indeed the position after 1 . . . B-K6 is a mirror image of the position after 1 . . . B-B5, taking the diagonal defined by the two Kings as a division of the board into two halves. Such repetitions of themes, even if not exact, are referred to as "echoes."

    4. Why then does 1 R-QKt4 work? Doesn't the Bishop already guard the mating square, QR3, analagously to variation 3a? Yes, but Black is in zugzwang, and must make a defensive error. 1 . . . B-Kt7 allows 2 RxB. The real point of the study surfaces with 1 . . . K-R2 2 R-QKt3! With the Rooks doubled, White has his choice of mates depending on the Bishop's position. Thus 2 . . . B-Q7 allows *only* 3 R-R3 mate, while the threat is 3 R-R4 mate. The King move has taken away the defensive square QR2, so that 2 . . . B-K6 no longer guards the Rook file.

These variations underline another "statement" that this study makes: In guarding a file, a Bishop has only three squares on which he can interpose (for whatever purpose). Many compositions have the effect of showing us what a small world the chessboard really is.

Fischer fell victim to another Kingside attack early in his career which well illustrates the power of doubling:

FISCHER

After 19 Q-Kt5

UNZICKER

Buenos Aires 1960

The threat of 20 QxRP+ is unanswerable, since Black cannot knock out both White pieces attacking his KR2, and he can't afford to bring White's QR into the game:

19 ...	KtxB+
20 RxKt	PxKt
21 QxRP+	K-Kt2
22 Q-Kt4+!	Resigns

Black will be forced to give up his Queen after 22 ... K-R2 23 R-KKt3, again because of mate threat on both files.

A Queen sacrifice at the enemy's R2 is always a possibility when Rooks are in "doubling position." The attacker must only calculate what interpositions by the defender are available. A famous illustration of this theme occurred in a blindfold "seance," as it was appropriately called, in Movieland:

BOROCHOW

After 23 ... P-K4

ALEKHINE

Hollywood 1932

24 Kt-K6!   Resigns

Alekhine comments drily in a style that has become fashionable for great players, "Not being a problem composer, I am not sure whether this actually *is* a 'problem move.' However, it is effective enough. . . ." The Knight move, in a problemist's readily understandable terms, simultaneously opens a line (guarding Kt8) and closes a line (of the Bishop, attacking the Rook), and thus threatens 25 QxRP+ followed by R-R3 mate. Does it help a player to think in terms of line openings and line closings? In a simple combination such as this, perhaps not. But I have found that a maze of variations can often be sorted out more efficiently, in the tension of a tournament game, if the rationale for each move under analysis is articulated. Too often a player laments, "I made the move I analyzed first, and rejected as a loser. But then I forgot why I had rejected it. . . ."

13 The Deadly Back Rank

My guess is that more mates are threatened, and actually occur, on the back rank than in any other general configuration. In spite of bad experiences with this simple ploy, masters and grandmasters continue to fall into trouble because of it, or actually get mated. Beginners are told to "make a hole" for their Kings at an early stage of the game. But something else always seems more pressing at the time. Fischer himself has overextended himself several times with a weak back rank, but he has been particularly cunning in exploiting this error in others.

There are many examples in this book in which back-rank problems are *hors d'oeuvres* for other combinations. Here they are the main course:

FISCHER

After 29 R-Q2

AARON

Stockholm 1962

29 . . .   **RxKt!**
        Resigns

White can interpose with Rook and Queen, but cannot avoid mate, after 30 PxKt Q-Kt8+.

At the very beginning of his astounding sweep of the U.S. Championship, Fischer allowed a neat combination based on his precariously walled-in King:

FISCHER

After 23 . . . R-Q2

MEDNIS

New York 1963–64

Fortunately, his opponent didn't see it, and neither did many commentators. As in the previous position, a Rook leaves the back rank and allows:

24 Kt-B5!   . . .

The Knight is immune because of Q-K8 mate, and the Queen is immune because 24 . . . RxQ 25 PxR R-K1 26 R-Q8 leaves Black no way to protect the Rook. Mednis lost a long endgame after:

24 Q-Kt5?   QxQ
25 KtxQ   P-B3

. . . forever ending any back-rank danger. Fischer went on to win eleven straight games.

Sometimes the back-rank weakness embarrasses the Queen because of the possibility of being pinned. Here, the result was merely a simplification which allowed Fischer's opponent to save a bad game:

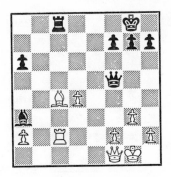

DONNER

After 29 . . . Q-KB4

FISCHER

Santa Monica 1966

Playing rather listlessly in the first half of the great Piatigorsky Cup tournament, Fischer failed to press his advantage in several winning games. Here he not only overlooks a combination that trades off Queens because of his weak back rank, but also fails to find an alternative based on his *opponent's* walled-in King:

| 30 B-Q3? | RxR! |
| 31 BxQ | R-B8 |

. . . and the players agreed to a draw because of the opposite-colored Bishops. Fischer could have kept his winning chances alive with 30 Q-Kt1, since 30 . . . RxB leaves the back rank insufficiently protected: 31 Q-Kt8+.

Incidentally, this was the second international tournament sponsored by Jacqueline and Gregor Piatigorsky, the type of patrons of the game who enriched the tradition of chess before the days when the Fischer aura created a broader base for financing tournament and match play.

"How the mighty have fallen" for weak back ranks is drastically demonstrated in this gamelet from the Interzonal tournament which launched Fischer's climb to the World Championship. His old rival Sammy Reshevsky, who owns the distinction of being the only man to have "won" a match from Fischer, misses not one but two typical back-rank ploys. (His match with Fischer, also made possible largely by the Piatigorskys, was even when Fischer withdrew over a dispute, and was technically awarded to Reshevsky.)

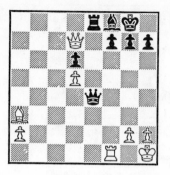

FISCHER

After 28 Q-Q7

RESHEVSKY

Palma 1970

28 ...   **Q-KB5!**

Doubly surprising, because this move also defends against the threatened QxP+ with mate to follow. As we have seen before, when a defensive move contains a threat there is a curious psychological tendency to overlook the force of the threat!

29 K-Kt1?   **...**

White should have admitted that his attack was a waste of time, and retreat his Queen to Kt5.

29 ...   **Q-Q5+**
30 K-R1   **Q-B7!**

This time there is no defending the first rank, since Q-Kt5 or R-KKt1 is crushed by 31 ... R-K8. White resigned.

Fischer was no doubt familiar with the following two classic examples of back-rank threats, as was Reshevsky. The difference is in sensing the danger when all the appearances indicate safe, calm positions:

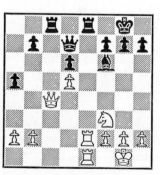

TORRE

After 19 Q-Q2

ADAMS

New Orleans 1925

All Black has to do is prevent a back-rank mate and his position is quite rosy. But that turns out to be a tall order:

20 Q-B7!!	Q-Kt4

The White Queen is protected by an invisible shield: both the Black Queen and the Black Queen Rook are needed to guard K1.

21 P-QR4	QxRP
22 R-K4!	...

A new twist: Now both the Black Queen and the Black *King* Rook must guard the back rank and hence cannot take the White Rook.

22 ...	Q-Kt4
23 QxKtP!	Resigns

The Black Queen has no squares from which she can continue to guard K1. The subtlety of such powerful pieces as the Queen and Rooks (see Chapter 7, "The Indelicate Queen") is one of the mysterious ironies of chess. Here, most players (and a computer) would probably play 36 . . . Q-Kt8+ 37 Q-B1 QxP, avoiding the trap 37 . . . R-Q8 38 R-B8 mate:

CAPABLANCA

After 36 RxR

BERNSTEIN

St. Petersburg 1914

Instead, the great Cuban forced resignation on the move with:

36 ...	Q-Kt7!

This is the only example I know of in which the Queen "forks" a Rook and the enemy Queen—in short, threatens both of them with capture when only one of them can be defended. If 37 R-B2, Q-Kt8+, or if 37 Q-Q3, Q-R8+, or finally if 37 Q-K1, QxR. For a practical game, it is about as precise and economical as any purist could ask.

IV Combinations

14 Two for One

Because chess is a game in which each player can make only one move at a time, the value of a particular move can be measured by a simple formula: Does it threaten more than can be *answered* in one move? It's a familiar situation. Wit may be defined as packing more than one meaning into ordinary words. In a tennis game, a pressing shot gives the defender a choice of a weak return or a wild gamble. In football, the defensive back must choose between covering a pass pattern or guarding against a run. In chess, of course, the situation is idealized. If there are two threats, even the average player can be expected to *execute* the one that is not defended against.

Basic though this may seem, chess players rarely give it any thought in an attempt to improve their play. They are victims of habit. They follow broad "strategic concepts," they mimic games of famous players, they search for traps and swindles. They seem to believe that combinations appear out of the blue.

A combination, in truth, can be defined as a sequence of moves resulting in an unanswerable double threat. It is not necessarily a sacrifice, or a series of moves which wins material, or a mating attack. The essential feature in any combination is that it *results* in a position which poses an unsolvable problem to your opponent.

The simplest combination on the board is the diagonal movement of the King to threaten something on both sides of the board at once. The geometry of the board is such that the King can travel just as fast from KR1 to KR7 via K4 as directly up the Rook file. This fact has made possible some startling studies by Richard Reti.

RETI (1928)

*White to play
and draw*

A glance at the board reveals that White has two potential threats: to advance his Pawn and to win the Black Pawn. Each threat separately is answered handily by Black. In case of 1 P-K7, the Bishop simply guards the queening square with B-Kt4, and gives himself up if the Pawn queens. Likewise, 1 K-B7 attacking the Black Pawn appears hopeless; the Pawn is always one move ahead. Yet White has a *combination:* With a single move he can combine an attack on the Black Pawn with an attack on the square QKt5, the Bishop's defensive post.

1 K-K7!   P-Kt4

The Pawn must run, since the White King threatens to get in its "square" (defined by the diagonal running from the Pawn to the eighth rank). It is much faster to visualize the square of a Pawn and to see if the opposing King can enter that square, than it is to count out each move by King and Pawn. It is not so obvious at this moment that the defensive post of the Bishop is irrevocably overrun by the King move, but look:

2 K-Q6   P-Kt5

Again the Pawn must advance, but now he blocks an alternate path for the Bishop to defend his King square, namely via R4. Now the double threat can be achieved in two moves:

3 P-K7   . . .

But not 3 K-B5, since the alternate defensive path of the Bishop can be opened up again with 3 . . . P-Kt6. The immediate threat forces the following sequence:

3 . . .   B-Kt4
4 K-B5!   . . .

The King is only apparently running away from the Black Pawn: he now threatens both the Bishop and to enter the square of the Pawn.

4 . . .   B-Q2
5 K-Q4

Draw

The King will approach the Black Pawn, and draw off the defending Bishop by queening the Pawn. In giving the full solution, Reti "bishoped" the Pawn in a little bit of poetic understatement. This dramatic example underlines three characteristics of a combination: (1) The first move contains inherently a double threat if each move is forced; (2) often the exact sequence of moves is critical, and must be forced by direct threats (3 P-K7); and (3) the final move poses an unanswerable double threat. When a combination is "speculative," no forced sequence exists and the first condition does not apply. The second condition is vital to a composition or study in most cases, but makes little difference to a practical player except when it is the only way to win!

If a general observation of Fischer's style can be made, it is probably that he sees more combinations inherent in moves, seizes upon them more often, and pursues them more accurately in their proper sequence of moves—than any other player alive. He plays very few speculative sacrifices (in contrast to Tal). He studiously avoids blocked positions in which the scope for combinations diminishes. He characteristically uses short, forced sequences of threats and double threats to secure even minimal advantages. He is especially adroit in the use of the Queen, pushing her to her full powers. In fact, several of his *few* losses in the major part of his career are directly attributable to his reliance on the recuperative powers of the Queen—as we shall see. Typical of his one-two punches is:

FISCHER

After 14 R-B1

RIVERA

Varna 1962

14 ...	Q-B3
15 P-B3	Q-Kt4

The mate threat after the first move allowed the Queen to put a double attack on the two Bishops, winning a piece. This simple example is no different in principle from the Reti position above: Both are double attacks preceded by a forced sequence of moves. In the following chapters we will examine Fischer's typical combinations under the usual categories: forks, skewers, destroying guards, pins, and so forth. These are useful analogies which help the student visualize what is happening. Yet even the "Zwischenzug," that "in-between move" which Fischer is so expert at, is really nothing but a double threat of a kind. In the long run, the insistence on analyzing moves *by what they threaten* will improve one's grasp of chess far faster than analogies to other games or to other mechanical phenomena (forks!).

Before going on to this delightful task—for Fischer's combinations are a joy to review—a few further points about double threats can be illustrated by two further "Reti" endgames similar to the first one in this chapter.

AFTER SARYCHEV
(1928)

*White to play
and draw*

The cast of characters is the same. The problems are pretty much the same for White: he threatens either to overtake the Black Pawn or to queen his own, but he is frustrated by (1) the fact that the Black Pawn doesn't have to move and endanger himself, and (2) the fact that the Bishop guards the queening square of his Pawn. For example, the direct approach 1 K-K6 B-B4 2 K-B5 B-B1 allows Black to hold the fort until the Black King can return to the scene. A new element of a combination enters the scene: not just how to overtake the Pawn (the King can enter its square at once), but how to disrupt *Black's* threat, the threat of creating an unassailable fortress with the Bishop at B1. The immediate queening of the White Pawn, of course, allows Black to run his own Pawn—1 P-B8(Q), B-B4+ 2 K-B7 BxQ etc. So we see that a double threat must often be set up, as in the Fischer example above, by a preliminary move which brings about the desired position. Only here it is most paradoxical:

1 K-B8! . . .

Strong medicine! In order to break up Black's defensive formation, the King not only blocks his own Pawn but also goes two moves away from the Black Pawn's square.

1 . . .	**P-Kt4**
2 K-K7	**P-Kt5**
3 K-Q6	. . .

. . . pursuing an attack against Black's Bishop's defensive post at his B4. But it seems that the Black Pawn is still too far gone.

3 . . .	**K-Kt5**
4 K-Q5	**B-B4**

. . . forced to guard the queening square. But now the White King has gained back two moves with his attack against the Bishop, and he re-enters the square of the Black Pawn!

5 K-K4
Draw!

A final example of how double attacks build up within a combination:

RETI (1928)

*White to play
and draw*

It looks hopeless! Where is the diagonal route which the King can pursue to help advance his own Pawn at QB6, and still watch three Black Pawns on the opposite wing (the Rook Pawn is enough!)? Yet the White King can parlay two double threats into an extreme time-saving combination:

1 K-Kt6 **P-R4**

Is it all over? The Rook Pawn can't be taken because then Black simply gobbles the Bishop Pawn.

2 KxP   ...

What's this? The King isn't even making progress to the Queen-side.

2 ...   **P-B4**
3 K-B6   ...

A glimmer of hope. The King now threatens to win both Pawns, and so forces one of them to move.

3 ...   **P-B5**
4 K-K6

Draw!

The White Pawn cannot be stopped from queening. All of which just goes to show that psychologically the King seems to travel more slowly across the board than down the board. Is this because all chessplayers view the board at an angle which tends to make the squares wider than they are deep?

15 Forks and Other Knives

The "fork" is the embodiment of a double threat. On the move, the defender finds two of his men—or perhaps we should say "persons"—impaled by one of the enemy. Forks are generally the final move of a combination, the point of it all. Any of the pieces can "fork," by this definition, but we consider double attacks by the King in the endgame section. When two pieces are attacked on the same line (by a Bishop, Rook, or Queen), the double attack is commonly called a "skewer," and when the King is involved as the second piece on the line, it is called a "pin." Essentially, they are all forks.

The Pawn fork occurs frequently in the opening, but it can be a threat anytime. Here Fischer tried to win a Pawn:

FISCHER

After 49 Kt-B3

BARCZA

Zurich 1959

49 ...	KtxP

The threat of a Pawn fork after 50 KxKt R-R5+ 51 K-K3 makes the Knight immune, but White upsets the idea with a sacrifice of his own:

50 KtxP+!   . . .

. . . and the game was drawn. The result was also inconclusive in the following position, but Black got the edge in the ending with a combination based on the possible Pawn fork at QB6:

SPASSKY

After 22 K-Kt2

FISCHER

Match, Reykjavik 1972

22 . . .   **RxP**
23 K-B3!   . . .

Again an active defense prevented a debacle: 23 RxR P-B6 leaves Black with the active pieces.

A battle for squares in the center in the opening stages of the game is the characteristic moment to watch out for a Pawn fork.

FISCHER

After 13 O-O

MINIC

Palma 1970

13 . . .   **KtxBP**

If the Knight is captured, 14 ... P-Q5 forks Knight and Bishop, not winning any material overall, but simply breaking up the center and mobilizing Black's game. Therefore, White chooses complications:

14 PxP	P-Q5!

Now the Pawn fork cannot be supported, but it blocks the line of the White Bishop temporarily and therefore enables Black to get both Knights into the game.

15 KtxP	KtxKP

... with a superior position for Black.

In the following position, Black is threatening KtPxP, with a discovery on the Queen. White's answer is devastating:

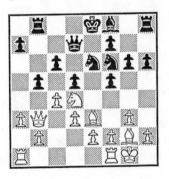

LAPIKEN

After 14 ... R-Kt1

FISCHER

Oklahoma City 1956

15 KtxQBP!	QxKt

The sacrifice must be accepted, since 15 ... KtPxP 16 KtxR! is a Zwischenzug, putting Black's Queen *en prise*.

16 PxQP	Kt-B4
17 Q-B3!	...

As an exercise in nomenclature, it is interesting to identify the strategy involved in the last two moves. Black's Kt-B4 was a Zwischenzug, attacking White's Queen. 17 BxKt QxB would have been a "comeback"—with two pieces *en prise*, one recaptures for the other. Now White's final Zwischenzug settles matters.

17 ...	Q-Q3
18 BxKt	QxB
19 QxKt	...

Black's Queen, in attempting to guard both Knights, was overloaded.

A Pawn fork typically can be speeded on its way by a single

threat against a piece, enabling the Pawn to advance without loss of time. Here Black was able to force a favorable exchange because of this possibility:

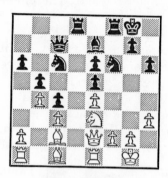

KHOLMOV

After 19 P-Kt4

FISCHER

Havana 1965

19 ...   Kt-Q5!

The Knight cannot well be taken because after 20 PxKt PxP the White Knight must move, allowing the fork P-Q6, and Black would end up with a protected passed Pawn at B5. It is interesting how many times Fischer has met unexpected trouble from doubled Pawns. In fact, there is a great difference between doubled Pawns which are exposed to attack, and those which, as here, give support and open lines.

The Knight fork has a particular magic, since it covers an unexpectedly large amount of ground—five squares on the horizontal and four squares on the diagonal. Adroit handling of the Knight is a sign of the master. Here is one of the most piquant examples of Knight wizardry:

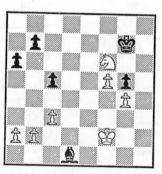

UNZICKER

After 40 ... K-Kt2

FISCHER

Siegen 1970

How can White save both the Knight and the King Knight Pawn?

41 Kt-Q7!   **P-B5**

41 . . . BxP is answered by 42 P-B6+ K-Kt1 43 P-B7+! KxP 44 Kt-K5+, forking King and Bishop.

42 K-Kt3   **Resigns**

Here a three-move combination based on a fork wipes out every White piece but the Queen:

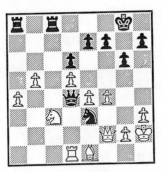

FISCHER

After 29 R-Q1

BISGUIER

New York 1960–61

29 . . .	QxKt!
30 BxQ	KtxR
31 Q-Q4	KtxB

. . . and Black wins.

The famous "family check" (King, Queen, Rook) is here shown in the rare case where the Bishop is also forked:

FISCHER

After 34 . . . BxP

TAL

Bled 1959

35 Kt-Q4!	Q-R5
36 RxB	. . .

Necessary to stop Black's mate threat. It seems that Black's KB5 is adequately protected:

36 ...	RxR
37 Kt-K6+	K-R1

Now it becomes clear: Kt1 is out because of the discovered check, and R2 is out because of KtxR+.

38 Q-Q4+	...

Now the Queen must interpose to prevent mate, when 39 RxR wins: 39 . . . QxQ 40 RxR+, etc.

Fischer had to extricate himself in the following position, where his opponent had several Knight forking possibilities:

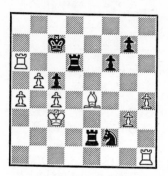

FOGUELMAN

After 38 . . . K-B2

FISCHER

Buenos Aires 1960

39 P-Kt6+	...

White's Bishop and King Rook are already forked. This move gains just enough time to survive, since the Pawn must be taken.

39 ...	RxP
40 RxR	KtxB+
41 K-Q3	KxR!

Black now has two different forks which hold his Rook. On 42 KxR, KtxP+ of course wins; but 42 R-Kt1+ K-R3 43 KxR allows the fork on the other wing. The game was drawn.

The Knight is the particular enemy of the Rook, when the Knight finds "soft" squares in the enemy camp:

SHERWIN

After 25 . . . K-B1

FISCHER

New York 1962–63

26 Kt-B5!   . . .

The threat is mate at the square K7, and it is soft indeed because none of the Black pieces can protect it. If 26 . . . R-K1, the fork occurs at Q6. Black had to resign after:

26 . . .   **RxP+**
27 K-B1   . . .

. . . because the fork at K7 will knock out the guard of the Rook after 27 . . . P-Kt3.

The Bishop fork is like a Pawn fork at long range, and of course has similarities with the Queen. Here is a textbook example:

FISCHER

After 35 Kt-B5

HEARST

League Match,
New York 1957

35 . . .   **RxP!**

. . . winning a Pawn because of 36 RxR BxKt+.
Here is a striking example of a fork of two pieces on a line, a

skewer. The black squares at Black's KB3 and QKt1 are easy prey for White's powerfully placed Queen and Queen Bishop:

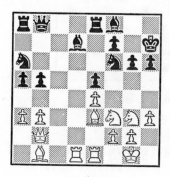

RESHEVSKY

After 25 . . . PxP

FISCHER

Sousse 1967

26 KtxP!   . . .

. . . and Black lost after a fitful struggle. Either the Rook is skewered to the Queen (after 26 . . . RxKt 27 B-B4 B-Q3 28 RxB!) or the Queen is skewered to the Knight (after 26 . . . QxKt 27 B-Q4). It should be pointed out that Reshevsky's equilibrium and tenacity were shattered in this game by a peculiar circumstance. Fischer had announced that he was leaving the tournament over a dispute, and Reshevsky waited patiently as Fischer's clock ran up to the hour mark, when he would be forfeited. At the last minute, Fischer rushed into the tournament hall, greeted his old adversary, and made his first move on time. This sudden reversal of fortunes, and the inference that Fischer had deliberately prolonged the wait, were psychological blows that Fischer could not have forgotten when he orchestrated his appearance in Reykjavik in 1972.

Fischer has always been alert to squeezing the last drop out of a position, remembering the maxim: "When you see a good move, don't make it—there could be a better one." Here he uses a Bishop fork just to achieve a better King position:

INCUTTO

After 39 . . . BxKt2

FISCHER

Mar del Plata 1960

40 B-R6!	RxR
41 BxKt+	K-R1
42 BxR	. . .

Rooks on their home squares are frequent targets of diagonal forks. Here Fischer uses it to win a Pawn:

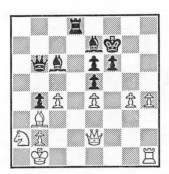

FISCHER

After 32 PxP

CARDOSO

Match, New York 1957

32 . . .	R-Q7!
33 QxR	BxP+
34 B-B2	BxR

. . . and Black wins.

Fischer was on the receiving end of the same type of fork at the U.S. Junior Championship in 1955, only here with the Queen:

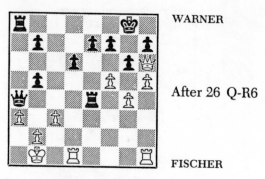

WARNER

After 26 Q-R6

FISCHER

Lincoln 1955

26 ...	R-K7
27 R-Q2	RxR
28 QxR	Q-K5+
Resigns	

The Queen, of course, has the greatest potential for forks. In Chapter 7, "The Indelicate Queen," we see how sophisticated she can be. Here are a few other examples of her broad powers:

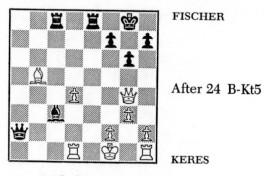

FISCHER

After 24 B-Kt5

KERES

Bled 1959

It is surprising how easy it is to overlook a fork by the wide-ranging Queen, even for such a careful tactician as Paul Keres:

24 ...	Q-Q4
25 BxR	QxR+
26 K-K2	RxB+
27 K-Q3	B-K8!

The final move, incidentally, is a good example of defense against a double attack: one defends the other. We examine this in detail in another chapter.

Another example of this clean-cut idea:

NIEVERGELT

After 16 . . . KtxP

FISCHER

Zurich 1959

17 RxP!	RxR
18 BxR+	K-R1

. . . for KxB would allow 19 Q-B4+, forking King and Bishop.

There is a geometrical quality about Queen forks, but in the following position, where Bishop and Knight forks are also illustrated, which is the most attractive maneuver?

BEACH

After 20 . . . BPxB

FISCHER

Western Open,
Milwaukee 1963

21 B-R6!	Q-B2

Avoiding the Queen fork after 21 . . . BxB 22 QxKt, when if Black tried to defend the Rooks with K-K2 he would soon be mated, and 22 . . . O-O would permit QxP+ followed by RxP.

22 Kt-Q6+!	K-Q1

. . . this time avoiding the Bishop fork after 22 . . . QxKt 23 BxB.

23 BxB	QxB
24 QxKt!	Resigns

He can't avoid the Knight fork (24 . . . QxQ 25 Kt-B7+). A re-markable demonstration of basic tactics.

Rooks occasionally fork King and Pawn or two Pawns in the ending, but their middle-game opportunities for double attacks are usually limited to what are commonly called "pins." Now a pin is nothing more than an attack on two pieces on one line. The lead piece is said to be "pinned" because it cannot move without allowing the capture of the piece behind it. When the King is the second piece on the line, the pin is of course absolute (the only absolute in chess is the imminent death of the King). The mechanism is in practice the same, for against a good tactician the loss of a piece is tantamount to the death of the King.

Here is a case of multiple pins in the middle game, in which White has just unpinned the Black Knight in order to pin the Black Bishop:

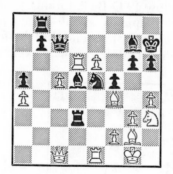

FISCHER

After 32 R-Q6!

WEXLER

Buenos Aires 1960

The threat is 33 RxB or 33 BxB. In the ensuing blood bath, Black comes out short:

32 . . .	BxB
33 RxR	BxKt

The Knight is pinned to the Queen by the mere fact that more of Black's pieces are *en prise* after 33 . . . KtxR 34 BxQ KtxQ 35 BxR.

| 34 BxKt | . . . |

. . . and White wins. Black cannot play BxB because of the final Rook fork, 35 R-Q7+, winning the Queen.

The common pin on the King file is decisive in many a game. Here Fischer gives it an unusual twist—a Queen fork for support:

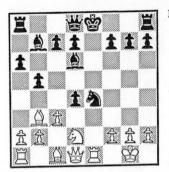

BISGUIER

After 11 Kt-Q2

FISCHER

Buenos Aires 1970

11 ...	BxP+

Black must gamble on an attack, since supporting the Knight by P-KB4 would seriously weaken his Kingside after 12 Q-R5+. 12 P-B3 in such positions must be looked at carefully because of the possible replies BxP+ and Q-R5.

12 K-B1!	...

Now there is no saving the Knight, as 12 . . . P-KB4 allows the Queen fork 13 Q-R5+.

Finally a basic example of how the King is prone in the endgame to forks when a key piece is caught behind him on a check:

KLING & HORWITZ
(1851)

White to play
and win

This position has been attributed to others, with the White Queen at QKt3, but it is so fundamental that Lucena might have discovered it:

1 Q-Kt4!	...

The idea behind this will soon become clear: Wherever the Black Queen goes on the diagonal, the White Queen will check in such a way as to force the Queen to the Knight file, i.e.:

1 ...	Q-R8
2 Q-R3+	K-Kt3
3 Q-Kt2+	K-R3

If 3 ... K-B2, then the same idea occurs: 4 Q-R2+! QxQ 5 P-Kt8(Q)+ followed by QxQ. If the King moves away, the White King breaks the pin.

4 Q-R2+	K-Kt3
5 Q-Kt1+!	QxQ
6 P-Kt8(Q)+	...

The winning fork, which could also be 6 P-Kt8(R)+. This is a beautiful elaboration of the simplest Rook fork of all, which occurs in this fundamental ending:

AFTER TROITZKY
(1896)

*Black to play and
draw. Reverse
Kings: White to
play and win*

With Black on the move, he must prevent the obvious threat of a Rook check, followed by P-R8(Q). The only move is:

| 1 ... | K-Kt2! |

If 1 ... K-K2, then 2 R-R8, and the Pawn cannot be taken because of the Rook fork 3 R-R7+. An amusing twist to this position is that if the Kings change positions, Black is lost even if he has the move, but for a curious reason. (I have adapted this from a Troitzky study.)

| 1 K-K5 | ... |

The threat is R-B8+. The Black King tries to hide behind the White King:

1 ...	K-K6
2 K-Q5	K-Q6
3 K-B5	K-B6
4 R-QB8!	...

A King and Rook battery!

| 4 ... | RxP |
| 5 K-Kt6+ | |

... and White wins.

16 Discovery

There is no mystery about it: A piece which opens a line (of a Rook, Bishop, Queen, or even Pawn) is capable by that very fact of making a double or triple threat. The "battery" piece gains new lines of attack (or defense, as we shall see). The "masking" piece can then choose whatever is its optimum square.

Line openings and line closings, which involve such things as pins, half-pins, focal points, checks, and cross checks, are the most powerful moves in chess. F. Vaux Wilson, a tireless advocate of reason in chess composition, has devised a score for the activity involved in each chess move. His question always is: What does it *do*? It is not surprising that discoveries "do more" than any other general type of move, and so score more in his "Method of Evaluation," or MOE, which has now been accepted as the best approximation of the relative force of individual moves.

Although line openings (which we will hereafter refer to generally as "discoveries") are essentially two moves in one, their effects are often not appreciated for what they are:

DI CAMILLO

After 39 . . . K-Kt2

FISCHER

Washington, D.C. 1956

40 B-B7! . . .

141

Forced, since there is no other way to defend the QP. But Fischer had to foresee this move much earlier in advancing his Pawn to this precarious position. Now, after a check by the Knight, Black must resign, since the check on the back rank cannot be stopped. The move itself, however, is not "brilliant" in depth or imagination. It is simply logical. The opening of the King file promises the win of the Queen. The only defense against this maneuver is to capture the Queen Pawn. So White places the Bishop on the only square which shields the Pawn from capture. QED.

The power of the discovery is naturally felt most strongly when the King is the object of attack. In the following composed ending, the Knight has no immediate win of material in sight, but he can threaten a series of checks, leading to mate or win of the Rook, by choosing the right first move:

KUBBEL (1912)

White to play

| 1 Kt-B8+! | K-K1 |

After 1 . . . K-B1 the King is driven to the wall: 2 R-B1+ K-Kt1 3 Kt-Q7+ K-R2 4 R-R1 mate.

| 2 Kt-K6 | R-Kt1 |

The Rook is lost if it goes to R2, and the King is mated if it goes to B2 (3 R-Q8+). But here the Rook fatally blocks a flight square for the King, and allows the same maneuver as in the note above.

3 Kt-B7+	K-B2
4 R-B1+	K-Kt2
5 Kt-K6+	K-R3
6 R-R1 mate	

Obviously, K6 was the key square for the Knight, but he couldn't reach it via B5, for that would block the Bishop file for the Rook.

Fischer's finest combinations have occurred against a King who has dallied too long in the center. As in his famous "Game of the Century" vs. Donald Byrne (see below), here in a U.S. Championship game he uses one discovery to set up a battery against the King, and the second discovery to reach a winning endgame:

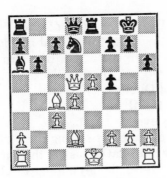

FISCHER

After 15 BxBP

SAIDY

New York 1965–66

15 ...   KtxP!

The Knight, incidentally, guards his KB2, a trivial but necessary consideration. In discovering on the enemy Queen, the Knight cannot be captured, because 16 PxKt QxQ 17 BxQ RxP+ wins back the piece.

16 QxQ	KtxB+!
17 QxR+	RxR+
18 K-Q1	KtxB
19 KxKt	R-K7+
20 K-B1	RxBP

The remarkable part of this combination is that Black arrives at an ending the exchange down. But the ending was won by Fischer with relative ease, because of the helpless state of the White Rooks and King.

A Knight can commonly open two lines, a double discovery so to speak. This was the justification for Fischer's last move:

FISCHER

After 18 ... B-R3

DAMJANOVIC

Buenos Aires 1970

White cannot reply 19 BxB because of KtxKP+. If there were only one discovery, on the King, this would not be fatal, since the Bishop or Queen could interpose at K3. But here the White Rook has also been "discovered on" by the Black Rook, and would be lost after an exchange of Queens. Therefore:

> **19 P-B4!**   . . .

. . . and the game was even.

A player often has the choice of setting up a battery, or simply moving the piece that would have masked the battery. The difference is considerable. Here, for example, Fischer could have avoided the threatened loss of material by playing 35 RxB followed by Q-R3, but it is not clear how he could have won. Instead, he set up a battery against the King which left his Rook the option of several damaging moves:

BOLBOCHAN

After 34 . . . PxP

FISCHER

Stockholm 1962

> **35 Q-QKt3!**   **RxKt**
> **36 R-K5+!**   . . .

A problem-like move, which earned Fischer the Brilliancy Prize. To defend the Rook, Black will run into a mate:

> **36 . . .**   **K-B1**
> **37 RxR+**   **Resigns**

Fischer could have announced a mate in three: 37 . . . KxR 38 Q-K6+ K-B1 39 Q-B8+ B-Q1 40 QxB mate. It is no longer the fashion to announce mates. But as recently as the historic game Capablanca-Marshall, New York 1918, in which Marshall introduced the gambit named after him in the Ruy Lopez, Capa announced a mate in six!

As the board becomes cleared of Pawns and pieces, a discovery against the King has awesome potential for picking up scattered and undefended material. A model for a Bishop-Rook battery is the following clear-cut study:

BIANCHETTI (1925)

White to play

1 B-Kt2	**...**

A player would make this move instinctively, yet it is not clear yet that the Black Rook is lost. The Rook must stay close to the King, or be swept up by the battery (1 ... R-B8+ 2 R-Q1+, for example). But the Rook can't go to either B2 or KKt3 because he would fatally block the King (1 ... R-B2 2 R-KR4+ K-Kt1 3 R-R8 mate). So he must try B1 or R3:

1 ...	**R-B1**
2 R-Q7+	**K-Kt1**
3 R-Kt7+	**K-R1**

Now what? The Rook can always be protected by the King.

4 K-R2!	**...**

The only move, since K-Kt1 allows 4 ... R-B8+. But now the Rook must move away from its haven, and will be won by the battery.

Even the lowly Pawn can mask a dangerous battery, especially as it threatens to queen after discovering. Fischer missed this possibility in the following exhibition game immediately after the Siegen Olympiad:

ANDERSSON

After 33 . . . Kt-K3

FISCHER

Siegen 1970

Fischer played 34 B-K5 and won easily enough, but elegant was:

34 RxKt!	PxR
35 R-Kt7	Q-B1
36 QxKt!!	RxQ
37 P-B7	. . .

The double check at Kt8 is fatal, as is 37 . . . QxR 38 P-B8(Q) mate. The famous Queen sacrifice that Fischer did *not* miss (which we have referred to several times) hinged on a common Bishop-Knight battery. It usually occurs with the King at Kt1, but its distinctive feature here is the same: The Knight can check endlessly either to gain time or to pick up material along the way, sometimes to mate.

FISCHER

After 17 K-B1

D. BYRNE

New York 1956

17 . . .	B-K3!

Like many brilliant moves, this is practically forced, since both Queen and Knight are under attack and 17 . . . Kt-Kt4 18 BxP+ KxB 19 Q-Kt3+ B-K3 20 Kt-Kt5+ is hardly appetizing. So the exclamation mark really belongs at several earlier moves where this possibility had to be foreseen. Another important feature of a Queen sacrifice should be mentioned here too. Because Black can take a perpetual check any time he wants if his Queen is taken, he keeps the draw "in hand." He can then decide, after grabbing all the material he can, whether he can play for a win. Many a spectacular combination is essayed with very little risk, and all the glory if it should work.

| 18 BxQ | ... |

A delightful point of the Bishop move is that if 18 BxB, Q-Kt4+ leads to the famous "smothered mate": 19 K-Kt1 Kt-K7+ 20 K-B1 Kt-Kt6+ 21 K-Kt1 Q-B8+! 22 RxQ Kt-K7 mate.

18 ...	BxB+
19 K-Kt1	Kt-K7+
20 K-B1	KtxP+

This wins a Pawn, but more important opens the long diagonal so the Knight will have a home at B6.

21 K-Kt1	Kt-K7+
22 K-B1	Kt-B6+
23 K-Kt1	PxB

Deciding to go for the win, which occurred on the 41st move. Incidentally, the recapture of the Bishop has the important feature of being a discovery on the Queen, thus gaining time to capture the Rook.

The Knight discovery on the King is often so powerful that heavy sacrifices can be made to set it up:

FISCHER

After 24 . . . Q-Kt4

SOBEL

Montreal 1956

Here Fischer finds himself on the wrong end of the gun:

24 P-KR4!	QxP
25 R-R1	Q-Kt4
26 RxP+!	K-B1

Taking the Rook would allow 27 KtxKt+ followed by Kt-K4+, winning the Queen. Fischer hopes for 27 KtxKt, when R-Q7+ would win White's Queen, but White now wins a piece the safe way:

27 QxKt	Resigns

Often there is a choice of capturing with check, or setting up a battery and eschewing check. This happens frequently at the square KB2 against a castled King, when either Rook or Bishop can capture there. The discovery is usually more damaging. A complicated example of this fact was overlooked by Fischer's opponent in the following position:

FISCHER

After 26 . . . PxKt

PARMA

Bled 1961

Here Parma cashed his check, 27 QxP+, but after K-Q1 28 RxR+ K-B2 Fischer's King escaped and the game was eventually drawn. The battery would have set up mating possibilities:

27 BxP!	R-KR1

If 27 . . . RxR 28 B-K6+ followed by QxB mate or Q-B7 mate. The Rook move is the standard defensive resource against a battery: Attack the battery piece.

28 Q-Kt7!	K-Q1

The battery piece can no longer be attacked, since the masking piece would capture it.

29 QxR+	K-B2
30 QxP	. . .

. . . and White has his pieces in play.

Batteries are naturally a favorite device in problem composition, since they compress so much action into a few moves. When line closings must also be reckoned with, the effects of battery play can be quite startling. Here is one of the most elegant two-movers ever composed:

ELLERMAN (1925)

Mate in two

1 R-Q7!   . . .

It is not surprising the Rook should move, to threaten 2 Q-B4 mate by relieving the Queen of the duty of guarding Q3. But this exact square is dictated by the variation:

1 . . .   **Q-KB7**

2 Kt-Q8 mate

The Knight must have a square to go to, once the Queen releases the pin. B5 and Q6 are out, because they give the Black King flights at K4 and Q5 respectively. These Knight mates occur when Black defends with the "self-blocks" 1 . . . Q-K4 and 1 . . . Q-Q5.

Another problem theme which can be quite useful to the practical player, as we shall see below, is the cross check—a discovery which simultaneously checks the enemy King and blocks a check on your own. Of the thousands of examples from problem lore, this is perhaps the clearest:

G. F. ANDERSON (1915)

Mate in two

1 K-Q6!   . . .

Discoveries abound: The King "discovers" the Queen, threatening 2 Q-Kt7 mate. If the Rook checks at Kt3 or Q6, he interferes with the guard of the Bishop on the battery piece—in effect, an "anti-discovery"—allowing 2 B-K6 and 2 B-Q5 mate, respectively.

It is clear from the preceding examples that a defense against a battery consists either in pinning the masking piece or attacking the battery "firing" piece, but only in such a way that the masking piece cannot in turn "shut off" or capture the attacker. Here Fischer turned a game completely around with an anti-battery move:

FAUBER

After 26 . . . Kt-B7

FISCHER

Milwaukee 1957

27 Kt-B4!   R-Q7

Only a double check can be safely used when the firing piece is under attack, and here 27 . . . Kt-Kt5++ 28 K-R3 leaves two pieces in take.

28 K-Kt1   . . .

. . . forcing Black to "discover" the White Rook.

28 . . .	Kt-Kt5
29 Kt-K6+	K-R1
30 KRxP	Resigns

In time pressure, the variety of discoveries, shut-offs, and cross checks that are possible are often difficult to calculate. Such was the case here:

FISCHER

After 34 K-R1

D. BYRNE

Cleveland 1957

White's last move has allowed a typical time-pressure "shot":

34 ...	P-B6
35 PxP	KtxKBP
36 R-Q1?	...

Attacking the firing piece, but Black has a shut-off. Even after the better 36 BxB+ KxB White must be wary of possible cross checks: 37 Q-B3+ Kt-Q5+ 38 K-Kt1 K-R3 39 B-B4 Kt-B6+ 40 K-R1 is relatively safe, but not 37 BxKt RxB 38 Q-Kt2+ R-B6+! 39 K-Kt1 Q-Q5+ etc.

36 ...	Kt-Q5+
37 R-B3	RxR
38 RxKt	RxP+

... and Black won in a few moves.

Sometimes the King can blithely walk away from a discovered check, because the masking piece simply has no targets. Here the array of force on the Queenside is impotent, since after any check the White King would simply run to K2 and KB1.

BENKO

After 30 ... K-R1

FISCHER

Curaçao 1962

In contrast, the White attack is aided by a forceful opening of the Knight file:

31 QxP+!   Resigns

It's mate next move.

An attack on the battery firing piece is usually met by simply moving the piece until it can no longer be attacked. Problem composers have shown how humorous the continued chase of the battery piece can be:

J. BREUER (1955)

Mate in four

1 B-B3!   . . .

One would automatically assume that 1 B-R8 would do the trick. But when Black has the artful defense 1 . . . R-R7 (not 1 . . . P-B4, for White mates in three, starting 2 R-Kt3+) 2 R-Kt3+ R-Kt2 3 RxR and now 3 . . . P-B4, forcing White to make one more move.

1 . . .   R-B4
2 B-R8!   R-B7

The Rook has blocked the Bishop Pawn from moving, and has only this defense left—to interpose at Kt7. But this move has also blocked the King (as in the Bianchetti study above), allowing:

3 R-R2++   KxB
4 R-R1 mate.

The idea contained in the defensive try above—interposing the Black Rook at the focal point of the Rook and Bishop, White's KKt2—can also be an attacking weapon:

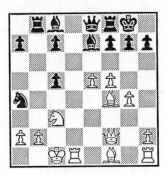

GERMAN

After 20 . . . Kt-R5

FISCHER

Stockholm 1962

21 B-QKt5!   . . .

This is the focal point of the Queen and Rook. In effect, by moving a piece where White is perpetrating an "anti-discovery" or interference (the usual problem term) on the Queen.

21 . . .	**RxB**
22 KtxKt	**R-Kt5**
23 Kt-B3	. . .

What has White accomplished with his little combination? He has removed one of his opponent's attacking pieces, gained time in clearing his back rank, and can now proceed with his Pawn-roller attack. This little combination is as exciting as any sacrifice.

Fischer has given us many examples of how the King can often ignore a battery aimed at him, as long as the King has safe squares to flee to:

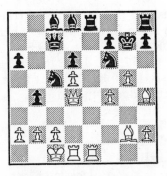

FISCHER

After 20 P-Kt5

BERNSTEIN

New York 1957–58

20 . . .	**B-B4!**

The King will have a haven at R3 as long as the White KBP can be blocked. Now also the threat of Kt-Kt6+ followed by mate forces a liquidation of heavy pieces.

21 PxKt+	K-R3
22 Q-B4	Kt-Q2
23 QxQ	BxQ
24 B-B3	B-Q1!

The thorn will be removed from his side, because the following battery play holds no terrors:

| 25 B-Kt5+ | K-Kt3 |
| 26 R-Kt1 | BxKBP! |

Against the same player, and in another U.S. Championship, Fischer again defused a battery bomb:

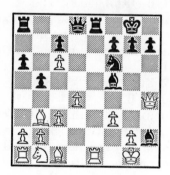

BERNSTEIN

After 15 . . . BxP+

FISCHER

New York 1959–60

| 16 KxB | Kt-Kt5+ |

Here the battery-masking piece checks, threatening the White Queen by discovery. But the King can protect her:

| 17 K-Kt3 | QxQ+ |

Black had to calculate 17 . . . RxR 18 QxQ+ RxQ 19 B-Q2! virtually forcing 19 . . . RxKt 20 RxR BxR 21 PxKt, when the threat of B-KB4 gives White the edge. Otherwise, 17 . . . RxR would gain a valuable tempo over the game:

18 KxQ	RxR
19 PxKt	RxB
20 PxB	R-Q1

. . . with an even game, which Black later lost.

A more complex discovery on the Queen was here answered by the same tactic, to no avail:

FISCHER

After 14 R-B1

LOMBARDY

New York 1960–61

14 ...	Kt-Kt5!
15 KtxKt	QxR+
16 BxQ	BxQ
17 Kt-Q5	B-R5+!

This interpolation leaves Black the exchange up after 18 P-Kt3
BxB. A discovery leading to another discovery (as in the Saidy-
Fischer game above) can occur with pieces as targets just as well
as with the King as the prize:

BERLINER

After 29 . . . P-B5

FISCHER

New York 1962–63

30 P-B6!	QxP
31 KtxP	. . .

A discovery on the Queen, and a second battery set up.

31 ...	QxP
32 Kt-R5+	. . .

Now a discovery on the Rook, winning the exchange.

32 ...	K-R1
33 QxQ	. . .

Black had a mate threat.

33 ...	BxQ
34 RxR, etc.	

Simple discoveries against minor pieces often have the purpose of forcing a favorable exchange, rather than winning material:

SHERWIN

After 15 . . . Q-Kt1

FISCHER

New York 1957–58

16 Kt-Q5!	PxKt
17 RxB	PxP
18 PxP	Q-Kt4

Black cannot play KtxP because of the fork after 19 R-Kt6 and 20 B-Q5, so White remains with a superior endgame. The following discovery has an equally simple idea behind it, *simplification*.

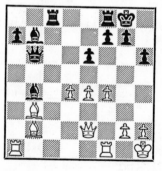

FISCHER

After 21 . . . BxKtP

PETROSIAN

Match, Buenos Aires 1971

22 P-Q5	B-B6!
23 BxB	RxB
24 B-B2	. . .

White's pieces are forced from their attacking positions, because 24 B-R2 is answered by PxP 25 PxP R-R6.

It is not always easy to visualize the results of line openings, even at the grandmaster level. The reason is probably that we are accustomed to inspect a discovery only as an attacking weapon. But it is not uncommon for line openings to have very subtle effects. Here are two good examples where Fischer missed his way:

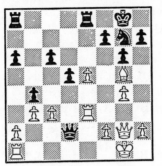

LARSEN

After 28 . . . P-Kt5

FISCHER

Santa Monica 1966

In the heat of battle Fischer has a hallucination. His battery of Rook and Bishop cannot attack the Queen; rather, it is the Rook that is under attack (29 PxP P-Q5 wins a piece). The only adequate defense is 29 P-B3 PxP 30 QxQ PxQ 31 R-Q1. Instead:

29 Q-R3?	PxP
30 Q-R6	Kt-K3
Resigns	

Only now does Fischer see that the intended 31 B-B6 P-Q5 32 QxP+ KxQ 33 R-R3+ does not mate because the Rook opens the line of defense for the Queen, and Black has 33 . . . Q-R3.

We have seen that the masking piece in a battery is generally immune from capture when it moves, if the battery attacks something else more valuable. This simple fact is the basis for the following combination, which Fischer (and just about everybody else) missed:

FISCHER

After 34 R-R2

PETROSIAN

Match, Buenos Aires 1971

	34 . . .	R-QB1?

Almost universally accorded an exclamation point—yet it doesn't win against correct defense! Black had an obvious advantage throughout the early part of the game, and here he could force the advance of the Queen Pawn by the use of a battery:

	34 . . .	R-Kt8+

(instead of 34 . . . R-QB1).

	35 K-Kt2	R-QB8

The point is that the QP can now advance to Q7 as long as the White Rook remains at QB7, when KtxP won't work because the Bishop is immune after BxKt. And if the Rook leaves the QB file after P-Q6, then R-B7 forces matters. Therefore, White must try to complicate life:

36 R-B6+	K-K2
37 R-B7+	K-K1

Studiously avoiding the Queen file, where he would be in check after the advance of the Pawn to Q7 and the capture there.

38 RxP	R-R4

And now the Queen Pawn cannot be stopped. Incidentally, the corollary to many effective battery openings, as here, is a little device which might be called a "comeback." In the above line, after the continuation

39 R-QB7	P-Q6
40 P-R4	P-Q7
41 KtxP	BxKt
42 RxR	BxR

. . . Black's last move wins a piece by coming back from an *en prise* situation to recapture. In the final position of the Sobel-Fischer game above, White's Queen and Knight were similarly defended, though both were *en prise*. This common type of combination is only one or two moves long, yet seems to be the hardest for the student to see. It is worth pointing out where it occurs on the following pages.

17 Destroying the Guard

To capture a piece which defends another piece is by definition a double attack. It is perhaps the most direct, the most understandable form of a chess combination. Its motif could be stated in a dozen other ways, but "destroying the guard" is obvious.

There is nothing peculiar to Fischer's style in this. But he has shown some fascinating variations on the main theme, which is illustrated here in simplest form:

FISCHER

After 24 K-R1

BERLINER

Western Open, 1963

24 ...	B-R3!

Here the *threat* to destroy the guard of White's KB3 is sufficient to win . . . a single Pawn.

25 Q-B2	BxB
26 QxB	QxP4.

159

Now a slight twist: A pin enables White to pick up his material—again with only a Pawn to show for the entire combination:

MECKING

After 18 . . . RxP

FISCHER

Palma 1970

	19 QxP+!	QxQ
	20 RxR	. . .

. . . and White gains a winning edge.

Here there are two guards on the White Bishop at Kt5. After eight consecutive captures Black emerges with a Pawn:

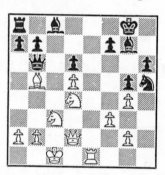

FISCHER

After 21 RxR

YEPEZ

Havana 1966

	21 . . .	BxP!

This preliminary is necessary because White would otherwise have a deadly check at K8 after the following captures:

	22 PxB	BxKt
	23 PxKt	BxKt
	24 QxB	QxB, etc.

A smorgasbord of combinational themes occurs in this game from the U.S. Championship, but it is all initiated by the attack at the base of the Pawn chain. (Chess manuals never fail to point out that Pawn chains should be attacked at their base—a form of guard destruction.)

FISCHER

After 19 Q-Kt2

KRAMER

New York 1957–58

19 . . .	KtxBP!
20 QxKt	KtxP!
21 Q-Kt4	Kt-K7+
22 K-R1	

. . . and Black won.

This neat sequence illustrates pins, Zwischenzugs, and finally the threat of a skewer, which prevented 22 K-B2 RxB! 23 QxR B-Q5+.

When the piece which destroys a guard also is immune from capture and threatens something additional, a triple threat occurs, as here:

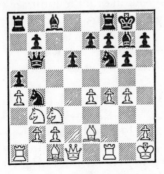

KORCHNOI

After 13 P-Kt4

FISCHER

Curaçao 1962

| 13 . . . | BxP! |

Quite a surprise for Bobby, who expected to break with P-B5 or P-Kt5 against any defense but this.

    14 BxB   **KtxB**
    15 QxKt   **KtxP!**

... attacking the Knight and the Rook simultaneously. The exclamation point is for seeing that the King Rook is loose after 16 Q-Q1 QxKt 17 R-R3 Q-B5! Black won handily.

In the same tournament Fischer missed an opportunity to pick up a Pawn immediately because he didn't see a one-move guard destruction:

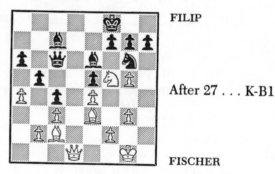

FILIP

After 27 ... K-B1

FISCHER

Curaçao 1962

Fischer now tried 28 Q-R1 in order to infiltrate on the Queenside, but he could have won in a hurry by going in just the opposite direction:

    28 Q-R5!   **K-Kt1**

Otherwise White will tear up the Kingside.

    29 QxKt!   **...**

The guard on Black's K2 is destroyed, permitting White to win a piece after 29 ... RPxQ 30 Kt-K7+, winning back the Queen.

A concept closely related to guard destruction is the "overloaded piece." A piece which must perform two duties will, in effect, have his guard dropped on the second duty when he is required to exercise his first duty. Often positions which seem to be massively overprotected are, on analysis, just one move shy of being able to hold everything:

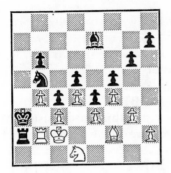

FISCHER

After 47 R-Kt2

ACEVEDO

Siegen 1970

48 ...	KtxBP!
49 KxKt	...

The Knight cannot recapture because it must also guard the Rook.

50 ...	R-R8!

Now the King would be overloaded if he tried to protect the Knight with 51 K-B2 (51 . . . RxKt), and the Rook cannot protect the Knight because of BxP+. So White resigns. In the initial position, the squares Kt2, Kt4, and B3 are all twice protected, but they fall one by one.

When guard destruction is the end point of a combination, it is particularly surprising, even to grandmasters. The following sortie was "seen" by the Northwestern 3.5 computer program (see Chapter 35, "Compute!"), but was underestimated by Larsen:

FISCHER

After 35 P-Kt4

LARSEN

Match, Denver 1971

35 ...	R-QR1

The strength of this move is masked by the apparent intention of attacking the RP. In reality, it attacks the Rook at Kt5!

36 PxP	PxP
37 B-B4	. . .

The Black Rook is not embarrassed for moves, but Fischer has a characteristically sharper idea:

37 . . .	R-R5!
38 R-QB1?	. . .

Even the computer saw that this was a waste of time. The Bishop will now be forced to capture Black's Rook.

38 . . .	BxP!
39 BxR	RxP+

Finally, the Rook at Kt5 is undermined.

40 K-Kt2	KxR

. . . and Black won.

18 Zwischenzug

This funny-looking, funny-sounding word (to those who speak only English) is also much misunderstood. The average player knows it means "in-between move," yet he also thinks of it, I'm afraid, as a rare ploy that occurs at the crucial moment of a combination, or as an unusual twist in the normal sequence of a game. In reality, the Zwischenzug, which I shall refer to as ZZ for short, is at the very heart of chess. And the abundance of games in which Fischer has employed it is ample evidence of its importance.

Fischer's surprise moves are rarely the speculative sacrifice of a piece, the long-winded redeployment of a Knight, or the bizarre and mysterious Rook move. Typically, he gets exclamation marks for ignoring threats when everybody else sees only the threats, or for delaying a recapture when it would leap to the mind of a master. This is the essence of the ZZ: it denies the expected, "knee-jerk" reply.

In "knee-jerk" chess, if your opponent captures a Pawn, you first see if you can recapture it. If your Queen is threatened, you first see where you can move it. If a mate is threatened, even in three or four moves, you meet the threat. Fischer is light-years ahead of the average player in this single respect: His nature seems to question the stimulus-response mechanism automatically.

One way of putting this is that the best defense is often a counterattack. But "counterattack" usually means a long-range plan of action. Here we are talking about thrust and parry; the ZZ makes its point in a single move. Every student of the game is familiar with the fulminations of theorists about space and force and mobility; about converting a spatial advantage into a material advantage. All of this makes sense, but far more basic is the concept of double threats. The ZZ is what it is because it essentially carries a double threat with it.

Take this clean little example:

FINEGOLD

After 47 B-K8

FISCHER

Western Open, 1963

White's advantage consists in King position, space, and having a specific target for attack, the King Pawn. Black, in fact, is hard-pressed for a move, and must threaten the Bishop in order to find a move that doesn't give the house away:

>   47 ...   K-K2
>   48 K-K5!   ...

But the King enters anyway. The double threat inherent in this move is (1) the attack on the Bishop, and (2) the intrusion of the King if the game reverts to a normal sequence of moves.

>   48 ...   B-Kt5
>   49 B-Kt6!   ...

Certainly not difficult to find, but again illustrating a ZZ: instead of the "expected" move by the Bishop to some safe square, which would allow the defense of the Pawn by B-B6, the Bishop makes a second attack, and the double threat against RP and KP wins handily.

The essential feature in a ZZ is to threaten something more valuable than whatever of your own is threatened. (It is more difficult to find a ZZ in which you threaten something only of *equal* value. Of this, more later.) A threat of mate on the move is, of course, the ultimate threat, and so it offers undeniable opportunities for ZZing. Fischer was hoist by his own petard in this double ZZ:

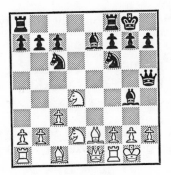

R. BYRNE

After 11 . . . B-Kt5

FISCHER

New York 1965–66

12 KtxKt?   . . .

Seemingly a move that requires a "knee-jerk" answer, since KtxB+ cannot be allowed. However:

12 . . .   **B-Q3!**
13 P-KR3   **BxB!**

The second ZZ. The Knight is allowed to escape, but Black will win the exchange. Essentially the same theme brought Fischer a sparkling win with a *two-move* mate threat:

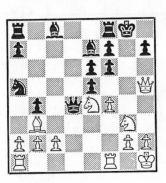

BENKO

After 17 Q-R5

FISCHER

Bled 1959

17 . . .   **KtxB?**
18 Q-R6!   . . .

Only the Black Queen can defend the threatened mate at Kt2 after 19 Kt-R5, since Kt-B6+ cannot be allowed:

18 . . .   **PxP**
19 Kt-R5   **P-B4**
20 QR-Q1!   . . .

Another little ZZ: The Rook is brought to safety before Fischer cashes his big check at B6.

20 . . .	Q-K4
21 Kt4-B6+	BxKt
22 KtxB+	QxKt
23 QxQ	. . .

. . . and White wins.

Sometimes the threat in a ZZ is only a device to gain time—time to remove a piece from a potential "skewer," for example:

LARSEN

After 18 . . . P-Q4

FISCHER

Match, Denver 1971

19 R-Kt3!	. . .

The threat of RxP+ followed by RxP+ (discovered) would win both Bishops, so it allows White time to get the Rook off a white square and to recover the Pawn:

19 . . .	P-KKt3
20 BxP	B-Q3?

Not satisfied with opposite-colored Bishops, Larsen gambles for more in view of the 4–0 score against him in the match.

21 RxB	BxR
22 R-K7	B-Q3
23 RxKtP	. . .

. . . and White has a winning edge.

Next to a mate threat, the possibility of interposing a mere check is quite common—if only to gain a Pawn. Trying to save the Pawn, many a player has lost his head:

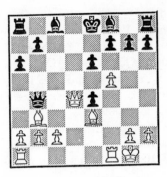

DELY

After 13 . . . Q-Kt5

FISCHER

Skopje 1967

| 14 PxP | BxP |

He cannot exchange Queens here or on the next move because the interpolation of a Pawn check or a Bishop check would, in the first case, win two Pawns, and in the second case win a piece.

| 15 BxB | PxB |
| 16 RxB+! | . . . |

A third ZZ forces the Black Queen out of action and allows the following murderous check:

| 16 . . . | QxR |
| 17 Q-R4+ | Resigns |

The Black King will be caught in the center after 17 . . . P-Kt4 18 QxKP and a check at either B6 or K6.

The in-between check is a frequent trick of the Knight, either to gain material or to improve the position of the Knight. The chess world was aghast when Spassky fell for one of the common garden varieties of this ploy in the eighth game of his championship match with Fischer:

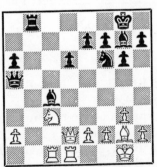

SPASSKY

After 19 KR-Q1

FISCHER

Match, Reykjavik 1972

White's last sets up the trap by protecting his Queen. Imagine Fischer's surprise when the World Champion played:

19 ...	Kt-Q2?	
20 Kt-Q5!	QxQ	

The usual way of backing out of the trap is Q-Q1, guarding the Pawn. But the Knight move also exposed the Queen Bishop to attack.

21 KtxP+	K-B1
22 RxQ	KxKt
23 RxB	...

... and Fischer won easily.

The identical idea, with a slightly different cast of characters, allowed Fischer to win a crucial last-round game against his "cousin" Arthur Bisguier. A draw would have meant a tie for the U.S. Championship between the two. Fischer lost the first game he ever played with Bisguier, and since then has drawn one and won thirteen!

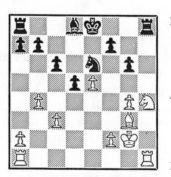

BISGUIER

After 23 . . . B-Q1

FISCHER

New York 1962–63

24 Kt-B5!	RxR
25 Kt-Q6+	...

The ZZ check allows the Knight to take up a commanding post, which was sufficient to win the ending.

An interpolation of a Rook check is somewhat less common than a Knight check, and therefore usually more surprising:

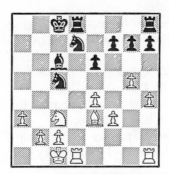

NAJDORF

After 18 . . . BxQ

FISCHER

Leipzig 1960

19 P-Kt4	Kt-R5
20 R-Q6!	. . .

The Black Knight at R5 is now hanging, since KtxKt is answered by the ZZ 21 RxB+. White is now able to win two pieces for the Rook, leaving him the exchange down for several Pawns.

20 . . .	K-B2
21 RxB+	KxR
22 KtxKt	. . .

Fischer failed to win the difficult ending.

Next in sequence as a likely candidate for ZZ attacks (after a mate threat or a check) is the Queen. Here Fischer was able to break out of a cramped position and trade off his "bad" Bishop because of the threat of an intermediary attack on the Queen:

FISCHER

After 20 QxKt

EVANS

New York 1965–66

20 . . .	P-B4!

The backward Pawn would successfully trade himself off after 21 BxB PxQP, so White must allow a disruption of his Kingside Pawns.

21 QPxP	BxB
22 PxB	. . .

. . . and Black also had an excellent post for his Knight at Q4, with White having the "bad" Bishop.

The same idea allowed Spassky to break up Fischer's Kingside in their first game at the second Piatigorsky Cup:

FISCHER

After 19 . . . Q-B2

SPASSKY

Santa Monica 1966

20 P-Q5!	PxKP

If 20 . . . PxQP, then of course White wins the KBP and has all the open lines.

21 PxP!	. . .

The first ZZ. White would otherwise lose the QP.

21 . . .	QxP
22 P-B5!	. . .

The second interpolation, while the Bishop hangs.

22 . . .	Q-B2

Black cannot afford the opening of the Knight file with 22 . . . PxP 23 KtxP! since the Bishop is still immune because Q-Kt3+ would win the Queen or mate. White went on to win a fine Bishop vs. Knight ending.

The Rook teams up well with the Queen in carrying off a ZZ. In the space of a few days at the chess Olympics, Fischer was both the victim and the beneficiary of this powerful maneuver. When a player's Queen is attacked, he almost instinctively looks for a square to move her to. But if he can afford a simplification, he can extricate himself without loss of time by in turn attacking his opponent's Queen. In the following position, Fischer was admittedly gambling in a bad situation, but it looks as if he finally has some kind of an attack:

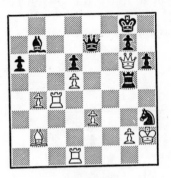

FISCHER

After 31 . . . R-Kt4

GLIGORIC

Leipzig 1960

32 R-K4!   . . .

But now Black must exchange Queens in view of 33 R-K8+ if the Black Queen moves, and so the game was soon over. Slightly more subtle was Fischer's Pawn grab below, made possible by a *quid pro quo* attack on the Queen:

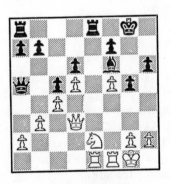

FISCHER

After 19 . . . Q-R4

SZABO

Leipzig 1960

20 R-B1?   QxP
21 R-B2   . . .

. . . hoping now to gain time for Kt-Kt3 and Kt-R5, with a Kingside attack. But Fischer keeps his Queen active, or forces an endgame, with:

21 . . .   R-K6!

Psychologically, the advantage is always on the side of the player who sees these relatively simple counterattacks. When the average player attacks the Queen, he says something like this to himself: "Well, he's got to move the Queen before he does anything else, and then I'll . . ." A superficially sound position can collapse in a matter of moves when a simple ZZ is overlooked:

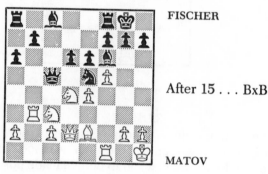

FISCHER

After 15 . . . BxB

MATOV

Vinkovci 1968

16 Kt-R4?   Kt-B5!

All of a sudden White's pieces are hopelessly *en prise* after any continuation: (1) If Queens are traded, the Black Knight forks the Rooks; (2) if 17 BxKt, QxB attacks both Knights and the King Rook; and (3) if the White Queen moves, QxKt forces an exchange at the end of which P-QKt4 forks two White pieces.

In recent years a Fischer trademark has been his willingness to place his Queen in apparent danger, relying on counterattacks to justify his daring. He was himself the victim of such a maneuver at the same Olympics mentioned above, and against an "unknown" in the preliminaries. In a standard Sicilian deployment, the first board for Ecuador "developed" his Queen at the very center of the board, where most masters would suspect she would lead a short life.

MUNOZ

After 16 . . . Q-K4

FISCHER

Leipzig 1960

Here Fischer calculated that the obvious 17 B-B4 Q-K3 18 Kt-Q4 KtxKP! was a saving ZZ, and the more subtle 17 P-B4 Q-K3 (or even 17 . . . KtxKP! 18 PxQ KtxKt+ 19 BxKt BxKtP) 18 P-B5 Q-K4 19 B-B4 QxKt! 20 PxQ KtxKP allowed Black a dangerous attack. So a Pawn race ensued, in which a typical ZZ again played a crucial role:

17	P-KR4	KR-B1
18	B-B4	Q-K3
19	P-R5	P-QKt4
20	PxP	BPxP
21	B-R6	B-R1
22	P-K5	P-Kt5!

When opposing Knights are fighting for squares in the center, typically the QKt at QB3 opposing the KKt at KB3, this sort of *quid pro quo* always has to be considered. A similar situation occurs commonly in King Pawn openings when White has his King Bishop at QB4, and plays P-K5, attacking the Black King Knight at KB3. White must always consider the rejoinder P-Q4 by Black. In any case, Black was able to get to the enemy King faster in this game by not having to answer 22 P-K5 directly.

A decade later, Fischer made the same risky-looking move Q-K4 on the Black side of a Sicilian Defense against Larsen, and again its soundness was based on the possibility of similar thrust and parry:

FISCHER

After 17 P-QKt4

LARSEN

Match, Denver 1971

17 ...	Q-K4!

It is obvious that the Queen is in no immediate danger of being trapped by 18 B-B4 because of KtxP, but what if White protects the KP?

18 QR-K1	B-B3!

Black proceeds to show that he will win the Pawn, in spite of the ominous lineup of White forces. A key consideration in a ZZ, as here, is that after Black is forced to play KtxP he does not have to worry about the White Queen moving to a safe square, since the White Queen Knight is under double attack by the Queen and Knight.

19 B-B4	KtxP
20 KtxKt	QxKt
21 B-Q3	...

... and this is the best White can do in "discovering," since he is jammed up by his own pieces. Otherwise, White would not have to allow the Black Queen either Q4 or the QBP. Fischer later managed to win this game with a late-hour swindle (see Chapter 35, "Compute!").

Playing fast and loose with the Queens can get one into trouble in a variety of ways other than by being trapped. When both Queens are *en prise*, a player must take into account the possibility of the one on the move becoming a "desperado," that is, selling her life as dearly as possible. It is indeed conceivable even for World Champions to overlook one-move combinations when the Queens are in heavy traffic:

FISCHER

After 17 P-K5

BOTVINNIK

Varna 1962

This epic encounter, the ending of which is discussed under "The Indelicate Queen" and "The Rook Distance," began rather humorously when the above position was arrived at in short order. It seems that Botvinnik had only to remember a variation he had prepared for his return match with Vassily Smyslov, and he reports ruefully that "at last everything was in order—on the board was the familiar position; then suddenly it was obvious that in my analysis I had missed what Fischer had found with the greatest of ease at the board." Fischer reports, "When I made this move, I felt sure he had overlooked it."

17 ...   QxBP!

The Queen becomes a desperado, instead of seeking refuge at KB4 or KR5, where Botvinnik had expected to harass her.

18 BxQ   ...

Both Queens could try to sell themselves dearly, but the difference is that the Black Queen would then have ZZ targets. E.g., if 18 QxKt, Q-K5 19 P-B3 Q-R5+! (or he could play Q-Kt5+ first—the idea is to decoy the White Bishop one way or the other) 20 B-B2 Q-Kt5+ and now the Black Queen is safe, and PxQ follows. Fischer impishly suggests 21 ... RPxQ! "(toward the center)."

18 ...   KtxQ

... and Black remained a Pawn up. This display of fireworks will remain a classic of Queen ZZs, on both sides, for as long as chess is played.

There is no routine way to foresee when a ZZ will come in handy; most likely, it is a matter of being in the right frame of mind for avoiding "knee-jerk" moves. Fischer's wily opponent in the following position, for example, foresaw that the vulnerable state of

Black's Rooks allowed him to force open diagonals to attack the Queen:

FISCHER

After 24 P-B5

JAUREGUI

Santiago 1959

24 ...   P-Q4

Naturally avoiding 24 ... QPxP 25 BxP and the Queen will be trapped by P-K5 and Kt-Kt5, in the right order. But White has a way to renew the threat of a Bishop attack:

25 P-B6!   PxBP

Black cannot trade Queens because on 25 ... QxQ White would interpolate PxR—a clear-cut example of the double threat inherent in a ZZ: White would threaten the Queen and would threaten *to* queen.

26 B-B5   P-QR4

Fischer tries to squirm out with a ZZ of his own, but White simply plays 27 Q-Kt3 and wins. 27 QxP would allow the further ZZ 27 ... R-R2.

Removing one's Queen from attack, as above, is what might be called an "anti-ZZ" and it can be especially effective when it contains an attack of its own:

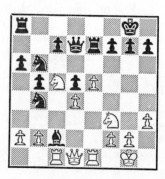

RESHEVSKY

After 19 ... BxB

FISCHER

Santa Monica 1966

20 Q-Q2!   . . .

Thus White is able to regain a full piece with a commanding position. This game, incidentally, was the beginning of a rousing comeback in the second half of the Piatigorsky Cup tournament, in which Fischer almost nipped Spassky at the wire.

A lowly Pawn move can often turn a game around as easily as a Queen ZZ. Typically, it is a matter of fighting for squares in the center. Here Fischer not only avoided a time-wasting retreat with his Bishop, but also opened the game to his advantage:

PORTISCH

After 14 . . . P-B5

FISCHER

Havana 1966

15 P-K5!   . . .

It is tit for tat as far as material is concerned whether Black now plays 15 . . . BxP or 15 . . . PxB.

"You first" is what Fischer says in the following game, in order to reserve his choice of squares for the Knight until after the Bishop moves:

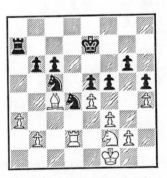

FISCHER

After 33 . . . P-B4

LARSEN

Monaco 1967

34 P-QKt4   **P-QKt4!**

In the simplest of positions, such ripostes are often the difference between an even position and a dead-lost game. Below, it appears that Black's Bishop has a choice between bad and terrible. 15 . . . B-K5 16 P-B3 actually loses the Bishop, and 15 . . . B-K3 allows a fork at QB2 which shatters Black's Pawns:

FISCHER

After 15 P-Kt4

PETROSIAN

Belgrade 1970

15 . . .	P-QR3!

Again the saving idea of "you first." In the openings, this little twist can mean that extra stitch in time that merely preserves the initiative. (Remember, "initiative" is nothing more than the ability to make threats that must be answered.)

MAROVIC

After 12 . . . P-K4

FISCHER

Zagreb 1970

Black has just made his break in the center. However, he is one move behind in development, and the center is subject to attack:

13 Kt-K3!   Kt-Kt3

The ZZ 14 KtxP precludes 13 . . . P-K5, so Black loses more time defending. White now gained a positional edge with 14 PxP KtxP 15 B-B4. Fischer's games are full of these nuances. In the following position from an important round of the 1970 Interzonal, he seized the first opportunity to avoid the "knee-jerk" move, PxP, and instead left this Pawn hanging for eight consecutive moves while he built up threats eventually leading to the discomfiture of the White King:

FISCHER

After 13 PxP

SMYSLOV

Palma 1970

| 13 . . . | Q-B3! |
| 14 Kt-B4 | Kt-B6! |

The momentum continues. The Queen is now attacked, and moving it will do little good: 15 Q-B1 KtxKt 16 KxKt QR-B1! with threats on the Bishop file.

| 15 KtxKt | QxKt+ |
| 16 K-B1 | KR-Q1 |

The series of ZZs goes on.

17 Q-B1	BxKt+
18 PxB	Q-Q6+
19 K-Kt1	QR-B1
20 PxP	PxP

. . . and although a Pawn down Black has a winning edge in his command of the open lines.

Finally, an example which shows that the ZZ can be as spectacular as a Queen sacrifice—because it *is* one:

SCHWEBER

After 22 . . . P-K5

FISCHER

Buenos Aires 1970

23 RxP!	QxQ
24 RxKt!!	. . .

The beautiful point: White can afford to interpolate this move because the Black Queen cannot find a safe square (24 . . . Q-B2 25 B-B4). She gives herself up on the only square where she gets the Rook in return, but White's two Bishops and the advanced Pawn proved to be more than enough compensation for the exchange. This combination is all the more surprising because it had to be foreseen several moves earlier when 22 . . . P-K5 became a possible Black threat. This entire conception, with its understatement, limited objective, and use of quiet threats, is in my opinion as pleasing as anything Fischer has created.

24 . . .	Q-Kt5
25 RxQ	BxR
27 BxKtP and won	

19 For the Defense

One of the first two books published in the English language was ostensibly on chess, *The Game and Playe of the Chesse*, William Caxton, 1475, and in the half-millennium since then more books have been turned out on the royal game than on any other subject. In all this literature, however, very little has been written on the defense against combinations and attacks. Grandmasters win most of their games against weaker opposition by finding the flaw in faulty combinations, by grabbing Pawns and warding off the attack that is supposed to result, and by reaping the positional fruits from an overextended attack. Fischer habitually beats *grandmasters* with such tactics.

Since the end result of any combination is a double attack, a successful defense consists in what might be called a double defense. A few examples will make this evident:

FISCHER

After 19 . . . Kt-R4

GLIGORIC

Palma 1970

183

                      20 Kt-Kt5   . . .
With this move White launches an ingenious combination, the
point of which is that after 20 . . . PxKt (practically forced in view
of the Knight forks at B7 and Q6) 21 BxP, White has the double
threat 22 BxR or 22 B-B3, trapping the Black Queen. But there is
a flaw:

              20 . . .   **PxKt**
              21 BxQKtP   **Q-K4!**
One attacked piece defends the other—the key idea in a double
defense. Fischer now wins two pieces for the Rook, since White
has nothing better than BxR.

The same opponent had a hallucination of an even more basic
type against Fischer, after obtaining a superior game up to this
point:

FISCHER

After 41 . . . P-Kt4

GLIGORIC

Monaco 1967

              42 BxP   **PxB**
              43 KtxP   . . .
Now both the Queen and the Queen Rook Pawn are threatened,
but the reply is simple enough:
              43 . . .   **Q-Q3**
. . . and Black guards both.

When two pieces are attacked at once, another form of defense
is for one of them to move making a threat of its own. Here a Russian grandmaster and contender for the World Championship
overlooks this one-move resource:

FISCHER

After 31 . . . KtxB

KORCHNOI

Curaçao 1962

32 R-QB1 . . .

Instead of the expected 32 PxKt, White seeks to win the piece without loss of the advanced Pawn. Note that the pin is a double attack, here on the Knight and the Queen.

32 . . . **Q-R2!**

The Queen moves out of the line of attack and attacks the enemy Queen. Note that the Black Queen is protected by a "comeback":

33 QxQ **KtxQ**

. . . and Black remains a piece up. The "comeback" is discussed more fully on page 158.

All Zwischenzugs are forms of defense, in the sense that they answer an attack by counterattack. Here are several ideas:

FISCHER

After 25 . . . RxP

JOHANNESSEN

Havana 1966

26 Kt-B4 . . .

Not only threatening 27 KtxP+ but apparently breaking the threat on the long diagonal with a "comeback" (26 . . . QxB+ 27 KtxQ).

26 . . .   **RxKt!**
                Resigns

Now 27 BxQ RxQ 28 BxB RxP! and the threat of 29 RxP+, winning the Queen Bishop, leaves Black the exchange or several
Pawns up. This might also be called an "anti-discovery" maneuver,
where the battery is defused by taking the battery mask. The following complex combination could have gone the wrong way for
Fischer if his opponent had seen a similar way to unmask a battery:

FISCHER

After 23 . . . B-R3

BENKO

New York 1966–67

Here Benko played 24 R-K1, and after 24 . . . KR-QB1! 25 KtxR
R-B7! the threatened discovery was sufficient compensation for
being a whole Rook down. The immediate threat is B-B6+, winning the KB. White had to play 26 RxB, and eventually Fischer won
the Knight and the game. But White could have won with:

24 KtxKR	BxR
25 Kt-B7	BxP
26 R-QKt1	R-QB1
27 Kt-Q5	R-B7
28 Kt-K3!	. . .

The attack on the battery *firing* piece takes out all its sting.

When an attack seems to be brewing, the rapid centralization of
the pieces can often be the only antidote. In several games, Fischer
has turned the tables with a redeployment of his Queen:

OLAFSSON

After 19 . . . P-K4

FISCHER

Stockholm 1962

20 Q-Kt5!   **. . .**

Retreating the Bishop would allow Black time for an advance of the Kingside Pawns. White's Queen now circles the board.

20 . . .   **P-QR3**

Protecting the Knight by 20 . . . KR-Q1 allows a further centralization: 21 Q-Q5, KR-B1 22 RxP!

21 QxKt   **PxB**

22 Q-B5!   **. . .**

The most basic winning device of all, which is also defensive: simplifying when you're ahead. White won the ending easily.

The answer to a Zwischenzug is to see it coming . . . and avoid it. Here Fischer does just this, even though the win of a piece looks tempting:

TAL

After 18 . . . RxP+

FISCHER

Leipzig 1960

The simple move 19 KxB looks so obvious Fischer had to give it a second look. It would threaten the Rook, regain the piece, and Black's Queen would still be *en prise*. But then would come the beautiful Zwischenzug 19 . . . RxP! 20 KtxQ RxQ and *White* would now have a double threat staring him in the face (KxKt or R-R8+). Therefore:

19 K-R1!	Q-K4
20 RxB	QxKt
21 KxR	Q-Kt5+

. . . with a perpetual check.

This game, incidentally, was the first of three of Fischer's "memorable games," on November 1, 2, and 3 — an eventful time!

Fischer has always taken considerable risks with his King, if in so doing he can win material. Here he thwarts a Kingside attack by getting three pieces for his Queen:

FISCHER

After 15 P-B3

PEREZ

Leipzig 1960

15 . . .	PxB!
16 PxP	B-Q3
17 Q-K1	Kt-K1
18 Q-R4	K-B1
19 Kt-B5	PxKt!
20 QR-K1	Q-K3!

. . . and Fischer won the ending.

One way of defending against a fork is to protect one of the attacked pieces by the other. Another way is to "fall" into the combination and show that it is just a way of simplifying the game:

GHITESCU

After 27 . . . P-K5

FISCHER

Leipzig 1960

28 RxP!   . . .

Fischer grabs the Pawn and proves it is the easiest way to win the endgame; after 28 . . . B-B3 one Rook defends the other (29 R7-K7) and the Rook ending is won easily enough.

An esoteric defensive stratagem was taught to Fischer in a famous game which has offered lessons for various sections of this book.

FISCHER

After 26 Q-K6

KERES

Curaçao 1962

26 . . .   **Kt-Q4?**

This allows a fine restrictive maneuver, which saves a middle-game catastrophe for White. Keres is able to keep the Black heavy pieces out of the game by bringing his Bishop to QB6. Fischer could have settled matters with 26 . . . Kt-B4, when the White pieces would be pinned down because of the threat of Kt-Kt6, e.g. 27 Kt-R2 B-K6+ 28 K-R1 Kt-Kt6 mate.

        27 Kt-R2!   **Kt-K6**
        28 B-B6!   . . .

In spite of Fischer's still-considerable advantage, Keres was able to hold his head above water to reach the following position, in which he again showed how to shield himself against the Queen:

FISCHER

After 56 Kt-B1

KERES

Curaçao 1962

Every book or article on Paul Morphy dwells on his "brilliance," his understanding of the importance of development, and his opening sharpness. Fischer is the first to put his finger on his greatest strength over his contemporaries: his accuracy. In this position, Fischer is hard on himself for missing the accurate line 56 . . . RxP; the idea is that R-R8 later will win an important tempo since Black would have to protect his Knight. As Fischer says, "Patzer sees a check, gives a check."

56 . . .	R-R6+
57 K-Kt1	RxP
58 P-Q5	P-Kt6
59 B-Q7!	. . .

This brilliant defensive move is now possible because R-R8 no longer gains a tempo, allowing the Rook to get to the KB file (if the White King were at R1, then R-R8 forces K-Kt2, and after R-R7+ and Q-B3 the Rook gets to KB7). The idea of the Bishop move is to block the Black Queen with B-B5, so that the QP can advance without allowing a Queen check at QB4. Complicated but logical, and it works!

59 . . .	R-R8
60 B-B5!	Q-B3

. . . with an eventual draw (see Chapter 7, "The Indelicate Queen," for the finish).

In the following interesting position, the Knight performs a similar shielding function in defending the Queenside Pawns, and it could have done even more:

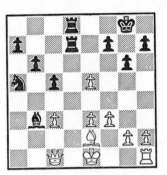

FISCHER

After 30 Q-B1

MECKING

Buenos Aires 1970

Fischer had made one of his rare speculative sacrifices to arrive at this apparent impasse. White cannot make headway against the Queenside because of the Knight at R4, and Fischer chooses to take a draw with 30 . . . B-B5 31 Q-B2 B-Kt6, repeating the position. The idea is that Black apparently cannot force an exchange which will allow his Rooks to penetrate. But there is a way:

30 ...	Kt-B5!	
31 Q-Kt1	Kt-Q7!	
32 Q-B1	B-B5	
33 Q-R3	...	

If 33 Q-B2, analogous to the game continuation, BxB forces the King to retake (the Knight masks the Queen from K2), when 34 . . . Kt-B5 would force an incursion by the Rook to Q7, with a win.

33 ...	BxB
34 KxB	Kt-B5

. . . and the Queen cannot afford to wander off without losing the Rook. A Fischer "might-have-been."

V *Ideas*

20 Nothing but Thinking

Chess without ideas is lifeless and, worse, unenjoyable. When a player becomes bored with chess, he is probably at a plateau of competence. The first move he sees usually turns out to be the move he makes. He feels he has mastered all the combinations, has a grasp of opening and endgame theory, but becomes impatient with the subtleties of position play and doesn't feel it is worth the time to try to extract something extra out of every position. The most damning criticism that can be made of such a player is that "he doesn't have any ideas." Fischer has often used this very characterization.

It is the ideas behind a chess position that are most difficult to define for a computer. Tactics are not ideas: They are the execution of ideas. An idea in this context is the consideration and weighing against each other of various tactical possibilities. In the following chapters we will consider such broad categories as the weighing of piece play against Pawn play, the value of space as against the possibility of becoming overextended, the material advantage of Pawn-grabbing against the loss of time, and so forth.

In this introduction I would like to indicate how the ideas behind Fischer's play can be just as concrete and demonstrable as a two-move combination. The reason why he chooses certain ways of handling a position can be stated in one sentence, rather than in a long list of variations. For example:

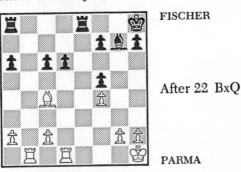

FISCHER

After 22 BxQ

PARMA

Zagreb 1970

Fischer has come out of the opening with a Pawn, but a quick inspection of the position seems to show that White has a draw or even more. His Rooks and Bishop enjoy open lines. The Bishop attacks two weak Pawns. The Bishops are opposite-colored, and there are no weak dark squares in the White camp. Most players on the Black side would now play 22 . . . P-Q4, "saving" the Queen Pawn and attacking the Bishop. Fischer's reaction is: Trying to hold everything won't work; I've got to create counterplay to keep the game alive:

22 . . .	R-K5!
23 BxBP	R-KB1!

. . . forcing the Bishop to choose diagonals. 24 B-Kt3 would block the Queen Knight file. Therefore:

24 B-R5	RxP

All of a sudden, the Queen Pawn is defended by the dangerous counterthreat of R-R5 followed by B-K4, when the KRP would fall. Even though Black's Queenside Pawns look hopelessly doomed, Black was able to win this game by Kingside threats.

What this game shows is the value of that intangible quality *initiative*. When things get complicated, the assessment of initiative can help guide the play better than a static positional evaluation.

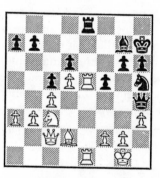

FISCHER

After 24 RxR

UHLMANN

Siegen 1970

24 . . .	BxR
25 Kt-Kt5!	P-R3

Fischer forces the following melee, basing his decision on the *idea* that he can get to the White King before he loses too much material.

26 KtxP!	B-Q5
27 KtxR	QxP+
28 K-R2	Kt-B5
29 BxKt!	QxR!

. . . but not QxQ, because the attack on the King is then over, and 30 P-Q6 would quickly decide the issue. Now White must give up the Knight to stave off the attack.

30 Q-B1	QxKt

. . . and although the game was difficult, it was eventually drawn.

The issue is clearly drawn in the following three positions, where counting material is not as important as counting tempi. In all three cases, the curious psychological impact of a *forced* defense is also illustrated:

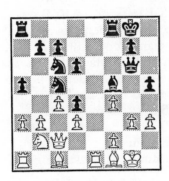

FISCHER

After 18 B-B1

SAIDY

League Match,
New York 1969

Black is fully developed, in return for the sacrificed Pawn. The simple idea Fischer had to consider is that White's only play consists in relieving the pressure on his Q3 by driving the Knight at Black's QB4 away. It will take two moves to play B-Q2 and P-QKt4. So Black has time to prevent that maneuver with:

18 ...	R-R3
19 B-Q2	R-Kt3!
20 BxP	RxP

. . . and Black won with continued Queenside pressure. Since Black's unusual development of the Rook was a forced defense, it had additional impact when White realized it was also an attacking idea.

Here, too, Fischer with Black must defend, against Q-B7:

FISCHER

After 18 Q-B4

TRINGOV

Havana 1965

18 . . .	Kt-QB3!
19 Q-B7	Q-B4+
20 K-R1	Kt-B3

Since this is the only move which prevents mate on the move, it is hard to give it an exclamation point. The idea is that if a piece must be returned to ward off the attack, this way is better than going into an ending (as was standard practice before this game) with 18 . . . QxP 19 QxQ KtxQ 20 BxB. Black regains the initiative:

21 BxB	KtxP
22 Q-K6	Kt4-Kt5!
Resigns	

Black threatens mate himself now starting with Kt-B7+, as well as RxB.

Fischer rarely speculates merely on the looseness of a position or on the difficulty of defense. When he sacrifices a piece, he visualizes concrete attacking possibilities. In the following position from a U.S. Championship, he again is seemingly forced to make the sacrifice, leaving his opponent with the feeling that he (Black) was calling the shots:

SAIDY

After 24 . . . P-K4

FISCHER

New York 1966–67

25 BxKRP! . . .

If the Knight had to retreat, Black could afford P-R5, or even P-Q4, when White's Kingside becomes very breezy.

25 . . .	KtxB
26 RxKt	PxKt
27 BxP	. . .

Now Fischer has two Pawns for the piece, but also absolute control over the Black squares on the Kingside. The threat of R-R6 gave White a winning game.

One of the rare times Fischer did speculate on a Kingside attack, without a definite objective, the defense carried:

DONNER

After 23 . . . Q-R2

FISCHER

Varna 1962

24 KtxP+	PxKt
25 R-Q4	P-KB4!

Black was able to hold on for the win: White simply does not have a preponderance of force on the Kingside.

Where Fischer does gamble is in allowing a menacing Pawn advance in the hope (or expectation) that the Pawns will become weak and will be an endgame liability. He has been smothered several times trying to win such positions, or to prove the idea a success:

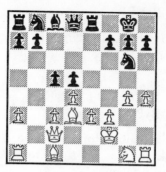

FISCHER

After 13 B-Q3

GHEORGHIU

Havana 1966

13 ...	Kt-B3
14 Kt-K2	B-K3
15 P-Kt5!	...

This game speaks volumes about the psychological pressures in master chess that have little to do with the "objective" situation on the board. Gheorghiu here offered Fischer a draw. This was the penultimate round in the Olympics, and Fischer held a clear lead over Petrosian for top honors at first board. A draw would have practically assured him of this important achievement at this point in his career, when he was out to prove himself against the Russians. Fischer also has shown a fine sense of honor at the chessboard: He does not accept draws when the position is obviously undecided. He declined the offer, and went on to lose the game and the first board prize by a quarter of a percentage point! The advance P-R5 and P-Kt6 broke up the Kingside and allowed White to win tactically in the center. Did Fischer really believe he had a superior or even equal position, or was he too stubborn to see that White's command of space was not a hollow shell? A curious footnote to the game is that Gheorghiu took only fifty-five minutes for the entire fifty moves, probably because he expected Fischer to play peacefully. This fact also had its effect; as players usually do in such circumstances, Fischer rushed his moves too.

A similarly overoptimistic appraisal of his King's safety almost cost Fischer the following game, in which he was willing to gamble that he could open lines on his opponent's King more quickly than vice versa:

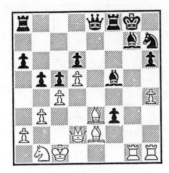

FISCHER

After 25 . . . KPxP

OLAFSSON

Zurich 1959

White now played 26 BxRP and Fischer went on to win another of his "memorable" games with the necessary defense 26 . . . R-R2. But White could have won a Pawn with the simple combination:

26 RxB+	KxR
27 BxP+	K-R1
28 BxR	. . .

. . . and now the Bishop at B8 must be retaken because of the mate threat on the long diagonal after 28 . . . PxB 29 BxP. There are several ideas behind this sequence. First, the matter of timing. Since White would not have wanted to block the position with 26 P-B4, Black should have taken the time to play 25 . . . R-R2, and then 26 . . . KPxP, arriving at the game continuation by a transposition of moves. Second, there is the old precept that the opening of a position usually favors the better developed party. 25 . . . R-R2 would have completed Black's development at a time when White could do little to improve the position of his pieces. Finally, there is the question of *counting*. When several pieces are *en prise*, the players must literally count the captures until a "quiescent" position, as the computer programmers call it, is reached. Here, for example, it is important to see that White's Queen Bishop can "eat" another Pawn after 28 . . . PxB or 28 . . . QxB.

Counting moves is quite common in the endgame, but is just as important in the heat of a combination. Here Black has three pieces attacking the Knight Pawn and White has three defenders:

FISCHER

After 30 P-B3

MEDNIS

New York 1959–60

30 ...	B-B8!
31 R-Kt2	...

Black brings a fourth to bear on Kt2, and so does White. But now the Rook at KKt2 is overloaded, having to defend the Knight as well as QKt2:

31 ...	RxP+!
32 RxR	BxR

Now the Bishop cannot be taken because after all the pieces are off the board Black has a won ending, even though a Pawn down. The passed, protected KP ties the White King down while the Black King goes after the Rook Pawns. Even then, it must be counted carefully, because White can play P-QR4 and threaten to play his King to R3, then Kt4, winning the QBP; after K-R3 Black would have to advance his King Pawn, but by that stage the Black King will have won the lead Rook Pawn and the Bishop Pawn just in time.

Counting the pieces *en prise* is the basis for this typical Fischer combination, which simply regains a Pawn with the better endgame:

FISCHER

After 17 Q-Q4

SZABO

Buenos Aires 1970

17 . . .   KtxQP!

The White Queen is overloaded, and so cannot take the Knight. And on 18 QxQ, PxQ the Pawn attacks the Rook, so again the Knight is immune.

Finally, a sparkling example of how a blocked position can be exploded open — with the help of a six-move countdown:

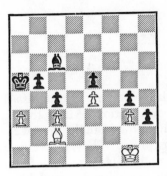

FISCHER

After 69 K-Kt1

BISGUIER

New York 1966–67

	69 . . .	BxP!
	70 BxB	K-R5

First, entry.

	71 B-B5	K-Kt6!
	72 BxP	P-K5

Next, advance. The White King is rooted to his square until the RP is captured.

	73 BxP	KxBP
	74 P-Kt4	K-Q7

Finally, counting. White resigned, since the QBP will queen with check in at most four moves. This is the type of sequence which a computer has great difficulty in finding: It is not easy to define the danger represented by the White passed Pawn in the final position, and it is harder to find the idea of marching in with the King.

21 Ploys

There are certain standard maneuvers in chess that are really not worthy of the name "combination," since they usually involve a single, unanswerable threat or a single line of action. For want of a better word, call them "ploys." They are ways of trapping pieces, of attacking or weakening the Kingside, of defending via a threat of a trap. The "Fool's Mate" is such a device, taking advantage of the weak KB2 square—it is in every manual of the game. When the KBP is gone, the check at QR5 on the King at K1 is another common ploy to watch out for. The questions to be asked are: Can a Pawn be interposed at Kt3? If so, is there another attacking piece which can take the Pawn? Or will a check at K5 win the Rook? This theme appears in countless openings.

The point is not that "ploys" are very deep—but they occur again and again. A complete player should be able to detect or use them as a reflex action. Here are some that come up quite often in grandmaster chess—and are sometimes missed even at that lofty level:

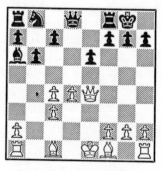

FISCHER

After 11 QxKt

PORTISCH

Santa Monica 1966

204

11 ...   Q-Q2!

A beautiful finesse: Fischer wants the Knight to go to B3 and
QR4. In any case, he can't defend the Kingside with Kt-Q2 and
Kt-KB3, because the pin B-Kt5 would be too strong. The finesse is
made possible by a common way of trapping the Queen: 12 QxR
Kt-B3, which actually occurred after the preliminary moves 12
B-R3 R-K1 13 B-Q3 P-KB4. White won two Rooks for the Queen,
but gradually drifted into a static position:

FISCHER

After 28 P-R4

PORTISCH

Santa Monica 1966

... where Fischer showed how Rooks are commonly trapped by
minor pieces:

28 ...   Kt-K6!

White now had to give up the exchange and soon lost.

Ironically, in the previous game between the same two players
in this tournament, Fischer missed a subtler but no less effective
Rook trap that cost him a vital half point. (See Chapter 26, "The
Exchange Sacrifice," for the first part of the game.)

PORTISCH

After 49 ... R3-Kt5

FISCHER

Santa Monica 1966

Here Fischer played the conservative 50 P-B3. The win was there with:

50 Kt-K3!	BxP
51 KtxR	RxKt
52 P-B4!	B-Kt7
53 Kt-Kt5!	...

. . . for after 53 . . . PxKt 54 K-B3 picks up the Rook.

The idea of trapping a Rook on the seventh rank with a Bishop recurs in master chess as a threat if not an execution. Sometimes the trapper gets a tiger by the tail. In the following position from the 1972 World Championship match, Spassky undoubtedly thought he couldn't effectively contain the Black Rook with B-Q3:

FISCHER

After 22 . . . R-Q7

SPASSKY

Match, Reykjavik 1972

23 BxP	RxQBP
24 R-K2	...

. . . and now we arrive at the famous ending that cost Spassky the final point. He had every reason to believe that the trading off of Black's last Queenside Pawn would assure a draw, but Fischer held White's Pawns in their tracks *by getting his Rook behind them,* and then penetrated on the Kingside with his King, and with a little help from his friend. He might well have tried to win this game with:

23 B-Q3!	RxKBP

White of course always has to calculate the chances after an exchange sacrifice: 23 . . . R-Q1 24 K-Kt3 QRxB+ 25 PxR RxRP (RxP+ 26 R-K3 is obviously in White's favor) 26 K-B3! R-Kt7 27 R-K8+ K-Kt2 28 R-Kt8 P-R4 29 R-Kt5, preventing P-R5. After K-K3 and the exchange of the outside Pawns, White's more active King should win.

24 K-Kt3	R-Q7
25 R-KR1!	R-Q1

The KRP is a goner, and the attempt to make something out of the other Rook Pawn is fruitless: 25 ... P-QR4 26 BxP+ K-Kt2 27 B-Q3 P-R5 28 R-R7+ K-Kt1 (the Black King is painfully tied down to two squares) 29 R-R4 PxP 30 B-R7+ (back again!) K-Kt2 31 RPxP, with a won game.

26 BxP+	K-Kt2
27 B-B5!	...

White now simply threatens to develop his Rook, after which he need not worry about an exchange sacrifice, and he can imprison the Rook for good with B-Q3. If now 27 ... QR-Q4 28 R-KB1 followed by R-B3.

The early stages of this game provided a standard example of how a Bishop traps a Rook by discovery. In this case, Spassky allowed himself to be trapped—or, rather, sacrificed the exchange —as the lesser of two evils. As we have seen from the above possibility, it might well have been a winning idea:

FISCHER

After 18 ... P-B5

SPASSKY

Match, Reykjavik 1972

Although attacked twice, the Black Queen Pawn is protected by the "discovery" BxP+:

19 KtxP	BxKt
20 RxB	BxP+
21 KxB	RxR
22 BxP	R-Q7

... arriving at the previous diagram. There is some merit in giving the positions in this sequence: If White did have a winning game after the exchange sacrifice, it seems hardly rational to give

Fischer's 18 . . . P-B5 an exclamation point, as most commentators
have done.

We have seen several examples of how the Bishop can be trapped
by Pawns, and the Knight by the Bishop. Here is a particularly
pungent case of how a Knight trapped by Pawns can be captured
at leisure — in order to take care of other necessities first. Also notice
in the diagrammed position a common way of restraining Pawns in
the opening; Fischer has allowed this ugly blockade at his Q3 just
to win a Pawn, and he must now try to extricate his Queenside:

MATULOVIC

After 11 . . . BxQ

FISCHER

Palma 1970

| | 12 K-Q1 | Kt-K3 |
| | 13 Kt-K1 | Kt-B5 |

The Knight cannot be driven away because of the curious mate
after 14 P-KKt3 B-K7+ 15 K-B2 Kt-R6 16 P-KB4? (to save the Pawn)
Kt-B7 17 R-Kt1 B-Q8 mate!

| | 14 KtxB | KtxKt |
| | 15 P-KB4! | . . . |

Fischer takes the bull by the horns: He will give up the exchange
to save his domineering Pawn at K5.

| | 15 . . . | B-R3 |

But Black declines to take it, not liking White's Pawn mass after
15 . . . Kt-B7+ 16 K-K2 KtxR 17 P-Q4. However, this might have
been his best chance in view of what follows. With 17 . . . P-KR4
18 B-K3 P-R5 19 K-B3 Kt-Kt6 20 PxKt PxP 21 Kt-Q2 the open Rook
file gives him a reasonable amount of play.

| | 16 K-B2 | KtxB |
| | 17 R-K1! | . . . |

. . . not just dramatics, since 17 KxB at once would *not* transpose
into the game line. Curiously, the Knight is equally well trapped at

QB1 as he would have been at KR1 in the above note. The point of the Rook move is that White must not allow a double threat when Black unavoidably plays BxP:

17 ...	O-O-O
18 KxB	BxP
19 P-KKt3	...

A remarkable recovery by Fischer: Such a Pawn grab would have cost a lesser player the game.

A player's repertoire must also include several ploys involving the attack and defense at certain weak spots in the King's field. When these become second nature to a player, his calculations can be speeded up considerably:

BISGUIER

After 25 ... Q-B4

FISCHER

New York 1957–58

Black threatens a standard mating configuration: P-B6 and Q-Kt5, when the defense P-Kt3 loses to Q-R6. There are three ways to defend against this: (1) guard Kt2 other than by playing P-Kt3; (2) be able to play Q-KB1 in answer to Q-R6; (3) be able to capture the BP in answer to Q-R6. Fischer first "threatens" the guard of Kt2:

26 Q-Kt4! ...

Another "Queen-around" idea Fischer has used so well: 26 ... P-B6 is now met by 27 QxKt Q-Kt5 28 QxKtP! holding Kt2.

26 ...	Kt-B1
27 Kt-R4	P-B6
28 Kt-B5+	K-Kt1
29 Kt-Q7+	K-Kt2
30 Q-Kt3!	...

Keeping an eye on the BP so as now to be able to allow Q-Kt5 31 P-Kt3.

| 30 . . . | Q-Kt5 |
| 31 Kt-B5+! | . . . |

This little intermezzo removes the Knight from the potential fork after QxP, which would occur in the event of an immediate P-Kt3.

| 31 . . . | K-Kt1 |
| 32 R-Kt3 | . . . |

Now if 32 . . . Q-R6, the Knight dances to its other safe square before the Queen gives up the pin on the Knight Pawn: 33 Kt-Q7+ followed by 34 QxBP. This was Fischer's finest display of tactical accuracy as a teenager.

The other weak Pawn that is often subjected to tactical ploys is KB2. Here is a sparkling example:

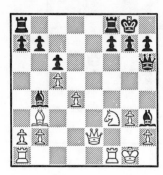

MINIC

After 19 . . . B-R6

FISCHER

Vinkovci 1968

| 20 Kt-K5! | . . . |

White willingly gives up the exchange, for he will get that and more by having a preponderance of force aimed at Black's KB2:

20 . . .	BxR
21 RxB	B-Q7
22 R-B3!	. . .

No exchanges, please, at White's K3.

22 . . .	QR-Q1
23 KtxKBP	RxKt
24 Q-K7!	Resigns

It's mate after 24 . . . R-KB1 25 RxR, etc.

In this seemingly placid scene, right out of a standard Ruy Lopez, a little Pawn loosens up Black's KB2, and in four moves the Kingside has crumbled:

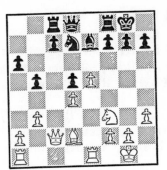

BARCZAY

After 19 . . . Kt-Q2

FISCHER

Sousse 1967

20 P-K6!	PxP
21 RxP	P-B4
22 B-R5!	. . .

A Fischer trademark: Reduce the defenders.

22 . . .	QxB
23 RxB	Q-Q1
24 Kt-Kt5	Resigns

White threatens 25 QxP mate, and if 24 . . . P-Kt3 25 R-Kt7+ K-R1 (KxR loses the Queen) 26 RxP+ and 27 QxP mate.

The move P-K6 is commonly used to open up KB2, to block the center and impede development in the opening, and, as below, to open up lines for the Bishops and Rooks:

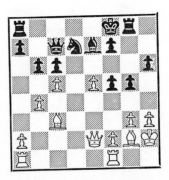

CARDOSO

After 22 . . . PxKt

FISCHER

Match, New York 1957

23 P-K6!	B-B3
24 QR-Q1!	Kt-K4
25 KR-K1!	. . .

Just a straightforward build-up of force wins material. If now 25 . . . Kt-Kt5+ 26 PxKt BxB 27 R-Q7, Black's KB2 will fall and he will soon be mated.

Combinations and sacrifices whip the blood, but many a fine game is merely an unerring application of ploys. As Fischer avers, "Over the board it is best not to make unnecessary sacrifices."

22 Zugzwang

Bobby Fischer once made the outrageous claim that a standard line in the King's Indian Defense was better for Black even a tempo behind, because White had nothing better than to commit himself to one of several unfavorable lines. White was at a loss for waiting moves. Fischer's approach to the openings was brash in those days, but he did have a point.

Zugzwang, the condition of having to make a move when one would rather pass, literally "move-bound," can occur throughout the game. Purists would argue that many middle-game positions created by the great master of Zugzwang, Aron Nimzovich, involved other complications. But the *idea* of putting your opponent on the move—asking, in effect, can you improve your position? even with the move—is closely related to the battle for squares, the maintaining of tension, and the general evaluation of threats and counterthreats. Often it's like opening a stuck window by first pushing it further closed.

First, a mixed example of move-exhaustion.

FISCHER

After 38 P-R5

PORTISCH

Bled 1961

213

38 . . .   **R-QR5!**

Black could not attack the KRP directly, with R-KR4, for then Kt-B4 is adequate. But now either 39 R-R2 or 39 Kt-B4 allows 39 . . . P-B3 mate! The threat then becomes clearer: 39 . . . P-B3+ followed by R-R4+, winning the Rook. So White had to play 39 Kt-B5, allowing 39 . . . R-R5 winning the Pawn.

The reduction of forces in the endgame makes the Zugzwang more clean-cut. Here are two previously unpublished positions which illustrate the idea strikingly:

ALEKHINE

After 70 K-B2

APSHENICKS

Buenos Aires 1939

The World Champion at the time, playing in the Olympics that left many masters stranded in South America when war broke out (seeds of a great awakening!), posed these problems for White:

1. Your King can't move, or the Pawn advances.
2. Your Rook can't move, or the Pawn is lost.
3. Your Pawn can't move, or my King gets to Kt2 and wins either the Rook or the Pawn.

White answers:

1. Your Rook can't move laterally without losing the KBP.
2. Your Rook can't move vertically without trading off your QBP: 71 P-R7! K-Kt2 72 R-QB8! KxP 73 RxP: drawn.
3. Your QBP can't move without allowing the same idea as above.
4. Your King can't move without allowing *me* the waiting move 71 R-R7.

Yet there is a way to break the deadlock, typical in the endgame: triangulation. The Black King can make three moves to leave Kt3 and return, whereas the White Rook can only make two moves (or an even number) to leave R8 and return:

70 . . .	K-R4!
71 R-R7	K-Kt4!
72 R-R8	K-Kt3!

. . . and White must lose, as he has no way to waste a move.

The triumph of Harry Nelson Pillsbury at Hastings, 1895, was such news that no one has noticed what happened to the second prize. Tchigorin had to win in the last round to come second alone, since the World Champion at the time, twenty-six-year-old Emanuel Lasker, half a point behind, won his last-round game early. A long struggle brought about this dilemma:

TCHIGORIN

After 59 . . . R-K2

SCHLECHTER

Hastings 1895

Carl Schlechter, the famous "drawing master," the Petrosian of his day, played:

| 60 R-QKt6 | K-B2 |
| 61 RxP? | . . . |

. . . and now Tchigorin performed a magnificent Zugzwang act:

| 61 . . . | K-B3 |
| 62 R-R5 | R-K1! |

As in the Alekhine game above, White's King and Rook are moveless. The subtlety of the situation is brought out by:

| 63 R-R7 | R-K3! |
| 64 R-R5 | R-K2! |

The parallel is complete: the Black Rook has lost a move so that it would now guard Kt2 after a repeated R-R7. But Schlechter could have done a waiting act of his own, instead of 61 RxP:

| 61 R-KR6! | . . . |

White now simply waits for Black to make the only move that changes the position, P-Kt5. Then, and only then, he plays R-QKt6. The difference is that he captures the Pawn on his fourth rank and is able to defend his Pawn from behind, instead of laterally. He is then un-Zugzwangable. To his dying day Lasker never knew that this little misstep cost him a second-place tie.

A curious example of Zugzwang in the middle game came up in the idea-filled Fischer-Spassky match, 1972. This, too, is a possibility that was passed over in the flood of publicity surrounding that epic event.

FISCHER

After 17 . . . Q-R4

SPASSKY

Match, Reykjavik 1972

Spassky demolishes the center with:

        18 KtxP!   **. . .**

. . . and Fischer replied, almost immediately:

        18 . . .   **B-Kt4!**

The Knight cannot be taken because of the undeveloped state of the Queenside: White would win another Pawn and break through with a Pawn roller. Now the Bishop prevents the Knight from retreating. Several commentators have suggested 19 P-R4 to draw the Bishop away, but after 19 . . . BxP 20 Kt-K3 Q-B6 followed by R-Q1, White's center comes under heavy fire. Yet White need not force matters. Instead of 19 B-R5 followed by a sacrifice at KB7, he could have placed the burden on his opponent with the waiting move:

        19 K-R1   **. . .**

Now all of the possible checks at K6 or Q5 by Black are gone, and he still cannot take the Knight. The King Rook must stand guard over his KB2, and the Knight is only a hindrance at Q2, e.g. 19 . . . Kt-Q2 20 P-KR4 BxP 21 Kt-K3 Q-B6 22 Q-K2! and QxQP allows 23 QR-Q1, winning the Knight.

Salo Flohr was once accused by Alekhine of making one waiting move after another to lure his opponents into making a mistake. This is perhaps a psychological Zugzwang. It is the opposite of initiative. But as these few examples indicate, it is an idea that even the great lights of the game have often failed to see.

23 Piece Play

Although Fischer's style has most often been compared to that of Capablanca, there is one respect in which he resembles Morphy and Lasker even more. He characteristically looks first at improving the position of his pieces rather than achieving a better Pawn formation. I think it is fair to say that Fischer has broken up more positions with the minor pieces than with a Pawn advance.

The difference between piece play and Pawn play is well illustrated in the following early game of Fischer's:

FISCHER

After 21 . . . Q-B3

PETROSIAN

Bled 1959

Here Petrosian was true to his style, and played the natural 22 P-K4. Fischer was able to hold the game because of his strong Bishop. If Fischer had been White, he probably would have tried:

22 Kt-K5!   **Q-R5**

The Knight cannot be taken because the Bishop is overloaded, having to guard Q1. Now another Knight move completely shatters the Kingside:

218

23 Kt-Q7 . . .

In his match with Spassky in 1972, Fischer showed again and again his willingness to give his opponent better Pawns in return for open lines for his minor pieces:

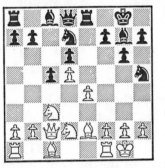

FISCHER

After 11 . . . Kt-R4

SPASSKY

Match, Reykjavik 1972

Fischer's last move goes as far back as a game of Boleslavsky's in 1950, the Russians were quick to remind us. But it must have surprised a lot of people, including Spassky, who now took thirty minutes before answering:

12 BxKt   PxB

Black's Kingside appears riddled, but in a few moves Black had his Queen at R5 and his Knight at KKt5, when White was forced to "straighten out" the Black Pawns by capturing there. This was Fischer's first victory over Spassky.

One sees centralization moves at critical junctures in many of Bobby's games. Here he is willing to give up two Pawns to restrict Black's Knight and infiltrate with his Rooks:

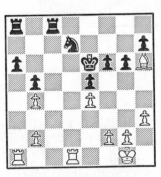

TAL

After 27 . . . R-B1

FISCHER

Portoroz 1958

28	B-K3!	R-B5
29	R-Q2	RxKtP
30	QR-Q1	Kt-B1
31	R-Q6+	K-B2
32	R-Kt6!	RxKtP

Black has only material to show for his discomfiture. White has a winning initiative.

33	QR-Q6	P-QR4
34	R-Kt7+	K-Kt1
35	RxBP?	. . .

Departing from his main theme. 35 R-K7 would have prevented the Knight from reaching the strong defensive post at K3. Now the game quickly became drawish after:

35 . . .	R-K1!

A timely centralization of the Bishop occurred in two crucial Fischer games, his first match game with Larsen, 1971, and here, the first game in the Russia vs. the World team match:

PETROSIAN

After 31 . . . R-B1

FISCHER

Belgrade 1970

Fischer won handily with 32 Q-K5 followed by B-B5, even though an immediate advance of Pawns on the Queenside seems more forceful. Fischer correctly realized that the Pawn advance would be that much stronger with all his pieces in play.

Here Fischer uses a tactical trick to centralize his Queen Knight:

JOHANNESSEN

After 17 . . . R-Kt1

FISCHER

Havana 1966

18 Kt-Kt6! . . .

The Knight cannot be taken because of the mate at Q7. The rest of the game is a lesson in the buildup of forces. First, the Knight goes to Q5. Then the major pieces double up on the Queen file. Finally, the King Knight goes to R5 via Q2, B1, and Kt3. When the break finally came, Fischer mopped up.

The minor pieces can break through an apparent wall of Pawns with surprising rapidity. Here are three drastic examples:

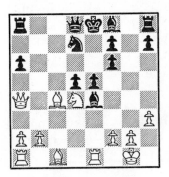

NAJDORF

After 13 . . . Kt-Q2

FISCHER

Varna 1962

In one of his rare displays of swagger, Fischer predicted he would demolish the Najdorf variation of the Sicilian, as played by its "inventor." He was right:

14 RxB! PxR
15 Kt-B5 . . .

At the cost of the exchange, White owns all the squares, and the Black King will be kept in the center:

15 . . .	B-B4
16 Kt-Kt7+	K-K2
17 Kt-B5+	K-K1
18 B-K3!	. . .

The final touch: Black's only developed piece is exchanged, and the Black squares are denuded.

Here in the space of three moves a Knight creates two mating threats:

FISCHER

After 22 K-Kt2

GLIGORIC

Bled 1961

22 . . .	KtxP!
23 KtxB	KtxR
24 Kt-Kt6	Q-B2!
25 RxKt	QxKt

. . . and the game was even.

Here the Black King is again forced to remain in the center, with his Rooks out of the game. In such situations, White has to look for a way of sacrificing a Rook for one of the Black minor pieces to increase his dominance in the center.

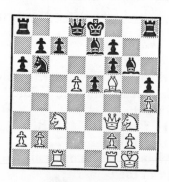

ADDISON

After 17 . . . Kt-Kt3

FISCHER

Palma 1970

	18 QKt-K4	KtxP

... and this gives him the chance. But if Black can't play this, he has no future at all.

19	KR-Q1	P-B3
20	Kt-B3	Q-Kt3
21	RxKt!	PxR
22	KtxQP	QxKtP

Black must gamble, as 23 Kt-B7 regains the exchange on any other move.

23	R-Kt1	QxRP
24	RxP	Resigns

The Black King would soon be mated after 25 BxB and 26 KtxP+.

Perhaps the best demonstration of Fischer's predilection for piece play is his willingness to sacrifice Pawns rather than submit to a blocked position. In the following important game, which cost Fischer a chance for first place, he didn't like the looks of a move that seems almost forced:

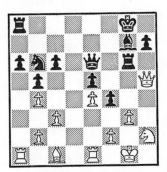

KELLER

After 25 ... R-Kt3

FISCHER

Zurich 1959

After the expected 26 P-Kt4, White's Bishop and Knight have limited prospects. Black could then restrict his adversary further with Q-Q2 or Kt-B5. Instead, Fischer gambled on:

26	Kt-B3	PxP
27	PxP	RxP+
28	K-R2	Q-Kt5
29	QxQ	RxQ
30	R-Kt1	RxR
31	KxR	Kt-R5!

With the loss of this game, Fischer could not catch Tal in the final round.

Queen position has also figured prominently in Fischer's games.

The centralized Queen is especially imposing when the board is open. Here Spassky shows that Pawns are often unimportant when the heavy artillery is given some range:

FISCHER

After 23 K-Kt1

SPASSKY

Mar del Plata 1960

23 ...   Q-Kt5?

Fischer misjudges the domineering position of the White Queen. He should have forced an ending with 23 ... Q-Kt6.

24 R-B2   B-K2
25 R-K4   Q-Kt4
26 Q-Q4   R-B1?

Hoping for 27 Kt-K5 RxR 28 QxR B-B4!, but Spassky doesn't fall for it.

27 R-K5!   Resigns

Too much material is loose. 27 ... Q-R5 loses the Queen (28 RxR+). 27 ... Q-Kt3 loses the Bishop (28 RxR+). And 27 ... R-Q1 also loses the Bishop (28 Q-K4, Q-R5 29 R-B4).

Here Fischer forgoes castling to make sure his Queen finds the right square for development:

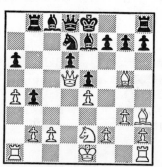

FISCHER

After 12 ... R-Kt1

MATULOVIC

Vinkovci 1968

13 BxB   KxB!

Fischer decides that the Queen belongs on the Queenside, at QR4 eventually. He can castle "by hand" if necessary with R-K1 and K-B1. In recent match games with Petrosian and Spassky, Fischer showed the unusual transference of the Queen from one wing to the other for defensive purposes. What was startling in both cases was that the Queen's route was through enemy territory, as in this earlier example:

FISCHER

After 16 K-R1

ROBATSCH

Havana 1965

16 . . .   Q-K6

A strange conception: Before making any Pawn advance, Fischer blunts a threatened Kingside attack (Kt-R5, R-B3 etc.) by preparing to station his own Queen there. The characteristic Fischer trait is the same: Whether it's a Knight or a Queen, his pieces find their best squares before he commits himself to a plan of action.

24 Pawn Grabbing

There are three general stages in the development of a player. As a novice, he takes material (especially Pawns) whenever they are offered, and checks out the consequences later. As a regular club player, he begins to resist the tendency to snatch Pawns as some kind of moral duty. Finally, at the expert or master level, he realizes that most Pawns are proffered without much more in hard analysis to back the sacrifice up than the dim memory that Alekhine or Tal once did something like it.

And the skeptical player soon learns that grabbing Pawns is often the fastest way to win games, at least against weaker opposition.

Fischer is the skeptic *par excellence*. In fact, a fair case can be made that Pawn grabbing has cost Fischer more lost games and certainly a lot more hard work than any other tendency. Most masters don't want to work that hard; Fischer seems to consider it a matter of honor to prove a sacrifice wrong if it *is* faulty.

Fischer was long infamous for his willingness to play either side of the "poisoned-Pawn" variation of the Sicilian. His most famous loss came in the eleventh game of the Spassky match, when he accepted the Queen Knight Pawn. In this chapter we will see some successful and some unsuccessful Pawn grabs. But in every case note the contortions Fischer has to go through to prove his point.

FISCHER

After 14 B-B4

BISGUIER

Bled 1961

226

	14 . . .	KtxP!

It is hard to believe that the success of this combination is based on the fact that Black's King Rook will attack White's Queen Bishop, gaining a tempo.

15	KtxKt	QxKt
16	QxKt	QxB
17	KR-Q1	Q-Kt3!
18	QxQ	BPxQ
19	R-Q7	B-B4

Black remains a Pawn up, even at the expense of allowing the White Rook to the seventh. In the following position, too, Fischer must pull out his whole bag of tricks to nail the extra Pawn:

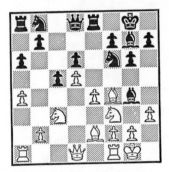

FISCHER

After 12 P-R3

UHLMANN

Palma 1970

	12 . . .	KtxKP!
	13 KtxKt	. . .

The rationale behind the moves explains more than a list of variations. The first point is that Black has an immediate threat of 14 BxB, followed by KtxP, forking the Queen and King Bishop, so he can ignore the attack on his Queen Bishop. Chess positions *do* repeat themselves; this line occurred in a similar position in the game Vladimirov-Yudovich, Gorky 1954 (!).

	13 . . .	RxKt

Again indirectly defending the Queen Bishop, by attacking White's.

	14 B-Kt5	Q-K1

Now attacking the King Bishop. See chapter 19, "For the Defense," for an elaboration of this basic defensive tactic: When two pieces are threatened (the Queen and the Queen Bishop), an adequate defense is to create a threat of one's own in removing one of the attacked pieces.

15 B-Q3   BxKt

Another defensive resource: the "comeback." Black is able finally to remove this piece from attack because 16 BxR BxB "comes back" from *en prise*. All of this for a Pawn!

People who don't even know the moves are probably aware of Fischer's most brazen Pawn grab of all—in the first game of the Spassky match:

FISCHER

After 29 P-Kt5

SPASSKY

Match, Reykjavik 1972

29 . . .   BxKRP

As we will see in Chapter 34, "Gordian Knots," opinion is divided on whether this is actually a losing move. Reshevsky gives it two question marks. I would say it deserves an exclamation point if only because it gave both players a chance to show their skill instead of taking an uneventful draw. Fischer's losing move was really a dozen moves later, at adjournment.

Fischer was luckier in the following two positions, where he allowed a fierce attack to gain a Pawn advantage:

SPASSKY

After 13 . . . P-R4

FISCHER

Match, Reykjavik 1972

Fischer's first game of the match with White—the fourth game, because he forfeited the second—almost ended disastrously when Spassky produced the new move 13 . . . P-QR4. P-Kt5 is threatened, and the Knight Pawn needs no support because of the attack on White's King Pawn. Actually, White now has little better than to take the Pawn, by first removing the King Pawn from attack:

14 P-K5	PxP
15 PxP	Kt-Q2
16 KtxP	Kt-B4!

Black's attack now moves along without loss of time, since the Knight fork cannot be tolerated.

17 BxKt	BxB+
18 K-R1	Q-Kt4!
19 Q-K2	. . .

Still unwilling to admit that Black's compensation for the Pawn is enormous, Fischer avoids Q-Kt3. As we will see in Chapter 31, "Themes," he was able to hold the draw only by a miracle.

Fischer's unheralded opponent missed a chance to capitalize on his weakened King position in this dangerously loose situation:

FISCHER

After 18 . . . QxP

NARANJA

Palma 1970

19 B-Kt5   . . .

White could have won at least the exchange with 19 Kt-Q5, since KtxKt is answered by 20 B-Q3! B-KB3 21 Q-R6 B-Kt2 22 BxQ BxQ 23 BxKB, when Black has three pieces in take and White only one.

19 . . .   P-KR3

Fischer now wisely decides to return the Pawn to relieve the pressure.

20 BxP	Q-R2
21 B-Kt5	QxQ
22 BxQ	. . .

. . . and the game was eventually drawn.

A common theme in these examples and those to follow is that Fischer's Queen is embarrassed or is shut out of the play in wasting the time to go after the stray Pawn. Here Fischer took time off to snatch a Pawn, when a simplifying line could have brought him a crucial victory:

SPASSKY

After 35 . . . K-Kt2

FISCHER

Havana 1966

36 QxRP	R-QB1

. . . and Black's counterplay saved the game. The attack would not diminish at all after 36 QxQ RxQ 37 R-Q6 R-QB1 38 R-K3! with the threat of R-B3. "The Pawn won't run away."

Here Fischer gave up his Queen for Rook and Knight rather than to submit to a repetition of moves at Q6 and K7:

POPOV

After 21 . . . Kt-Kt5

FISCHER

Skopje 1967

22 QxQR   RxQ
23 KtxB   Q-Kt3
24 P-QB3   . . .

Fischer's active Bishops were enough to draw, but was it worth the Pawn grab? Like Lasker, Bobby is willing to take the chance that his opponent will overplay his hand. Here he didn't:

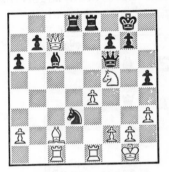

PACHMAN

After 27 . . . Kt-Q6

FISHER

FISCHER

Mar del Plata 1959

28 BxKt   RxB
29 Q-B4   . . .

The trouble is there just aren't any good squares to bring the Queen back to. So Fischer tries a swindle:

29 . . .   P-KKt3
30 R-B5   R-K3!

The Knight will now fall, because the Black Rook at K3 can now interpose at KKt3, ending all counterplay.

The difference between a Queen in play and out of play is dramatically spotlighted in this two-move sequence:

FISCHER

After 27 B-Kt5

RESHEVSKY

Match, Los Angeles 1961

| 27 . . . | QxRP? |
| 28 Q-Q7! | . . . |

The Queen hits three targets at once, winning immediately.

The score of the Fischer-Larsen match made so much news (6–0, following on the heels of 6–0 against Taimanov) that the merits of the final game have been largely neglected. Fischer went a-Pawn-grabbing, and got away with it:

FISCHER

After 30 . . . P-B4

LARSEN

Match, Denver 1971

Here Larsen played the tame 31 Q-B6, a move he could have had without loss of time after:

| 31 Q-Kt5+ | K-R1 |
| 32 Q-B6+ | . . . |

But he could win outright with:

| 32 Q-Q8+ | K-Kt2 |
| 33 KtxBP+! | RxKt |

White has an intermediate check to hold the Knight after 33 . . . PxKt 34 Q-Kt5+, before retaking the Rook.

34 RxP+	K-R3
35 R-R4+	R-R4
36 R-KB1!	. . .

And now all White's force enters the final attack. On his thirty-first move, Fischer could play either K-B1 or K-B2 also. The latter is met 32 Q2 QxKtP!, opening lines for the Rook, since the Queen has a check in hand for 32 . . . RxKt. The former allows 32 R-KB1, finally freeing the Knight for attack, since the Queen again has a Zwischenzug check to answer 32 . . . RxKt. What might have been!

25 Room, Please!

There is an undercurrent of tension in every game of chess in the struggle of the minor pieces — the Bishops and the Knights — against the Pawns for access to good squares. Sometimes this struggle takes the form of a Pawn storm, in which the pieces are simply overrun. Sometimes it involves the unexpected sacrifice of a Pawn to open a square for a piece. Sometimes it is simply a search for the only way to get from here to there, a logistical problem.

The artist in Bobby Fischer is revealed in his choice of square-freeing moves in this position:

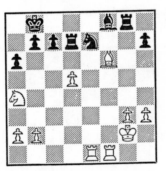

JIMENEZ

After 28 . . . R-Q2

FISCHER

Havana 1966

Problem: how to win a piece at K7. The direct 29 BxKt, BxB (note that RxB won't work because of the guard-destroying move 30 RxB+, the check being the point) 30 R-B7 looks good enough. But then there is some untidiness after 30 . . . P-Kt4! 31 Kt-B3

(Kt-B5 is met by the Zwischenzug 31 ... RxP) RxP+! 32 K-R2 (K-B2 allows 32 ... B-R5) B-Q3 33 RxR RxKt+! 34 RxB R-B7+, drawing. Diabolical. But Fischer finds a simple way to enter with his Knight, and end all complications:

29 P-Q6!   ...

The right sequence. A square at Kt6 is reserved for the Knight.

29 ...   **PxP**

30 BxKt   **BxB**

Note also that the Black Pawn at Q3 now inhibits the Black Bishop, forestalling any of the complications mentioned above.

31 R-B7   **Resigns**

After 31 ... R-K1, 32 Kt-Kt6 R-B2 33 Kt-Q5 wins a full piece.

A drastic example of the value of access to squares was missed by Fischer and his opponent both in this touchy position:

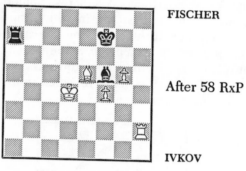

FISCHER

After 58 RxP

IVKOV

Zagreb 1970

Fischer was making another great attempt to save a lost cause, but now, instead of checking the King away on the fifth rank, he played:

58 ...   **R-Q2+?**

59 K-B5?   ...

The whole point is getting the King into the fray. This could have been accomplished magnificently with 59 B-Q6! RxB+ 60 K-K5, winning back the piece with a won Rook and Pawn ending. After White's lapse his King could never get back to the Kingside.

The bread and butter of the positional player is the following "square-expanding" idea—a Pawn sacrifice that would be valid even if the Pawn were never regained:

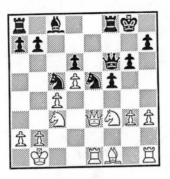

FISCHER

After 22 KtxP

SUTTLES

Palma 1970

22 ...	P-B5!
23 PxP	KtxKt
24 QxKt	Q-R5!

Before he plays B-B4+, the point of the Pawn sacrifice, Fischer seizes the black squares as well. He will play RxP perhaps before getting the Bishop into play. The single Pawn move created squares for Queen, Rook, and Bishop.

Now some examples of how Fischer had to take it on the chin because his opponent found the room to operate:

UHLMANN

After 30 QxR

FISCHER

Buenos Aires 1960

30 ...	P-K6+!
31 K-Kt1	...

The first point: If the Pawn is taken, the Queen enters the White camp with check.

| 31 ... | RxQ+ |
| 32 KxR | P-K7! |

Another square-gobbler. The Pawn will never queen, but it ties up the White pieces after 33 R-K1 Q-K5, to be followed by Q-K6. Equally devastating was this break:

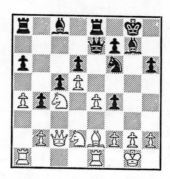

FISCHER

After 20 . . . PxB

NAJDORF

Santa Monica 1966

| 21 P-K5! | PxP |

The White pieces now gain access to all the central squares, including the Queen to KB5:

22 B-B3	Q-B1
23 KtxP	B-Kt2
24 Kt2-B4	QR-Q1
25 Kt-B6	RxR+
26 RxR	R-K1
27 R-Q1	R-B1
28 P-R3	Kt-K1
29 Kt6-R5	R-Kt1
30 Q-B5	Kt-Q3?
31 KtxKt	Resigns

The search for squares is a purely geometrical problem in the following three positions, but the key moves are nonetheless startling for that reason:

DARGA

After 26 . . . K-B2

FISCHER

Berlin 1960

Fischer describes the position with characteristic brashness: "Problem: White to play and win." The retreat of the Bishop to find a new diagonal does have a problem flavor:

27 B-B1! ...

. . . and after B-B4+ followed by Q-Kt5 Black had to resign. There was something almost mystic about this problemlike move:

FISCHER

After 21 Kt-B3

GHEORGHIU

Siegen 1970

21 ... **B-R8!**

Is the exclamation point for shock or brilliance? It did not accomplish more than a draw, but it was logical enough. The Bishop could not retreat to the Queenside because it would then be blocked by the Knight when it moved to B3. And at Q6 or B6 it would allow White to gain time as the White King advanced to K3. The same move in another position was not enough to find freedom for the Bishop:

FISCHER

After 36 P-R4

KALME

Milwaukee 1957

| 36 . . . | RxB |
| 37 PxR | B-R1 |

Young Bobby's idea is to break through with his Pawns. He fails—simply because even this square is not safe:

38 K-B2	P-Kt6
39 R-B1	P-Q4!
40 PxP	P-B5
41 RxP	P-Kt7
42 R-K1	P-Kt8(Q)
43 RxQ	RxR
44 R-B8+	. . .

The fly in the ointment. Not only does the Bishop go, but also the Rook Pawn.

Fischer's losses have tended to result from cramped positions— a reliance on the resilience and counterattacking possibilities of the boxer in a crouch. The player with greater freedom of movement, which is to say *room*, can usually get his threats in first, even against a Fischer:

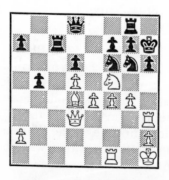

FISCHER

After 29 P-Kt4

RESHEVSKY

New York 1965–66

29 . . .   KtxKtP

Rather than submit to P-Kt5. But now the Knight is lost, since
30 Q-KKt3 Kt-B3 would allow Q-Kt5, threatening QxP+ or RxP+.
Equally cramped was this position:

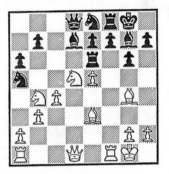

FISCHER

After 19 B-Kt4

BISGUIER

New York 1956

In most cramped positions there is simply too much *en prise*
when a combination begins. For example, 19 . . . BxP won't work
because 20 BxR BxR 21 BxB leaves White a piece up. What follows
is just as bad:

19 . . .	RxP
20 B-Kt6	Q-B1
21 BxB	QxB
22 BxKt	. . .

. . . and White won. Some accounts say Bisguier never beat
Fischer. Others say this was the last time Bisguier beat Fischer.
Well, it *was* the first time, and who knows if it will be the last?

26 The Exchange Sacrifice

It is part of the chemistry of chess that a Rook and Bishop work almost as well together as two Rooks. The position of the Pawns, the scope of the Bishop, the King position are of course all-important. But, "all things being equal," the sacrifice of a Rook for a Knight or Bishop, especially if a Pawn is won in the bargain or the enemy's Pawns are disrupted, is not as surprising a trade as most chess players customarily believe.

Many a man has "won the exchange" only to find that he has lost the game. The most likely time for an exchange sacrifice is when the position is out of balance, and this can occur as easily in the middle game as in the endgame.

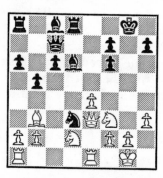

PORTISCH

After 18 . . . Kt-Q6

FISCHER

Santa Monica 1966

Here the sacrifice is virtually forced, since Black threatens B-B4, B-B5, and KtxKtP as well as the Rook. Fischer had to foresee that he would get a lot of play on the weakened Black Kingside squares several moves before:

19 Q-R6!   **B-B5**

The best defense. After the immediate KtxR 20 RxKt, Black could not afford to take the time to defend the KBP anyway.

    20 QxP   **R-Q3**
    21 Q-B3   **KtxR**

Fischer went on to achieve a winning position, and then threw away the win through a later miscalculation. That was one of the few times Fischer made a sacrifice without a clear follow-up. In the following position, Fischer has his choice of how to make the sacrifice, and he naturally chooses the way that will preserve his dominance on the black squares:

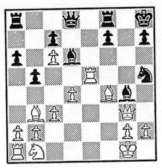

SEIDMAN

After 16 . . . Kt-R4

FISCHER

New York 1960–61

    17 RxKt!   **BxR**
    18 Kt-Q2   . . .

Simple development, plus the two-Pawn advantage, gave White an excellent game. (17 QxB KtxB 18 QxKt P-B3!)

Fischer's artistic nature shows in the way he prepared for the exchange sacrifice in this Olympiad game:

FISCHER

After 43 Kt-B1

GLIGORIC

Siegen 1970

43 . . .   RxP!

He could have preceded this with R-B7+, since 44 K-Kt3 RxRP
45 RxB KxR transposes back into the game line. But this capture
is certainly more pleasing to the eye.

44 RxR   R-B7+

45 K-Kt3   RxKt

. . . and the White Kingside Pawns all fall.

Rook and Bishop are ideally suited for advancing passed Pawns.
When the defending Rooks are in front of the Pawn, they are particularly helpless:

BERTOK

After 30 . . . Kt-K4

FISCHER

Bled 1961

31 BxP!   KtxR

32 RxKt   R-Kt1

33 P-B5!   . . .

The Pawn will cost Black a piece. Below, Bishop and Pawn
bottle up both Rooks, allowing White to destroy Black's Queenside:

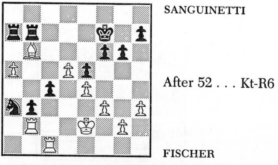

SANGUINETTI

After 52 . . . Kt-R6

FISCHER

Mar del Plata 1959

51 R-QR1	Kt-B7
52 RxKt!	PxR
53 R-QB1	...

The important difference is that Black wins only one Pawn by returning the compliment with 53 . . . RxB. White's King now marches to QKt5 for an easy win.

In fully a third of the games between Fischer and Spassky in their World Championship match, both players had to weigh the compensations for the exchange sacrifice. This was one of the critical areas where Fischer's judgment proved to be superior. In the seventh game, however, he nearly lost from the adjourned position by not taking advantage of a possible exchange sacrifice:

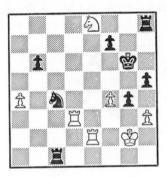

FISCHER

After 40 . . . K-Kt3

SPASSKY

Match, Reykjavik 1972

41 P-R4!   . . .

Spassky sealed this move after considerable thought. It is a fine example of an option-preserving move, since P-R4 must be played in most lines. For example, the immediate 41 R-Q5 allows 41 . . . P-B3 42 P-R4 R-B7, because of the Knight fork. Now Black must commit himself to a line of play. Curiously, opinions were widely divided about the outcome. Fischer expressed confidence that he would win. Petrosian saw a draw. Bronstein felt Spassky had the chances.

41 . . .	P-B3
42 R-K6	R-B7+
43 K-Kt1	K-B4(?)

White would have a perpetual check after 43 . . . K-B2 44 P-B5 RxKt 45 R-Q7+. But since Black is now just about committed to a forced draw, one wonders what Fischer had in mind. His real chance for winning was the exchange sacrifice 43 . . . RxKt 44 RxR

K-B4 45 R-QB8 K-K5 46 R-Q6 P-Kt6 with some nasty mating threats. He certainly had little to fear with his great King position.

44 Kt-Kt7+   KxP(?)

Now he should be content with a repetition of moves 44 . . . K-Kt3 45 Kt-K8. The Black King is soon in hot water.

45 R-Q4+   K-Kt6

46 Kt-B5+   K-B6

47 R6-K4   . . .

This nails down the draw (which Fischer took by perpetual check), but White had all the chances with 47 R-Q3+ K-B5 48 Kt-Kt3 with the immediate threat of Kt-K2+, winning material. And all of this only seven moves after overnight analysis!

Fischer could not resist a great gamble in the following position, which stunned the onlookers. Perhaps here he played to the crowd:

FISCHER

After 21 RxR

KORCHNOI

Sousse 1967

21 . . .   BxRP

He takes a Pawn rather than the Rook! Psychologically, one is always tempted to play a combination that works so well in all other lines: for example, the fork after 22 RxP B-QB3.

22 RxR+   KxR

23 R-R2   . . .

White must go through contortions to develop his Rook, but Black's Bishops and Queenside Pawns did not turn out to be so vicious as they look. A well-fought draw resulted. The game of chess would not be the same without that uncertain balance known as the exchange.

27 Simplify!

The middle-game idea that seems to come most naturally to the world's great players has always been the possibility of simplification. A chess game, in this sense, is like a mathematical theorem. To construct a proof is to reduce the complex problem to more manageable terms. For all of his combinational cunning, Fischer seems to prefer wherever possible to reach a comfortable ending rather than to try to force a middle-game decision that is not clear.

Obviously, no player can dictate the type of game he wants against any opposition. But Fischer is particularly skilled in the simplifying combination, even when tempting alternatives beckon for brilliance. Here is a classic example:

TAIMANOV

After 19 R-K1

FISCHER

Match, Vancouver 1971

$$19 \ldots \qquad \text{RxP}$$

Otherwise Black merely concedes a Pawn.

245

20 RxP+!   **K-Q1**

An intriguing position! Pawns are equal, but the Black King appears vulnerable. First, is a Queen sacrifice possible? 21 QxR+ KtxQ 22 RxKt+ K-B1 23 R-B4 K-Kt1! 24 R5xP Q-Kt3 25 K-R1! QxP 26 P-KR3! R-Q1! 27 R-B7 Q-Kt8+ 28 K-R2 R-Q7 just holds everything. Another attacking possibility is 21 R-K8+ RxR 22 BxR KtxB 23 QxKt+ K-B1 24 Q-B5+ R-K3 25 R-Q5 P-QKt3 26 Q-R7! and Black Pawns must fall: 26 . . . P-Kt3 27 P-B5! PxP 28 RxP; or 26 . . . R-K8+ 27 K-B2 R-B7 28 Q-Kt8+ K-Kt2 29 Q-K8! Instead of this line, which promised to end it in a hurry, Fischer chose a Rook-and-Bishop versus Rook-and-Knight ending:

<table>
<tr><td>21 Q-K2</td><td>RxR+</td></tr>
<tr><td>22 QxR+</td><td>Q-Q2</td></tr>
<tr><td>23 QxQ+</td><td>KxQ</td></tr>
<tr><td>24 R-K5!</td><td>P-QKt3</td></tr>
<tr><td>25 B-B1</td><td>. . .</td></tr>
</table>

. . . and White's Bishop gained full command of the white squares. The ending required considerable finesse to win, but Fischer obviously felt this type of game was the safest and surest way to a full point. (See Chapter "Reach.")

There is no hesitation when simplification leaves a book win:

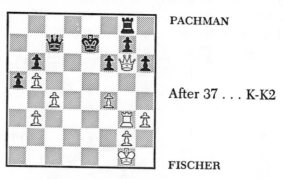

PACHMAN

After 37 . . . K-K2

FISCHER

Leipzig 1960

<table>
<tr><td>38 QxKtP+</td><td>RxQ</td></tr>
<tr><td>39 RxR+</td><td>K-Q3</td></tr>
<tr><td>40 RxQ</td><td>. . .</td></tr>
</table>

The same idea leaves White a good Pawn up:

REE

After 16 . . . Kt-R4

FISCHER

Nathanya 1968

17 QxB+! QxQ
18 BxP . . .

In the same tournament Fischer found this opportunity to trade Bishop for Knight, along the way weakening the Black center:

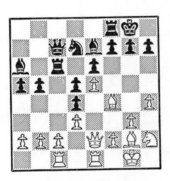

U. GELLER

After 16 . . . B-R3

FISCHER

Nathanya 1968

17 BxP! PxB
18 P-K6 . . .

Fischer is alert to the smallest gain, here the exchange of White's King Bishop, giving him the Bishop pair:

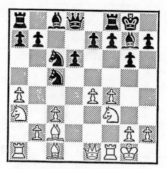

FISCHER

After 12 B-B2

MARIC

Skopje 1967

| 12 ... | Kt-Kt6! |
| 13 BxKt | Q-Kt3+ |

A common form of simplification occurs after the move Kt-Q5, involving either a Pawn fork to regain the piece, or threats against the King to save it from capture:

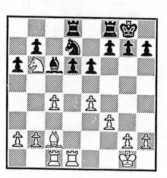

ROSSETTO

After 18 . . . Kt-Q2

FISCHER

Mar del Plata 1959

19 Kt-Q5!   ...

After either PxKt or BxKt, no material is gained or lost, but the White Bishop is released from his Pawn prison. Typically, the threatened check at K7 in such positions makes the move somewhat forcing.

SOFREVSKI

After 14 . . . PxB

FISCHER

Skopje 1967

15 Kt-Q5!   KR-K1

The Knight cannot be taken because of 16 RxP, when Black has no defense against Q-R6 and R-KR5. Now Black loses his Bishop pair.

The other important use of simplification is to break an attack. Sometimes it takes a strong will to return material in order to weather a storm, as these two examples show:

FISCHER

After 21 B-Q1

KAVALEK

Sousse 1967

Fischer is three Pawns and a piece up—but what Pawns! In order to parry the threat of QxP, Black could try 21 . . . B-B4+ and 22 . . . B-Q5, but then 23 Q-Kt3 allows the Queen to infiltrate. Taking courage in his hands, Fischer challenged the attackers:

21 . . .	R-B1!	
22 BxP+	K-Q1	
23 R-Q1+	B-Q2	
24 Q-K3!	Q-R4	
25 R-Kt7!	. . .	

White takes a draw with perpetual check against 25 . . . B-B4 26 KRxB+.

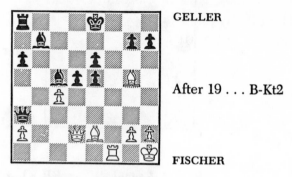

GELLER

After 19 . . . B-Kt2

FISCHER

Monaco 1967

On the other side of the same heavily analyzed variation of the Sicilian, Fischer overlooked a simplifying idea by his opponent. Instead of threatening a winning Queen infiltration with 20 Q-B2 P-Kt3 21 B-R5! he gave Black time to force a Queen exchange:

| | 20 B-Kt4? | PxP |
| | 21 BxP | Q-Q6! |

This loss in the last round did not knock Fischer out of first place, but it must have been particularly galling to lose in his own tactical backyard.

VI *Just for Fun!*

28 Opening Adventures

One look at a copy of a book on the openings is enough to terrify anyone but the chess fanatic. One has to have a special incentive to wade through column after column of variations—perhaps to beat your archrival at the club or to prepare a trap for the next round of a tournament. Too many good players, in my opinion, spend their time studying opening theory when their tactical abilities and endgame skill are undeveloped.

Yet openings can be an adventure, and Bobby Fischer enjoys the discovery of a new line as much as an astronomer finding a new star. After thousands of treatises and millions of magazine articles on the openings, it is no less than amazing that new ideas can still be turned up in the first ten moves of a game. If you are the one who makes the discovery, you have the feeling of adding to the general body of truth—a short step but nevertheless a step toward that dream that has always hovered over the thirty-two pieces lined up in their starting positions: White to play and win.

Thousands of players, including nonmasters, have left their names on opening variations. Perhaps that too is some incentive. The use of proper names to identify opening lines is quite a ritual, the incense of chess. When Mikenas played 1 ... P-KKt3 against Alekhine's King Pawn opening at Folkestone 1933, the World Champion called it simply the "King's Fianchetto" and commented, "This move is rightly considered as inferior . . ." As it gained new adherents over the last thirty years, however, it has been called variously the Pirc Defense, or the Robatsch, and now simply the Modern Defense. Curiously, Capablanca alone among the chess greats did not leave his name on even a subvariation, but not because he failed to innovate. I think it is more a tribute to the Cuban's great versatility and abhorrence of pet lines, and in this Fischer is now showing a like maturity.

The best use of opening compilations is for reference after you have played a game rather than before. Where did he/I go wrong? Did I improve on some great game of the past? Looking up an opening in advance is not only a wearisome exercise, but it is something like studying the dictionary or looking at the solution before you try to solve a problem. Reuben Fine's advice is that the excessive preparation of opening lines can tend to stultify your thinking during the game. A good trial lawyer can tell you that nothing brings out the truth like the adversary system.

Besides, where is the fun in relying on your memory? In 1969, the magazine *Informator* awarded a game of Fischer's the honor of being the second-best game played anywhere in the world in the first half of the year. Four years later, at Madrid 1973, the game Karpov-Bellon followed the Saidy-Fischer game through White's twenty-third move, including seven moves given exclamation points by R. G. Wade in his book on Fischer. When Julio Kaplan analyzed the Karpov game in *Chess Life & Review* in March 1974, no mention was made of Fischer's winning line, which Bellon missed starting with his twenty-third move. Wade went so far as to say that this would have been the *best* game of 1969, first half, except for Fischer's doubtful opening gambit. Karpov not only failed to take advantage of this supposed opening lapse; he kept right on walking into a lost game constructed, unbeknownst to him, by the World Champion he hopes to dethrone.

It is noteworthy that Fischer does not play opening gambits the way Alekhine or Tal used to. The above-mentioned example is an exception:

1 P-QB4	P-K4
2 Kt-QB3	Kt-QB3
3 P-KKt3	P-B4
4 B-Kt2	Kt-B3
5 P-Q3	B-B4
6 P-K3	P-B5?!

. . . as played by Fischer and Bellon. As Wade mentions, this move fits Spielmann's definition of a real sacrifice (or gambit): The consequences are incalculable and the compensation intangible. The idea is to open lines toward the KB2 square, to block the prospects of White's Queen Bishop, and to create a target at

White's Q3. At the cost of a Pawn, Fischer achieved all of this when his opponent (as did Karpov) failed to react aggressively:

7	KPxP	O-O
8	KKt-K2	. . .

Here there was nothing to fear after 8 PxP R-K1 9 P-B4 P-Q3 10 BxKt PxB 11 P-Q4! The adage goes: The way to refute a gambit is to accept it, all the way if possible.

This opening line also illustrates the well-known trick of trying a marginally successful formation with colors reversed. In this case, the defense to the English opening here becomes an attack against the Sicilian Defense, if tried from the White side. It might interest theorists to know that the extra move seldom is enough to alter the basic values in such positions. In the above case, for example, White has played P-Q3 on his fifth move. If Black avoids that move in the Sicilian (that is, with colors reversed), then at the end of the refutation noted above (11 P-Q4) the position is identical whether it is played as White or Black.

Another rare example of a Fischer gambit came at Buenos Aires 1960, against Korchnoi's Sicilian:

1	P-K4	P-QB4
2	Kt-KB3	P-QR3
3	P-Q4	PxP
4	P-B3	. . .

Late in his career, Alekhine pronounced this his last word on how to deal with the Sicilian, but preceding P-Q4, in order to control the center with Pawns. If Black fails to take the gambit, this is exactly what will happen. After 4 . . . PxP 5 KtxP it is a real gambit. Korchnoi held on to the Pawn for twenty moves, then returned it to obtain an equal game—which the student should know is the standard theme in meeting a sacrifice.

Other than these two examples, Fischer's gambits tend to come later in the game. He is characteristically the one who tries to refute Pawn offers, as in his announced "bust" of the King's Gambit based on hanging on to the Pawn. Incidentally, many so-called gambits (the Queen's Gambit, the King's Gambit) are not sacrifices at all in most of their lines—certainly not by Spielmann's definition.

There are two major themes running through Fischer's choice of openings, in addition to his skeptical opinion of gambits. First, he delights in cultivating discarded variations and milking them for original twists. Second, he relies on piece play rather than a powerful Pawn center to fight for an opening advantage.

Before becoming serious, I would like to present what might be called the control of the center with Pawns, *in extremis:*

FISCHER

After 24 K-K1

PACHMAN

Santiago 1959

This is perhaps the wildest, if not the funniest, position of Fischer's career. The absolute "control" which White exercises over the center is of course meaningless—except that the Pawns prevent a frontal attack on the King. Quite incidentally, it is interesting to see how Fischer could have won, even though a piece down, by not pressing the attack too soon:

24 ...   Q-Kt8+?

"Patzer sees a check, gives a check," as Fischer himself would say. First 24 ... Kt-K2 preserves more options, since once the Queen says "A" she must say "B." Black gains a move, since 25 B-B4 is answered by R-R8+, forcing B-B1; and Black's threat is to proceed as below without losing another piece:

25 K-Q2   ...

White is mated upon 25 B-B1 QxB+.

25 ...   QxP+
26 K-B3   ...

... and now Q-Kt6 is met by 27 Q-Q3 Kt-K2 28 B-B4!

Fischer has related with pride that his study of the "old masters" has given him several opening novelties. He shows himself in this respect to be the realist rather than the sentimentalist. Chess is no less subject to the whims of fashion than women's clothing: It is "smart" to be seen reeling out the latest lines of the "Sozin" variation of the Sicilian (who Sozin is nobody knows, I suspect). In rehabilitating old lines from the nineteenth century, Fischer is merely playing moves for their objective value rather than for their reputation, or for the reputation of their adherents.

Here he dusts off a move of that opening eccentric Steinitz:

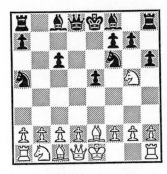

BISGUIER

After 8 . . . P-KR3

FISCHER

Poughkeepsie 1963

This normal line from the Two Knights' Defense gives Black a temporary initiative for the Pawn after 9 Kt-KB3 P-K5. Fischer essays the bizarre:

9 Kt-KR3 . . .

Fischer played this twice in the New York State Championship; the idea is to develop faster at the expense of returning the Pawn:

9 . . .	**B-QB4**
10 O-O	**O-O**
11 P-Q3	**BxKt**

. . . followed by Q-Q2. It is fascinating to see Fischer quoting Gottschall from an 1892 issue of the *Deutsche Schachzeitung* to demonstrate various combinational possibilities for White and Black. He won both games, but not necessarily because of the opening. The opening did accomplish one thing: It placed both players on an equal footing for the struggle to follow.

In other notes to this game, Bobby is particularly flamboyant. Of his first move, P-K4, he takes the liberty of writing "best by test." After 1 . . . P-K4 2 Kt-KB3 Kt-QB3 3 B-B4 Kt-B3 4 Kt-Kt5 P-Q4 5 PxP, he says "5 . . . Kt-Q5!? (Fritz) . . . [is] interesting but unsound." I doubt one player in a thousand could tell us who Fritz was, but the line is not played enough to know for sure if it is unsound or not. The shortest game on record that Fischer has lost, to my knowledge, followed this variation: 6 P-QB3 P-Kt4 7 B-B1 KtxP 8 PxKt (Fischer has also played 8 KtxRP) QxKt 9 BxP+ K-Q1 10 Q-B3 B-Kt2 11 O-O PxP 12 QxP? Kt-B3 13 Resigns, since there are threats of mate, QxB, and B-Q4, winning the Queen. It should be pointed out that this was a simultaneous game from Fischer's 1963 tour, and not a clock game.

Although he has not traced the following opening specifically back to Morphy, Fischer has used a system against the Sicilian many times which first appeared in the unofficial World Championship match between the New Orleans genius and Adolph Anderssen:

1	P-K4	P-QB4
2	Kt-KB3	Kt-QB3
3	P-Q4	PxP
4	KtxP	P-K3

Now called the Taimanov variation, this is of course of ancient lineage, and was part of the original idea of the Sicilian.

5	Kt-Kt5	. . .

. . . an attempt to force weaknesses at the expense of a lot of time.

5	. . .	P-Q3
6	B-KB4	P-K4

Curiously, Black often chooses this move with a will in the Sicilian, but here White actively tries to induce it. A good alternative is Kt-K4 (Fine), although neither Najdorf (at Santa Monica 1966), nor Taimanov (second and sixth games, Match, Vancouver 1971), nor Petrosian (first game, Match, Buenos Aires 1971) thought so.

7	B-K3	Kt-B3

Here Anderssen played 7 . . . P-B4!? against Morphy in Paris 1858(!), and came a cropper: 8 QKt-B3 P-B5? 9 Kt-Q5! winning in a few moves.

8	B-Kt5	. . .

The laborious maneuvering of the White Bishop is one of the few examples of one player being able to waste several moves with one piece just to obtain a positional edge. That apparent edge here is the threat to secure the square Q5.

8	. . .	Q-R4+
9	Q-Q2!	. . .

Outdoing Morphy, he gives up a Pawn for pure development. For 8 . . . P-QR3, etc., see Fischer-Petrosian in Chapter 33, "The Reason Why." We are now following Fischer-Taimanov, second Match game.

9	. . .	KtxP
10	QxQ	KtxQ
11	B-K3	. . .

The fourth move of this Bishop in the first eleven moves by White leaves Black with a difficult game.

11	. . .	K-Q2
12	QKt-B3!	. . .

A characteristic touch: Black's only developed piece is traded. In such positions the gambiteer must not worry about winning back his Pawn quickly.

12 ...	KtxKt
13 KtxKt	K-Q1
14 Kt-Kt5	...

Back again. Fischer has ample play for the Pawn. (For the ending, see Chapter 29, "Grandmaster Gaffes.")

Suetin is credited with finding a flaw in Fischer's treatment of this line, and passing it on to Petrosian. However, the Latvian master Vitolins apparently published the same idea five months before the Fischer-Petrosian match. It's difficult to keep up!

As an alternative to this way of handling the Sicilian, Fischer is more famous for his 6 B-QB4 line, the so-called "Sozin." It was once thought that developing the Bishop on this square was asking it to "bite on granite" when Black played P-K3. Indeed, Fischer was able to pull off some flashy attacks when Black stayed with the "Dragon," characterized by P-KKt3:

RESHEVSKY

After 11 Kt-K6

FISCHER

New York 1958–59

White has sacrificed his Bishop at KB2, and whether the Rook or King had taken it Kt-K6! would follow. The Queen is lost, for KxKt soon leads to mate. The position loses some of its luster when we learn that this entire trap had been published in a Soviet magazine a few months earlier—Reshevsky was the only one in the tournament room who hadn't seen it!

On a later occasion Fischer had a similar opportunity and let it pass:

1 P-K4	P-QB4
2 Kt-KB3	Kt-QB3
3 P-Q4	PxP

	4 KtxP	P-KKt3
	5 Kt-QB3	B-Kt2
	6 B-K3	Kt-B3
	7 B-QB4	Kt-QR4

... and here Fischer played B-Kt3 (Fischer-Leopoldi, Western Open 1963). This time Black hasn't castled, and so after

	8 BxP+!	KxB
	9 Kt-K6!	Q-Kt1
	10 Kt-B7+	...

... Black doesn't lose his Queen, but his game is a shambles.

When Black sets up a Sicilian with P-K3 instead of P-KKt3 to develop the King Bishop, the idea of the Sozin is to play P-KB4, B5 and break up the Pawn phalanx. Black's counterplay consists of an attack on the King Pawn, undermining the natural support of the Knight at White's QB3 with P-QKt4, Kt5. At Zagreb 1970, Korchnoi played P-QKt4 without the support of a Pawn at R3, and got away with it. This game no doubt gave Spassky ideas. In the first Sicilian of their 1972 match at Reykjavik, Spassky threatened to play the Pawn to Kt5 by playing P-QR4, giving up the support of the QKtP. White's pieces are typically overloaded in this type of position: That is, the pieces that can win Black's QKtP are the same that are supporting the King Pawn. So to win a Pawn, White must advance his King Pawn and thereby give Black's Queen Bishop a lot of scope. This game is discussed in detail in other chapters, but it is important here to see the general ideas behind the choice of an opening system.

Another famous Fischer "revival" occurs in the exchange variation of the Ruy Lopez. This is the opening that Lasker used to beat Capablanca in their dramatic final encounter at St. Petersburg 1914. But Fischer found something slightly different—in the order of moves:

	1 P-K4	P-K4
	2 Kt-KB3	Kt-QB3
	3 B-Kt5	P-QR3
	4 BxKt	QPxB
	5 O-O	...

In this most logical of openings, in which White systematically strives to put pressure on the King Pawn, every student learns at an early age that the Pawn cannot be taken without giving up his own KP (5 KtxP—instead of O-O—Q-Q5!). And if the White KP is defended by 5 P-Q3, Black can go about his business with B-QB4, because now 6 KtxP Q-Q5 threatens mate and the Knight. It was customary to play 5 P-Q4 and head for an ending in which White had better Pawns but Black had the two Bishops. Fischer's O-O (not that it hadn't been played often before) was aimed at embarrassing Black in defending his King Pawn. When he won three straight games with this new weapon at the Havana 1966 Olympics, there was talk of a "bust" of the Steinitz Defense deferred. Since then, the defense has been bolstered, and Spassky nearly beat Fischer with Black in one of the latter's favorite lines, at Reykjavik.

What is consistent in Fischer's approach to the openings—and it is the basic lesson of this chapter—is that a player should strive to fight at the earliest moment for an edge. The majority of chess players either ape well-known lines, or develop in a routine way, or create some kind of a Pawn formation in the abstract. The game of chess really doesn't begin until one of the players makes a threat. A "conversation" then begins to shape up, in which threats are answered with counterthreats, defenses are tested, goals are established. Most of Fischer's games (and those of the masters) have no central theme; the play follows the lead of tactical opportunities. Great symphonic build-ups tend to be crashing bores.

In this position, for example, where the opening is about over, Fischer is not content with the obvious P-R3, or O-O, to be followed by Kt-Kt3, B5. He strikes out at once at a target:

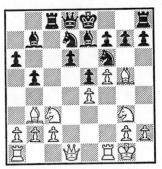

FISCHER

After 13 O-O

R. BYRNE

Sousse 1967

13 ...	P-KR4!

The idea, of course, is P-R5, undermining the King Pawn. The only way to stop this is to create another weakness—at R4:

14 P-KR4	P-Kt5
15 BxKt	...

The logic of Black's plan is this: BxKt is forced, in order to maintain the King Pawn, when Black plays P-Kt5. So Black's KRP will fall:

15 ...	BxB
16 Kt-Q5	BxP
17 KtxRP	Q-Kt4!

This is the rub. The White Knight must fight for its life, first ingeniously, then hopefully, finally futilely.

18 P-B6	P-Kt3
19 Kt-Kt7+	K-Q1

Black was able to win in ten more moves.

The openings offer an adventure of another kind—the opportunity to indulge in a little amateur psychology. When Spassky came up with a surprise move in the eleventh game of the 1972 match (14 Kt-Kt1, attempting to embarrass the Black Queen which had eaten the poisoned pawn in the Sicilian), it was a foregone conclusion that reams of Russian analysis were behind it. Yet Spassky hesitated over the move for a considerable time, as if making a spur-of-the-moment decision. Although these little tricks are quite common, I can't recall an instance where Fischer has done the same. When he makes a rapid move, it's because he has made up his mind. When he deliberates, he hasn't made up his mind. Bobby's objective behavior at the chessboard goes a long way to excuse his shenanigans as a chess politician.

29 Grandmaster Gaffes

There are scores of examples in this book of "how the mighty have fallen." Although Fischer does put fearsome pressure on his opponents, there is no reason to believe they blunder against him any more than against anyone else. Or do they overlook the obvious, when faced with perhaps the most accurate player in history? In any case, here are some glaring examples of chess blindness:

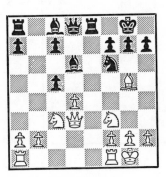

FISCHER

After 13 . . . P-B4

GHITESCU

Leipzig 1960

       14 PxP??   **BxRP+**

White loses his Queen in the first thirteen moves of the Olympiad. Perhaps he wasn't warmed up.

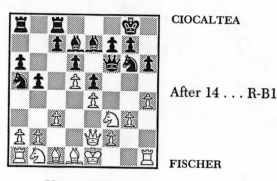

CIOCALTEA

After 14 ... R-B1

FISCHER

Varna 1962

15 B-Kt5!   ...

At the next Olympics, another Queen bites the dust in a hurry.

Both Taimanov and Spassky were said to have felt some "sinister force" when they met Fischer in their matches. Whatever the reason, they sprinkled their games with absolute bloopers—at the same time showing a general level of chess equal to any World Championship series before them.

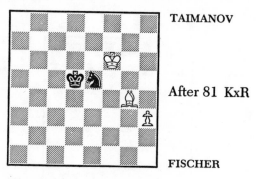

TAIMANOV

After 81 KxR

FISCHER

Match, Vancouver 1971

81 ...   K-K5?

Some of Fischer's *Sitzfleisch* must have got to the Russian. There are two fairly easy drawing ideas, the most basic of which is that all Black has to do is get his King to KR1, since the White Bishop does not control the queening square. Therefore, 81 ... Kt-Q6 82 P-R4 Kt-B5 83 K-B5 K-Q3! does the trick. For the record, Fischer finished as follows:

82 B-B8!   K-B5

Now 82 . . . Kt-B6 is no good because of the Bishop check, forcing a won King and Pawn ending.

83	P-R4	Kt-B6
84	P-R5	Kt-Kt4
85	B-B5!	. . .

Zugzwang.

85	. . .	Kt-B6
86	P-R6	Kt-Kt4
87	K-Kt6	Resigns

Taimanov followed this with an oversight that would be horrendous for ten-second chess:

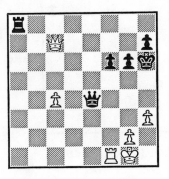

FISCHER

After 45 . . . K-R3

TAIMANOV

Match, Vancouver 1971

46 RxP?   Q-Q5+

The Rook goes after 47 R-B2 R-R8+.

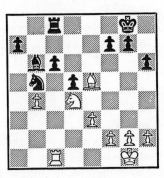

SPASSKY

After 27 Kt-Q4

FISCHER

Match, Reykjavik 1972

27 . . .   P-B3?

Black gives back the Pawn when he could have traded off the minor pieces with an easy win: 27 . . . KtxKt 28 BxKt BxB 29 PxB R-Kt1 etc. In fact, what did Fischer have in mind with 27 Kt-Q4?

28 BxP . . .

Since Black has a piece *en prise*, the unprotected Knight, the Bishop becomes a "desperado." The game was drawn lamely.

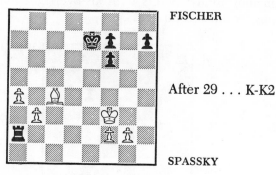

FISCHER

After 29 . . . K-K2

SPASSKY

Match, Reykjavik 1972

Spassky's last series of moves as World Champion had two lemons in the space of five moves.

30 P-KKt4? . . .

The only threat a doubled Pawn poses is generally that it will advance and trade itself for a better Pawn. Spassky sets it up:

30 . . .	P-B4!
31 PxP	P-B3
32 B-Kt8	P-R3
33 K-Kt3	K-Q3
34 K-B3?	. . .

His last chance was to close the door at K5 with 34 P-B4, when Black can make no headway. Now it's over.

For some unexplained reason, one of the soundest players of this era has stumbled repeatedly against Fischer. Svetozar Gligoric is also one of Bobby's great friends among the masters.

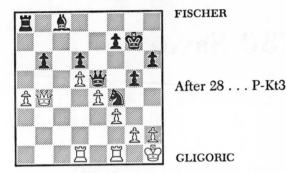

FISCHER

After 28 . . . P-Kt3

GLIGORIC

Palma 1970

29 R-B2?   Kt-Q6!

"Played like a shot," was the report from the tournament hall. The fork works, because after 30 RxKt White has three pieces that can get back to the first rank, but no two on the same square!

It is good to know that the grandmaster and the novice share the same humanity.

30 Saves

There are "saves" and there are "swindles." Frank Marshall, the great American Champion roughly between Pillsbury and Kashdan, which is rough enough, gave meaning to the word "swindle." Even the great Alekhine paid grudging respect to Marshall's ability to rescue draws from losses and wins from draws. The element that distinguishes a swindle from a save, however, is not ingenuity or diabolical cleverness, but *tenacity*. When it counts, this is what Fischer has.

Only Lasker before him has shown what tenacity can accomplish. The game that admirers of Lasker find most typical is the clash with Capablanca at St. Petersburg 1914, where Lasker defended an ending with Rook against two pieces when he needed not merely a draw, but a win. He drew! He went on to win the second encounter with Capa to overtake him and win the tournament. We have yet to see such drama in any of Fischer's tournaments, but the tenacity is there—and perhaps is all the more worthy of the man for that reason.

At Zagreb 1970, where Fischer was fighting for his big comeback on the international scene, Walter Browne had won the exchange and it looked as if he would turn the endgame into a rout. But Fischer fought on, sixty, seventy, eighty moves. In the following position, Fischer's advanced Pawn seemed worthless, his Knight immobile, his King in a mating net.

268

FISCHER

After 87 . . . K-B1

BROWNE

Zagreb 1970

88 P-B7? ...

A forceful move, but Fischer finds a "swindle" that saves the game. The difference is that the Black Knight is allowed to make a threat, which would not be possible after virtually any Rook move—R-KR7 being doubly safe.

88 ... **Kt-Q2!**

Strangely reminiscent of the Lasker-Lasker endgame of 1924 (see below). The Rook on the rank can't adequately defend the advanced Pawn if the Knight is allowed to "mask" it.

89 K-B6 **P-R8(Q)!**

To draw the Bishop away from protecting the Rook.

90 BxQ **Kt-K4+**
91 K-Kt6 **B-B4+!**
92 KxB **KtxR**

... and the Knight will be able to immolate himself for the Pawn. A problemist would also find satisfaction in the fact that the queening move "decoyed" the Bishop to a square where he could not give a good check.

One of the great sagas of chess is the New York 1924 tournament, which brought together virtually all the leading masters of the day. Other tournaments may have been more important, or more closely contested, but none had the dramatic inevitability of this one. The World Champion was Capablanca, and such was his popularity that the newborn *Time Magazine* carried his visage on the cover as the tournament began. (It was the last time a mere chess player was to have a *Time* cover to himself.)

Emanuel Lasker entered the tournament an emotional favorite. Was his loss of the championship to Capa three years earlier really decisive? The American Master Edward Lasker has written several loving and witty accounts of the battle for first place, in which he himself played an important role. In both of his games with the World Champion, Edward Lasker had a winning advantage, only to draw the first and lose the second. Then came his turn to throw a scare into his namesake. Just before the following position was reached, Capablanca and other contestants were heartily congratulating the American as he waited outside the tournament room for Lasker to make a move:

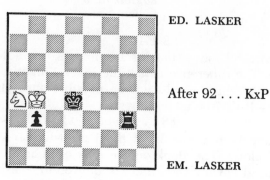

ED. LASKER

After 92 . . . KxP

EM. LASKER

New York 1924

Upon his return, Black quickly realized that the Knight is a stout defender. It simply shuttles between Kt2 and R4. If the Black King tries to approach on the second rank by going around the Rook (93 . . . R-K6 followed by K-K5, K-B6, etc.), then White has time to play K-R3, K-Kt2, and Kt-B3, masking the Rook from the Pawn and winning it. So Emanuel Lasker chalked up another half-point on his way to first place.

Incidentally, the King and Knight can always draw against King and Rook as long as the King avoids the corner and keeps the Knight nearby.

Fischer has long had the reputation of not becoming discouraged in apparently hopeless positions, and, on the other hand, of being patient against a tenacious defender. With White, Fischer would have won the following position, if only by not committing himself too soon. With Black he was able to draw it!

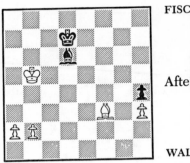

FISCHER

After 53 . . . K-Q2

WALTHER

Zurich 1959

54 P-R4? ...

It seems strange to give this natural-looking move a question mark, but it throws away a half-point. Bishops of opposite colors are notorious for their drawing possibilities, but only when the Pawns can be "fixed" by the King and Bishop working in unison. A further complication here is that Black can give up his Bishop for both Pawns, as long as his King can reach KR1. The White Bishop cannot oust him from the corner. (Compare this idea with the draw Fischer missed in his first match game with Spassky, 1972. See Chapter 34, "Gordian Knots.")

54 ...	K-B2
55 P-Kt4	K-Kt1!
56 P-R5	K-R2

White could make no headway, since the Bishop will take up a position on the R2-Kt8 diagonal and sacrifice himself for both Pawns when P-Kt6 is played. The point is that the White King cannot support this advance from any square except B6, and he can't get there because B-B2 will force the Pawns to move. The winning line therefore consists in getting the Pawn to Kt6 before this defensive alignment can be set up. 54 P-Kt4 just does the trick: 54 . . . K-B2 55 K-R5 K-Kt1 56 P-Kt5 and P-Kt6 cannot be stopped.

Fischer has also found himself on the receiving end of some "saves." If, as Capablanca said, a player learns far more from his losses than from his wins, Fischer had some early tutoring that has stood him in good stead.

CIOCALTEA

After 42 RxP

FISCHER

Havana 1965

With his Bishop pinned and P-Kt6 staring him in the face, it would appear that Black has lost the Pawn race. However:

42 ...	P-K6+!
43 K-B2	...

If the King retreats he not only allows a Rook check, releasing the pin, but gets in a mating net. But now the Bishop is unprotected:

43 ...	BxP!
44 RxR	BxB
45 R-KB7	P-B6!

The final point. With the Knight Pawn liquidated, the Bishop and King can draw much as in the Browne-Fischer and Lasker-Lasker positions.

In middle-game positions, ingenuity rather than tenacity is the mark of the successful "save." Robert Byrne got a lesson in swindling in the following exciting U.S. Championship game:

FISCHER

After 24 ... R-B6

R. BYRNE

New York 1959–60

25 Kt-Kt5 ...

This is apparently a killer, since the KBP cannot be defended. Fischer's rejoinder, which was obviously planned when he made his previous move, could hardly have been fully anticipated by White, or he would have tried the more complicated 25 Kt-B6! The Black Rook at Q2 is threatened, so the ultimate threat against the BP is the same. The difference is that Black does not have the same defense as in the game (sacrificing his Queen) because of the loss of the Rook, e.g.: 25 . . . RxB 26 KtxR R-Q7 27 RxP RxP+ 28 K-B1 Q-Q1 29 Kt-B6! threatening the familiar Rook and Knight mate beginning QxP+! (See Chapter 8, "Mate in the Afternoon.) And if Black takes the time to defend his Rook with 25 . . . R2-B2 26 Kt-Kt4! gets there first: 26 . . . RxB 27 KtxP PxKt 28 QxP+ K-Kt1 29 R-B4, or 26 . . . Q-B1 27 B-Kt6, winning without risk.

Now, however, Fischer is allowed to reveal his saving clause:

25 ...	RxB!
26 RxP	R-Q7!!
27 P-K4	...

The exquisite point is that Black defends by the back door after 27 Q-Kt6 RxP+ 28 K-B1 RxKt.

27 ...	QxR
28 KtxQ+	RxKt
29 QxR	BxP

FISCHER

After 29 . . . BxP

BYRNE

30 R-K1 ...

Fischer has only two Bishops for the Queen, but White cannot afford to let them have a free rein. After 30 QxKP, a move most players would leap at, Fischer had worked out a neat drawing line: 30 . . . B-Kt7 31 R-K1 BxP 32 R-Q1 (or the Bishop check would be embarrassing) BxP+ 33 K-R2 BxP+! 34 QxB RxR 35 KxB R-Q7+ followed by RxP, and White is out of Pawns. The Rook can't be picked up with a check, and he will simply sit at QR4. Few players have explored as fully as Fischer the drawing chances in reducing the Pawns on the board. In his only loss to Reshevsky in a U.S. Championship, he played with a Rook against Queen for twenty moves in a similar ending before succumbing.

30 ...	RxP+
31 K-B1	B-Q4
32 R-K2	R-Kt5?

In exchanging Rooks the draw was assured, since the QRP must fall. After almost going astray, Fischer soon repeated the position three times and claimed the draw.

Not long before this game was played, Fischer pulled a rabbit out of the hat in the following desperate position:

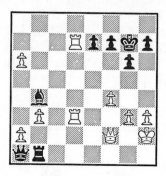

FISCHER

After 38 . . . B-Kt5

REDOLFI

Mar de Plata 1959

Who would recognize the Black position as Fischer's? With his last move he allows 39 Q-Q4+, exchanging Queens and ending all resistance. Hoping against hope, Fischer tries a "Marshall" and his gullible opponent falls into a mate. Time trouble?

39 P-R7?	B-B4
40 QxB?	...

He could still win in a walk with 40 Q-Kt2 B-Kt8+ 41 QxB.

40 ...	R-R8+

. . . and mate next move.

There is an area of composition in which artful "saves" are the *pièce de résistance:* stopping Pawns on the verge of queening. (No "swindles" seem to have ever been composed, perhaps because they seem to work out over the board quite readily.) Like

;aving the heroine from going over the waterfall, the rescue of an
ipparently lost cause is full of melodrama:

DOERNTE

White to play

RICHTER

Berlin 1939

Two connected passed Pawns on the sixth can't be stopped by
a Rook unless one of the Pawns is already under attack. What has
Black to fear?

1 K-Q6!	P-Q7
2 K-B7	P-Q8(Q)
3 R-R6+!	. . .

And now it is White who will queen a Pawn, only this time it's
mate:

3 . . .	PxR
4 P-Kt6+	K-R1
5 P-Kt7+	K-R2
6 P-Kt8(Q) mate.	

31 Themes

Chess problems and studies are the idealization of what can happen on the board. The themes which problemists explore are not foreign to the practical player; it's just that themes are only the means to an end for the player.

The study of problems, therefore, and especially endgame studies, can be quite helpful to the player in improving his technique. But such a study should not be considered a substitute in any way for practical over-the-board experience.

It will be interesting to see if Bobby Fischer turns his hand to an occasional chess composition, as many of the greats of chess have done before him. Lasker and Capablanca even collaborated in a joint endgame study. Botvinnik, Keres, and Smyslov have all published problems and endings. Alekhine apparently did not, but he enriched the theory of many endgames (Rook vs. Knight, for example) with intensive analyses of his own games and annotations for several major tournament books.

Fischer has ample material in his games so far to demonstrate quite a number of problem themes. And I suspect he has enjoyed those games the most in which he was able to create something that will live in chess history, rather than the occasional game that sprang full-blown from a prepared variation, or fell into his lap because of a blunder by his opponent. It is this natural preference on the part of most players which gives the lie to the common complaint that the competitive element in chess is destructive.

Fischer's forceful style has produced many fine examples of the interference theme. In this basic tactic of line-moving pieces, one piece moves onto the line of another, preventing the first from reaching a critical square. If the second piece is an enemy piece, the effect can be quite simple:

LASKER (1890)

*White to play
and win*

1 P-Kt5+!   KxP

The result is the same if the Pawn is not taken: the line of the Bishop on the diagonal KR3-QB8 is obstructed.

2 P-R5   ...

. . . and now the Bishop has no way to guard the square QR2 in two moves, where he has to head the Pawn off at the pass.

The most common type of interference is the so-called "Grimshaw," where a Bishop steps in the way of a Rook and the Rook steps in the way of the Bishop—on the same square. In the two-move problem, the result is checkmate; in over-the-board play, the result can simply be the loss of a Pawn. Fischer's strange-looking move in the following position from the seventh game of the Petrosian match had the effect of inducing either an interference or a favorable endgame:

PETROSIAN

After 11 . . . B-K2

FISCHER

Match, Buenos Aires 1971

12 Q-R4+   . . .

Apparently a meaningless check, since Black "develops" his Bishop with a tempo after 12 . . . B-Q2. However, this is just the point. The Black Queen Pawn has then one less guard, since the Bishop has interfered with the Queen. The result of this is that after 13 Q-B2 Black cannot castle: 13 . . . O-O 14 B-KKt5, and by capturing the Knight White would win either the Queen Pawn or the King Rook Pawn. (14 . . . P-Q5 fails because of the "comeback" after 15 BxKt PxKt 16 BxBP.) Black must therefore offer a Queen exchange.

12 . . .   **Q-Q2**
13 R-K1!   . . .

Instead of going for immediate gain with 13 B-Kt5, winning the exchange at the cost of getting his Queen out of play, Fischer forces a Queen exchange which brings his Knight to control over his QB5. White won a delicate endgame.

Rarer and more striking is the so-called "Holzhausen" interference, between like-moving pieces. Spassky set this one up as if he were working with Fischer on a joint composition:

FISCHER

After 27 Q-B2

SPASSKY

Match, Reykjavik 1972

27 . . .   **BxP!**

The White Queen has cut the line of the Bishop, and so has assumed the guard of both the QRP and the KP. White resigned, for 28 QxB allows the double threat 28 . . . QxP.

When the pieces in question do not interfere by choice, but find their critical square blocked by an enemy piece, the problem world refers to the interference as a "Plachutta." An unbelievably clearcut example occurred in the following consultation game:

ALLIES

After 30 . . . K-Kt4

TARRASCH

Naples 1914

White has two potential threats: Q-Kt7+ and RxP+, both leading to mate. The former is prevented by the Black Queen, the latter by the Black Queen Rook. But there is a critical square, QB2, through which each Black line of guard must pass. Therefore, logic dictates:

31 B-B7! Resigns

If the Rook takes, then Q-Kt7+; if the Queen takes, then RxP+ (in full, 31 . . . QxB 32 RxP+ QxR 33 Q-Kt7+ KxP 34 R-R1 mate).

The following position illustrates a Holzhausen and a Grimshaw on the same square, with a few pins thrown in for good measure:

KERES

After 26 . . . PxB

FISCHER

Curaçao 1962

27 QxP Q-Q3

Threats on the back rank allow White to maneuver his pieces into overwhelming positions.

28 Q-R4 Q-K2

First, the Holzhausen, blocking the King Bishop.

29	Kt-B6+	K-R1
30	Kt-Q5	Q-Q2
31	Q-K4!	Q-Q3
32	Kt-B4	R-K2

Now a Grimshaw interference on the Queen, allowing 33 B-B8. Fischer chose to take the interference on the Bishop to play 33 B-Kt5, trading off the minor pieces and the Queens for a won Rook and Pawn endgame.

A Grimshaw often has defensive purposes: By causing an enemy Rook and Bishop to fall all over themselves on their critical square, a player can find necessary "flight" squares for his King.

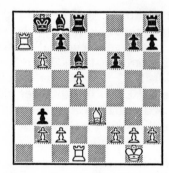

ANASTASOPOULOS

After 19 . . . B-B1

FISCHER

Clock Simultaneous, Athens 1968

20	PxP+	BxP
21	P-QB4!	. . .

. . . and Fischer soon won. He saw the defensive interference after the plausible 21 R-Q3 PxP 22 R-Kt3+ B-Kt3! and the Black King gets out at R2. This idea is often used in the two-move chess problem to prevent "cooks"—unwanted solutions.

Line-moving pieces are subject to errors, even while they remain on their main line of guard, by choosing a square which allows another type of threat. This complicated-sounding maneuver is best defined by example. In the following position the Black Queen Rook is comfortable at R1, guarding the back rank. White threatens Q-Kt4+, winning the Knight, which must interpose. But then Black would still have some play left. Fischer ends all doubt by luring, or decoying, the Queen Rook to a less comfortable square:

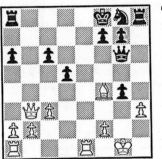

GELLER

After 19 . . . PxP

FISCHER

Bled 1961

20 Q-Kt7!	PxP+
21 B-Kt3	R-Q1
22 Q-Kt4+	. . .

Black resigns, as he loses both Knight and Rook after 22 Kt-K2 QxKt+. Generally called a decoy, or "Roman" after an early example, this theme can also involve a forcible luring of the defending piece to an unfavorable square:

SHOCRON

After 38 . . . Q-Q1

FISCHER

Mar del Plata 1959

| 39 RxKt | Q-QB1! |

Black has relied on this pin to win the Rook, for obviously 39 . . . PxR 40 QxP+ followed by QxKP leaves the Bishops a wide swath.

40 B-Q7! . . .

An elegant reply, decoying the Queen to an unprotected square. For if now 40 ... QxB 41 RxP+ wins the Queen. The decoy is equally a defensive weapon against a series of checks. A piece can often be thrown in front of a checking Queen either to divert the Queen on the following check, or to gain time for development. The first of these reasons is well illustrated by Fischer:

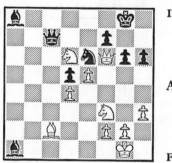

IVKOV

After 40 ... Q-B2

FISHER

Palma 1970

41 BxP!	...

This is easy enough to see; what is surprising is the defense to Black's counter:

41 ...	Q-B8+
42 Kt-K1!	...

Black counted on 42 K-R2 Q-B5+, exchanging Queens and avoiding an immediate debacle. But after the Queen is diverted to K8, Black has no further checks and the attack proceeds:

42 ...	QxKt+
43 K-R2	Kt-Kt4
44 BxP+!	Resigns

After 44 ... KtxKt 45 Q-Kt6+ mates next move. The forlorn position of the two Black Bishops shows once again that the basis for an attack is bringing superior force to bear.

One of the most famous positions in the history of the game involved a decoy which fell just short of working. There are many other combinational themes here, but this is the most piquant:

LASKER

After 18 . . . R-R6!

PILLSBURY

St. Petersburg 1895–96

19 PxP+   . . .

Controversy has raged for eighty years over whether or not Pillsbury had a better defense. The Black Rook must be taken, but can White improve his chances with either of the Zwischenzugs PxP+ or P-K7? The most recent suggestion is to leave the Pawn where it is, to block the King file, and try to run to the Kingside with the King. For example, 19 PxR Q-Kt3+ 20 K-B2 R-B1+ 21 K-Q2 QxP+ 22 K-K1 Q-B6+ 23 K-K2! But Black can improve here with 22 . . . Q-K6+ 23 B-K2 PxP, taking advantage of the threats of R-B1 and the general advance of the central Pawns. Actually, Pillsbury's move almost rescues the game:

          19 . . .   **RxP**
          20 PxR   **Q-Kt3+**
          21 B-Kt5!   . . .

If the King wants to hide in the corner, White must divert the Queen from the attack on the QP, and also develop his King Rook; for example, the immediate 21 K-R1 allows BxP+ 22 RxB QxR+ 23 K-Kt1 R-B7, etc.

          21 . . .   **QxB+**
          22 K-R1   **R-B2?**

But now 22 . . . Q-B5 would have forced the win of the QP, because the Queen has no squares for maintaining the guard after 23 Q-Kt4 P-KR4. After a later inaccuracy Lasker won this titanic struggle and turned the course of the tournament around. Pillsbury lost the next four games in a row and dropped to third place, after scoring 2½ out of 3 in the first three games with Lasker.

A position that is likely to gain the same notoriety over the years is from the famous fourth game from the Fischer-Spassky match, 1972.

We have seen the opening innovation of Spassky's (see Chapter 28, "Opening Adventures"), which leads directly to this after a series of relatively forced threats and defenses:

SPASSKY

After 29 . . . R-R1

FISCHER

Match, Reykjavik 1972

The best way to appreciate the complex alternatives which follow is to see how Fischer now defends against direct threats:

30 Kt-B3	BxKt
31 QxB	B-Q3
32 Q-B3!	. . .

This little resource transposes an overwhelming attack into an equal ending. Note that if White had to run with his King, 32 K-Kt1 R-R5 would threaten both RxB and Q-R7+ followed by R-KB5, winning the Queen.

The annotators all jumped on 29 . . . R-Q1 as the winning move (Smyslov, Reshevsky, etc.), with the idea that White must now block the square QB3 with his Pawn, whereupon Black can force the above line with 30 . . . R-R1, since the White Queen can no longer go to QB3, as happened in the game.

Robert Byrne then pointed out that by allowing White time to support the Knight, Black also allows the White Rook to defend against 30 . . . R-R1 with 31 R-KB1! Before going into these complications, it should be pointed out that White's main defensive idea is to obtain a perpetual check by getting in Kt-B5+ at the proper time—that is, when the Black Queen is tied down to Q3 or, barring that, when the Rook is loose at Q1. Also, an essential element of Black's 29 . . . R-Q1 is that the White Knight cannot make any good discoveries because of the weakness of the back rank. E.g., 30 Kt-B5+ K-B3! 31 RxR Q-K8+ 32 K-R2 B-Kt8+ 33 K-R1 B-B7+ 34 K-R2 Q-Kt8 mate. Going back to the original position, then, let us assume that White's Pawn is at QB3. There could follow:

31 R-KB1	R-R5
32 Kt-B5+!	QxKt
33 RxQ	RxQ
34 RxB	RxP

. . . and now White must take the draw with 35 RxP, but not 35 B-Q5 (an attempted interference!) BxB 36 RxB PxR 37 KxR P-R5! (one unit holds two) with a winning Pawn endgame.

The win, however, is still there for Black just before the diagrammed position. Instead of 29 . . . R-R1, start with

29 . . .	R-Q1
30 P-B3	B-Kt3

If Black has time for this, his attack goes ahead smoothly. By protecting the square Q1, Black forever avoids the threat of Kt-B5+ followed by QxP+, with a perpetual. The question is, does he have time for this, or can White now regroup?

31 Q-K2	Q-Kt6
32 R-Q3	. . .

The first interference: The Bishop now no longer protects KB1, a fact which is important in the following.

32 . . .	Q-B5

And now the White Queen cannot persist in following her opposite number: 33 Q-Kt4 Q-B8+, etc. The threat is B-Q3, forcing K-Kt1, when the Black Queen penetrates with checks at R7, R8, and Kt7. 33 Q-K3 allows Q-B8+ 34 Q-Kt1 BxP+, etc. Finally, if White follows the previous idea of getting his Rook to KB1 (after 30 . . . B-Kt3):

31 R-KB1	B-B2
32 K-Kt1	R-R1
33 Kt-B3	Q-K6+
34 K-R1	B-B5!

. . . and it's now the White *Queen* that's trapped—there's no defense to P-B4. There are few positions which show so richly the themes of self-block (P-QB3), pins and unpins (by the Knight at Q4), and interferences (35 B-Q5, 32 R-Q3) as does this simple-looking situation.

A prominent two-move theme is the half-pin, in which two Black pieces are on a line with their King, and one cannot leave the line without allowing a fatal pin of the other. It's a highly technical performance most of the time. To see it over the board is a rare delight:

ROBATSCH

After 12 ... R-Q1

FISCHER

Varna 1962

13 P-KKt4!   **...**

On PxP, the KR file would be opened, and on:

13 ...   **KtxP**

14 QR-Kt1   **...**

... is the half-pin which protects the Queen Bishop.

Perhaps the most practical benefit that comes to the chess player from a knowledge of problem themes is the sense of the importance of mating threats. Time is all-important in a problem. Material means nothing if mate can be averted before the prescribed two or three moves. Accordingly, when an exact calculation of the timing of a mating threat as against a material loss is necessary in a practical situation, a well-rounded player has an edge. Here, for example, is a position in which it appeared highly unlikely that the Black King was in any danger:

LASKER

After 50 K-K5

LOVEGROVE

Exhibition Game, San Francisco 1902

The circumstances surrounding this game deserve an explanation. In this age of jet travel, it is difficult to imagine European chess masters of the last century traveling by steamer, railroad, and buckboard to the Far West for chess exhibitions. Yet Zuckertort came to the Nevada gold fields in 1884, and the World Champion, Emanuel Lasker, hit San Francisco right after the turn of the century. It had become customary by this time for the supporters of the local champion, Dr. Walter R. Lovegrove, to raise a sizable stake for individual encounters between the touring masters and their hero. And a hero he often turned out to be:

| 50 . . . | P-Q5?! |

Lasker presses for a brilliant win, but a problemlike defense turns the tables.

| 51 KxR | P-Q6 |
| 52 K-K5! | . . . |

Two connected Pawns on the sixth cannot be stopped, unless the King can be threatened with mate.

| 52 . . . | P-Q7 |
| 53 R-Kt8+ | K-R5 |

After 53 . . . K-R3 54 K-B6 K-R2 55 R-Kt7+ K-R1 (K-R3 56 R-R2!) 56 R-Q7! P-B6 57 K-Kt6 forces mate in two.

54 K-B4	K-R6
55 R-Q8	P-B6
56 K-K3	Resigns

The pawns are stopped and will be won after K-K2 and K-Q1.

32 One-Liners

Now, just for fun, a panorama of great moves, great positions, crowd-pleasing eye-popping combinations. Fischer has yet to match the greatest thriller of them all:

MARSHALL

After 23 R-B5

LEWITZKY

Breslau 1912

23 ...   Q-KKt6!!

Harold Schonberg says that the story that the crowd "showered the board with gold pieces" is probably apocryphal. Frank Marshall says in his autobiography that yes, it "literally happened." *He* was there.

You can be sure that when the opportunity comes, however, Fischer will find the big move, as he has already clearly shown:

FISCHER

After 23 KxR

LETELIER

Leipzig 1960

23 . . .   QxP+!

Too bad the Black King Knight is on the board, or it would be a model mate—every square in the King's field guarded only once.

MIAGMASUREN

After 28 . . . R-R2

FISCHER

Sousse 1967

29 B-Kt2!   PxP?

He should have smelled a rat, but it's nice that Black didn't see the combination and play the prosaic 29 . . . Q-B1. Then White would have had to work for the win with 30 B-K4, ganging up on the King Knight Pawn. Now Fischer could have announced mate in seven (allowing for three useless checks P-B8(Q)+, etc.):

30 Q-R6   Q-B1
31 QxRP+!!   Resigns

After 31 . . . KxQ 32 PxP++ KxP 33 B-K4 is mate!

BENNETT

After 37 . . . BxP

FISCHER

San Francisco 1957

38 R-Q8+!   ...

Winning the U.S. Junior Championship with style. The same
diversionary tactic appears in R. Byrne-Fischer (See Chapter 36,
"The Immortal Games"), and here:

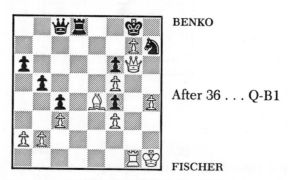

BENKO

After 36 . . . Q-B1

FISCHER

New York 1965–66

37 Q-K8+!

Nor does Fischer save his fire and brimstone for the second half
of the tournament table:

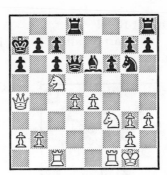

GLIGORIC

After 17 . . . K-R2

FISCHER

Havana 1966

18 KtxRP! ...

It's curtains after 18 . . . PxKt 19 RxP.

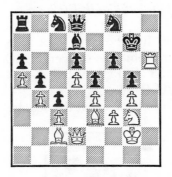

GLIGORIC

After 34 . . . K-Kt2

FISCHER

Zagreb 1970

35 RxP! ...

Black has his choice of being forked (35 . . . QxR 36 Kt-R5+), or skewered (35 . . . KxR 36 BxP+).

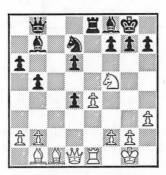

KERES

After 39 . . . PxKt

FISCHER

Zurich 1959

40 Kt-R6+!   ...

Black's Pawns are in disarray after 40 . . . PxKt 41 Q-Kt4+,
winning back the Knight.

SPASSKY

After 37 . . . Kt-B3

FISCHER

Match, Reykjavik 1972

38 RxKt!   ...

There is no shelter from the converging Queen, Rook, and
Bishop. For example, 38 . . . PxR 39 RxP K-Kt1 40 B-B4 (holding
the Rook to K2) K-R1 41 Q-B4.

Some positions seem to fly apart at the seams:

FISCHER

After 26 K-B1

UNZICKER

Varna 1962

26 . . .   **RxBP!**

Neither Rook can be taken without allowing the other one to
enter the attack on the King.

Finally, one of the more unlikely positions from Fischer's career.
Who would believe that with all this Queen power the issue would
be decided by a Knight fork?

PETROSIAN

After 41 . . . K-Kt6

FISCHER

Bled 1959

42	Q-QR1	Q-R6
43	QxQ+	KxQ
44	Q-R6	Q-KB2
45	K-Kt2	K-Kt6
46	Q-Q2	Q-KR2
47	K-Kt3?	QxP!

This is it! Petrosian was so happy to have escaped with his life six moves earlier that he accepted a draw after:

48 Q-KB2?   Q-R8!

An unforgettable position. A brilliant game, a witty position, a spectacular move don't show up in the crosstable, but they make chess worth playing.

VII The Logic of Chess

33 The Reason Why

If the average player were to be given the solution, without comment, to the following problem, I believe he would not realize what happened, why it happened, or why a dozen other solutions could not happen. Yet it is among the simplest of chess positions:

E. ZEPLER (1937)
(*Chess Review*)

*White to play
and mate in five*

Here is the main line of the solution:

1	B-Q3	B-Kt3
2	Kt-B3	BxB+
3	K-B2	B-K7
4	Kt-K4	any
5	Kt-Kt3 mate	

Why doesn't any other Bishop move at the first turn work? Why doesn't Kt-B3 immediately work? The solver begins to ask himself some basic questions, and outlines this sequence of facts:

297

1. White can never take the Bishop without allowing stalemate.

2. White will never succeed in mating with the Bishop, because he can always be challenged by his opposite number.

3. Therefore, White must mate with the Knight.

4. The mate must occur at Kt3, since the White King must take refuge at B2 on the inevitable check from the Bishop.

5. It will take three moves for the Knight to get to Kt3. If he goes via QB1, he can always be prevented from reaching Kt3 because the Bishop can guard the only gate to that square, K2.

6. The Knight *must* reach Kt3 in three moves, because he can reach it in either three or five moves, but not in four. Such is the geometry of Knight moves, from white squares to black. (And remember, White must always spend one move in moving his King to B2 on a check.)

7. Therefore, the Knight must try the route B3, K2 or K4, Kt3. However, can't the Bishop also guard the gates K2 and K4 from either White's Q3 or KB3?

8. Yes, but the Bishop can be put into Zugzwang at either square for lack of other moves. His main defense, stalemate, is also his main weakness, Zugzwang.

9. This is the hardest point to visualize: White must have his Knight at QB3 and Black's Bishop at his Q3 when it is Black's turn to move, when the Bishop must relinquish either of the two gates, K2 or K4.

10. Therefore, White must force the Bishop to his Q3 on the second move. This can only be done by first playing the Bishop to Q3 and then playing the Knight to QB3, using the King move in answer to check to throw Black on the move. Note, for example, that if White tries to vary the sequence of moves with:

| 1 B-Q3 | B-Kt3 |
| 2 K-B2? | B-B4! (or R2) |

. . . successfully wastes a move, so that 3 Kt-B3 BxB puts White in Zugzwang.

11. White cannot vary the first move, either. 1 B-R6 B-B3 2 Kt-B3 B-Kt7+ 3 K-B2 B-B6 successfully guards both gates, with White on the move.

12. The above revelation makes one wonder why 1 . . . B-B3 followed by the check at Kt7 is not a sufficient defense to the "key" move as well. So we examine 1 B-Q3 B-B3 2 Kt-B3 B-Kt7+ 3 K-B2 B-B6. Ah! but now 4 Kt-K4 forces the Knight through, since the White Bishop is in a position to recapture, with mate, on BxKt.

If we had only gone as far as the official solution, we would have accepted this as a "tempo Roman," a decoy in which White lures a Black piece to a square on which he will be "tempoed." But then we see that Black's B-B3 is a defense to any key move of the White Bishop on the KB1–QR6 diagonal . . . except when the White Bishop is able to retake at K4. And moves on the other diagonal are answered simply by BxB. The motive of the key move B-Q3 is mixed: The logic of the solution is dictated by either the fact that the Bishop must be able to retake at K4 or the fact that the Q3 square is the Zugzwang square for the Black Bishop.

The result in either case is the same: White mates in five moves. But the purpose of a chess problem, to illustrate a logical skein in a sequence of moves, is blurred irrevocably. (A big question, the purpose of a chess problem: This is only one of many suggestions for an answer in this book.)

This study nevertheless is a striking illustration of the kind of reasoning that underlies the choice of a move. The first game of the Fischer-Petrosian match is one long (and still unended) example of the logical patterns of spectators, commentators, and the players themselves, all attempting to make sense out of a chess position.

We begin from the famous position in which Petrosian varied from the sixth game of the Fischer-Taimanov match, 1971. Instead of the innovation 11 . . . P-Q4, Taimanov had played Kt-Q5 and obtained an inferior ending.

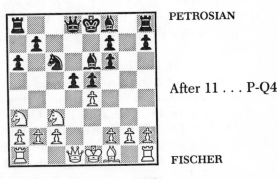

PETROSIAN

After 11 . . . P-Q4

FISCHER

Match, Buenos Aires 1971

Fischer's characteristic stubbornness in wanting "to be shown" if and where his previous winning openings were faulty almost cost him this game. In the match with Spassky, he was careful not to repeat variations even if they had won for him before.

Petrosian's 11 ... P-Q4 has been played with Black even a tempo behind this position. White has wasted so much time to obtain a positional edge that Black can attempt to solve his problems tactically.

12	PxP	BxKt
13	PxB	Q-R4
14	Q-Q2	O-O-O!
15	B-B4	KR-Kt1

PETROSIAN

After 15 ... KR-Kt1

FISCHER

A nearly forced sequence of moves brings about a position in which White is embarrassed on all fronts. He can't castle Kingside because of B-R6, winning the exchange. His Queenside is a shambles. And he has at best an uneasy truce in the center, where Black threatens to win the Queen Pawn if the White Queen leaves the file, and White cannot threaten to fork Black's minor pieces unless she *does* leave the file.

16 R-Q1   ...

Fine gives this a question mark, Byrne and Korchnoi an exclamation point. Fine's suggestion B-Q3, here or on the preceding move, works out poorly after 16 ... BxP 17 KtxB QxQ+ (instead of RxKt or QxKt) 18 KxQ RxKt 19 K-K3 R-R4 and Black will be a Pawn up with an excellent position. 16 R-Q1 is a courageous move, typical of Fischer, primarily to guard his Queen and threaten B-Q3. Petrosian is bluffed.

16 ...   B-B4

The groans were heard all the way to Moscow when Petrosian failed to take the Knight Pawn. 17 B-Q3 was not that much of a threat, since 17 ... BxP 18 KtxB RxKt! is now the answer to 19

B-B5+. It is no doubt true that 16 . . . RxKtP would give Black all
sorts of winning chances. All Petrosian had to do was calculate
whether the Rook could be trapped after 17 Kt-K4. But Black can
either play the safe 17 . . . R-Kt3 (White's Bishop is in take after
18 QxQ KtxQ, thus saving the Black Bishop), or the aggressive
17 . . . Q-Kt3, with all sorts of attacking ideas involving Kt-Q5, etc.

Here is where the commentators start to lose the logic of the
game. Perhaps 16 . . . RxP is a sufficient way of winning; is it also
the necessary way? Only if both conditions are true can 16 . . .
B-B4 be condemned; as we shall see, it also should win as easily
as 16 . . . RxKtP. (In the Zepler study above, 1 B-Q3 was both the
sufficient and necessary winning move, but the "tempo Roman"
motive was only one necessary motive. The solution was therefore "singular," but the motivation was not.)

Perhaps Fischer was aware of the unsuspected force of the
threat of 17 B-Q3, as his commentators have not been. In any event,
16 . . . RxKtP is ingeniously answered by 17 B-Q3 BxP 18 KtxB
RxKt 19 K-B1! The King move simultaneously releases the pin on
the Queen, threatening B-B5+, and also attacks the Rook.

17 B-Q3   . . .

PETROSIAN

After 17 B-Q3

FISCHER

Petrosian can now win quite simply with 17 . . . P-K5, since the
pin on the King file would win a piece if the Pawn is taken. White
would then be forced to play a hedgehog defense with 18 B-B1
B-Kt5 19 R-QKt1 Kt-K4 20 R-Kt3. The incredible part of this
scenario is that the critics who condemned 16 . . . B-B4 and showed
that 17 B-Q3 was forced now claim that 17 . . . P-K5 wins! Korchnoi
and Furman, on the other hand, fail even to mention 17 . . . P-K5.
Gone are the days when Lasker could say, in his introduction to
his notes in the St. Petersburg 1909 tournament book, "The glos-

sary was meant to be both necessary and sufficient. Nowhere will
it be found lacking in supplying information needed, but it has no
superfluities."

17 ...	BxB
18 QxB	Kt-Q5
19 O-O	K-Kt1

Now threatening 20 ... QxKt. White just has time to stave off
immediate disaster.

20 K-R1	QxRP
21 P-B4	...

White must create threats of his own or the Queenside will kill
him in the endgame. But the following forced sequence leaves
doubts:

21 ...	R-QB1
22 Kt-K4	...

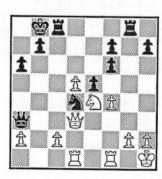

PETROSIAN

After 22 Kt-K4

FISCHER

22 ...	QxQ

Petrosian opts for an equal endgame, just when he could show
for the last time that his middle game was demonstrably won. The
variations are complex but instructive, involving a King hunt, pins
and counterpins, an exchange sacrifice, and back-rank mates.

The winning idea begins 22 ... QxP, winning the Queenside
Pawns for future reference, and embroiling White in fatal complications when he tries to get compensation. There are two main
ideas:

1. 23 KtxP RxKtP! 24 KxR RxP+ 25 K-Kt3 R-Kt7+ 26 K-R4 RxP+
27 K-Kt5 P-R3+ 28 K-Kt4 Q-Kt7+ 29 Q-Kt3 P-R4+ 30 KtxP P-B4+
31 K-Kt5 RxKt+, etc. (Fine's analysis). Most players would not
bother to calculate the outcome of the King hunt after 25 K-Kt3,

knowing that there "must be something there." In this line, the attempt to counterattack with 24 Kt-Q7+ K-R2 25 KtxP (Fine) or 25 PxP (Korchnoi) is met in both cases by the fine problem idea 25 . . . KtxP, maintaining material and the attack because of the Knight discoveries and the denial of the diagonal checks to the White Queen.

2. Korchnoi's suggestion 23 R-Q2 leads to more branches, but Black gets a won endgame: 23 . . . RxBP 24 RxR KtxR 25 Q-K2 (Korchnoi stops here, but the pin is meaningless) PxP! 26 KtxP R-Q1! 27 RxP R-Q3 (now possible since the White Queen cannot play 28 Q-Q5 because of the mate on the back rank) 28 R-B1 Q-Kt7 29 Q-B2 Q-Q5! simplifying to a won endgame. Black has enough Pawns to be able to sacrifice the exchange in the line 27 Q-K7 (instead of 27 RxP) RxP! 28 KtxR QxKt. Another pin fails after 28 QxP Q-B5.

If, as the above indicates, Black still has a win on his twenty-second move, then something must be wrong with White's previous play. We would have to look at the universally praised 21 P-B4, since the moves following that are forced. It would seem that White cannot afford to give away his Queenside, and must instead play 21 Kt-K4. In this case, Black must exchange Queens, since 22 P-QB4 would leave White with a solid game. But back to the game:

23	PxQ	R-B7
24	R-Q2	RxR
25	KtxR	P-B4
26	PxP	R-K1
27	R-K1	Kt-B7
28	R-K2	Kt-Q5
29	R-K3	Kt-B7
30	R-R3	. . .

Fischer now decides to make a game of it, as Petrosian was in time trouble. After a series of moves in which Black fails to find the right squares for his Knight and Rook, Fischer's advanced Pawn creates another critical position:

30	. . .	RxP
31	Kt-B3	RxP
32	RxP	RxP
33	P-KR4	Kt-K6
34	RxP	R-Q8+
35	K-R2	R-R8
36	P-R5	. . .

PETROSIAN

After 36 P-R5

FISCHER

Here Fine comments, "White does not have better." Actually, the Pawn advance wins, so why does he need better?

36 . . .	P-B5

This loses in a hurry: 37 RxP RxP 38 R-K4! KtxP (the Knight and Rook work poorly together, and one will be tied down to the defense of the other, in either case losing the Knight) 39 K-Kt3! R-R4 40 Kt-K5 Resigns. The commentators have claimed that 36 . . . P-B5 was a blunder, throwing away the draw. Actually, the advanced Pawn can still be driven through:

36 . . .	RxP
37 R-Kt7	P-B5
38 R-Kt5!	. . .

Instead of Fine's 38 P-R6, when R-R4 holds the Pawn from behind. Black's defense hinges on the fork by the Knight at Kt5. Once the White King can advance, he can avoid this possibility and support the united Pawns, whereas the Black Pawns cannot advance without either being lost or allowing a fatal exchange of Rooks because the Black King lacks shelter.

38 . . .	R-B7
39 Kt-Q4	R-B2
40 K-R3	R-R2
41 K-R4	P-Kt4
42 R-Kt6	P-Kt5
43 P-R6	P-R5
44 R-Kt8+	

. . . followed by R-Kt7+.

Many an opening variation has been condemned because of the outcome of the game rather than because of its own merits. Lines are continually being re-evaluated on the strength of "missing links" between supposedly won positions and a minute alteration in the early part of the game that could have changed the outcome.

The key move in a composed ending ideally hinges on a slight change in the final position. The circumstances of the mate dictate the first move; the child is father to the man. In the following study, White is apparently faced with a choice of which Pawn should capture:

R. BURGER (1969)
(*The Problemist*)

White to play
and draw

But a little background brings the endgame into focus. If White tries 1 P-B6+ K-B2 2 P-R6 K-Kt1 he is thrown on the move. It is well known that if neither side can waste a move on the other wing, whoever has to move in this position is lost. The position goes back to Greco, but it has been used over the years by chess hustlers who, willing to take either side with the Black Pawns in a less advanced position, will bet they can capture all the Pawns with White or queen with Black. For example, Black to move (after the above preliminaries) cannot play 3 . . . P-Kt6 4 K-Kt2, nor 3 . . . P-B6 4 K-B2 P-R6 5 K-Kt3 (and similarly after 3 . . . P-R6). But if White has to move, he is lost: 3 K-Kt2 P-Kt6 or 3 K-B1 P-R6 and in both cases all the Pawns go to the sixth rank and then walk in.

Therefore let's try:

1 RPxP   . . .

Whether the Bishop or Rook Pawn should capture, let's hold in doubt for the moment—it seems that in such a symmetrical array there is no difference.

1 . . .   K-Kt1

Neither side can touch the right side of the board, as we have seen above. But this has to be checked later.

2 P-B6   K-B1
3 P-Kt7+   K-B2

Of course 3 . . . K-Kt1 4 P-Kt6 puts Black in Zugzwang.

4 P-Kt6+   K-Kt1

Now what? Strangely enough, White can construct a stalemate

position for his King at R1, but only by forcing the Black Pawn to move first on the Rook file:

5 K-B1!	P-R6

We have seen in the long note under the diagram that P-B6 is answered by K-B2 and P-Kt6 by K-Kt2. Therefore this is forced.

6 K-B2!	. . .

Again the only move. White must be able to play to Kt1 only after P-Kt6, as we shall see; P-R7 also transposes to a variation shown below.

6 . . .	P-Kt6+
7 K-Kt1	P-B6

If 7 . . . P-R7+ 8 K-R1! P-B6 bringing about the same position as:

8 K-R1!	P-B7

Also 8 . . . P-R7 places the White King in stalemate. Now if White can liquidate his own Pawns it's a draw.

9 P-B7+	KxP
10 P-B8(Q)+	KxQ
11 P-Kt7+	K-K2!

. . . and Black mates in two: 12 P-Kt8(Kt)+ K-B1, etc.

This last possibility, that the Black King can run away from the last Pawn to approach the queening square, leads us back to the first move. If instead of 1 RPxP White had played 1 BPxP, the entire sequence would have been the same, except that White's ninth move would have been:

9 P-R7+	KxP
10 P-R8(Q)+	KxQ
11 P-Kt7+	K-R2
12 P-Kt8(Q)+	KxQ

Stalemate. The difference is that the edge of the board prevents the Black King from running away on his eleventh move. The key is therefore 1 BPxP (capturing away from the center).

But we have to take one last look at the possibility of 1 . . . P-Kt6 (instead of K-Kt1). Can White still bring about the stalemate position?

2 K-Kt2	K-B1
3 P-R6	K-Kt1
4 P-Kt7	K-R2
5 P-Kt6+	K-Kt1
6 K-R1	. . .

If K-B1, P-B6 and P-B7 wins.

6 ...	P-B6
7 K-Kt1	P-B7+

. . . winning as in the main line. What if Black takes the opportunity to advance the Bishop Pawn first? 1 . . . P-B6! forces 2 K-B2, and after the White Pawns are advanced as far as they can, White must retreat his King and allow P-Kt6 and P-B7. There is no stalemate with the King on B1. Alas! the preliminary moves are meaningless. The study had to be revised with the starting position as in the first line shown, after 4 . . . K-Kt1. Then White can draw as shown — but the tantalizing choice on the first move is lost. A simple resetting of the Queenside in the opening position — Black King at QR1, Black *Bishop* at QKt2, and White Pawns at QR6, QKt5, and QB6 — saves the study's key move dilemma. Which Pawn must take the Bishop, and why?

34 Gordian Knots

Whenever there is a discussion of whether chess is an art or a science, it is helpful to reflect on the fact that there are thousands of positions which seem to defy definitive analysis. And these are not necessarily complex middle-game positions or amorphous opening positions. Cheron once published an entire book on the subject of a few similar positions involving only King and two Pawns on each side. Not one player in a million, I'll wager, understands the analysis.

The word that cautious annotators favor in such circumstances is "chances." In the following position from the first game of the 1972 World Championship match, Fischer probably realized that his Bishop could be trapped, but he knew that in any case he would get fighting chances. Chess is a science when it follows a demonstrable rule, such as Rook Pawn and Bishop cannot oust the defending King from the corner if the corner square is not controlled by the Bishop. Chess is an art when various rules are placed in the balance, and a specific relationship between the rules in an individual case is found.

FISCHER

After 29 P-Kt5

SPASSKY

Match, Reykjavik 1972

29 ...	BxKRP
30 P-Kt3	P-KR4
31 K-K2	P-R5
32 K-B3	K-K2

Here everyone has presumed to read Fischer's mind: He intended, supposedly, to play 34 . . . P-R6, and while the White King is capturing the Pawn (33 K-Kt4) escape with the Bishop via Kt8, B7, and Q8. The flaw in this idea is that White can still imprison the Bishop with B-Q2 at the appropriate moment, leading to just about the same position as what follows in the game.

The main Russian chess journal *Shamati*, however, claimed that Black could draw here with 32 . . . P-Kt4, e.g., 33 K-Kt2 P-Kt5 34 KxB P-R6, tying up the King. White seems to be a move too slow. After 35 P-B3 P-B4 36 P-K4 K-K2 37 PxBP KPxP 38 PxP PxP the following position is reached:

FISCHER
(Analysis)

After 38 . . . PxP

SPASSKY

Now it's a matter of counting. White will play his King to KB1 and his Bishop to K3, Kt1, and then his King around to KB4, winning the Knight Pawn. Meanwhile, Black must play P-Kt3 (in answer to B-K3) and his King to Q3, Q4, B5, etc., winning both Pawns. That's seven moves on each side. Black's King is now at R6 and White's at KKt4. To get his Pawns moving, Black must decoy the Bishop off the diagonal with P-R7, BxP. Now we have:

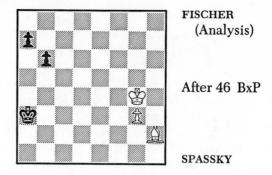

FISCHER
(Analysis)

After 46 BxP

SPASSKY

46 . . .	P-Kt4
47 B-Kt1	P-R4
48 K-B4	P-Kt5
49 B-B5	K-Kt6!
50 K-K3	K-B7!

But not 50 . . . K-B5 51 B-Q4 P-R5 52 P-Kt4 P-R6 53 P-Kt5 P-Kt6
54 P-Kt6 P-Kt7 55 P-Kt7 P-Kt8(Q) 56 P-Kt8(Q)+, winning the
Queen next move. Nor 50 . . . P-R5 51 P-Kt4 P-R6 52 P-Kt5 P-R7
53 B-Q4 K-B7 54 P-Kt6 P-Kt6 55 P-Kt7 P-Kt7 56 P-Kt8(Q), and
whichever Pawns queen White mates in a few moves. Now the
game is drawn because Black will get his Rook Pawn to the seventh
when White queens. The White King is one move too far away to
obtain the "book" win against the Rook Pawn.

Yet all of this is futile! All White has to do to win is to leave the
King Pawns on the board. Instead of 37 PxBP, White simply plays
38 PxKtP BPxKtP 39 P-K5! and the Black King is shut out. White
transfers his Bishop to KKt1, as above, and proceeds to pick up
everything. Vis-à-vis the Black King, the White King always wins
a stand-off because the Bishop can make waiting moves.

Therefore, Fischer took his best chance with 32 . . . K-K2. Now,
after a series of pretty much forced moves (White had to try to
infiltrate the Kingside via KR4), Fischer sealed a blooper, however, bringing about this position:

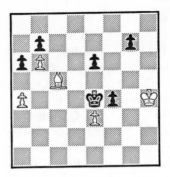

FISCHER

After 40 . . . P-B5

SPASSKY

The Pawn advance looks forceful, since it trades off the last White Kingside Pawn. Yet it also moves the Black King one square too far away from the Queenside. With 41 PxP KxP 42 K-R5! White was able to win the Black Pawns because the threat of running the King to QB7 is faster than Black's counterthreat of advancing the King Knight Pawn. Fischer here had his first and last chance to draw the game with 40 . . . K-Q4. (Incidentally, if this is true, the annotators have to go back and change their question marks and exclamation points earlier in the game. Fischer's Bishop sacrifice becomes merely a noble adventure instead of the "elementary blunder" the analysts have tried to pin on him.)

The idea of 40 . . . K-Q4 (instead of P-B5) is to force the exchange of the last White Kingside Pawn with his *Pawns,* so that the Black King will have time to attack the Queen Rook Pawn. Then, when this Pawn is forced to go to R5, the King returns to QB1 and just sits there. The position is then one for the books: The White Bishop and King cannot oust the Black King from QB1 any more than they could from the corner. It's a sub-case of the general rule mentioned in the second paragraph of this chapter.

Whether or not Black can accomplish this plan of action, however, has been clouded in the dust of a dozen annotators. Botvinnik says, "Tougher was 40 . . . K-Q4 41 B-B8 P-Kt3. . . . Analysis convinced me that Black's position is already lost." If chess is a science, is there any room for such characterizations of moves as "tougher"? Actually, Black has little trouble drawing in this line:

| 40 . . . | K-Q4 |
| 41 B-B8 | P-K4! |

To the point: Black need not save his Kingside Pawns — just trade off the King Pawn.

42 K-Kt5	P-B5
43 PxP	PxP
44 KxP	K-B3

If the Bishop had taken the Knight Pawn, the move here would have been K-B4, with the same result: the Queen Rook Pawn must move, locking up the position.

45 P-R5	K-Q2, etc.

White can make a much better try for the win with either 41 B-K7 or 41 B-Q4, in both cases wishing to defend the Knight Pawn with the Bishop. The former is a particularly tough Gordian knot, as far as differences of opinion go:

41 B-Q4	P-K4
42 B-B3	P-B5
43 PxP	PxP
44 K-Kt4	K-B4
45 B-R5!	P-Kt4!

. . . and now the White King can make no progress, since 46 KxP P-B6 wins the White Pawns. Or:

41 B-K7	P-K4
42 K-Kt5	P-B5
43 PxP	PxP
44 KxP	P-R4!

The difference between this and the losing position in the game is ever so slight: There, White had his Bishop at KB2 (and a Black Pawn was at K5, a meaningless cipher). Black could not then attack the Rook Pawn with P-R4 and K-B5 because the White King would simply follow him across the board and trap him at White's R4. Then tempo moves by the Bishop (QB5, Q6) would force the King Knight Pawn to his doom. So in the game Fischer had to try to sacrifice the Knight Pawn to drive the King away, but White still had time to reach QKt7. Here, the Bishop loses a move getting to KB2:

45 B-R4	K-B4!
46 B-B2+	K-Kt5
47 K-K5	KxP
48 K-Q6	K-Kt4
49 K-B7	K-R3, drawing

Various other "unsolved" positions from the Fischer-Spassky match are mentioned elsewhere in this book (and, I hope, solved). I have saved a particularly intriguing one for now. During this game and after adjournment, no one seemed to be sure who was winning. It seems to me that Fischer, even though a Pawn up, was delighted to see his rival repeat moves and tacitly offer the draw.

SPASSKY

After 44 Q-R6

FISCHER

Match, Reykjavik 1972

White has serious back-rank problems. If Queens were traded, Black would win in a walk by pushing the King Pawn. The threat is apparently 47 Q-K3+, although there is nothing to fear after 47 . . . R-Q5 except another repetition of moves with 48 Q-R6. The game proceeded:

44 . . .	Q-KB6
45 Q-R7	. . .

Supposedly threatening 46 R-R7, and forcing the Queen to return. After further repetitions, the game was agreed drawn. However, Black can afford to try for a win with:

45 . . .	R-Q8!

Krogius gives this a question mark, but Black wins by "falling" into the trap:

46 RxP+	QxR
47 RxR	Q-B6!

The weak back rank severely restricts the Queen and Rook, even though White is now two Pawns up.

48 R-QKt1	. . .

The Queen would have to play nursemaid to the King after 48 R-Q6+ R-B3 49 RxR+ QxR 50 Q-Kt1 P-K5, and it is not difficult to see who will win the Pawn race.

48 . . .	P-K5
49 Q-R6+	R-B3
50 Q-Kt5	Q-Q6!

... and Black will only have to weather a few checks before getting his Pawn to the seventh and playing QxR+. This possibility is all the more surprising because it came at a time when Spassky desperately needed a full point, and he and his "team" had the benefit of a night of analysis from about the diagrammed position.

Perhaps eighty years from now these and other mysteries of the Fischer-Spassky match will be solved by eager historians, as was the famous Pillsbury-Lasker fourth game from the dramatic St. Petersburg tournament from the Gay Nineties. An attempt to show an escape clause in Lasker's great combination (see Chapter 31, "Themes") recently led to a controversy over the following position, which is forced when the White King attempts to flee to the center:

LASKER
(Analysis)

After 23 . . . PxP

PILLSBURY

St. Petersburg 1895–96

Black threatens 24 . . . R-B1, since he can always drive the King to the Bishop file with B-B6+. The main line goes:

24 Q-R3	B-B6+
25 K-B1	R-B1+
26 B-B3	P-K4
27 Q-Kt3	. . .

Otherwise B-Q5 will be impossible to handle.

27 . . .	P-K5
28 Q-B2	Q-B5

... and the pressure mounts. The soundness of the combination depends on lines like this, where Lasker is playing a Rook down. And since Lasker considered this his finest game, it is worth trying to collect all the loose ends and be able to say once and for all, "It works."

35 Compute!

One gets the impression from watching computers play chess that their main function is to provide jaded college students with a game on a hyped-up pinball machine. The dream of a thinking machine that can plan, conceptualize, correct its errors, and teach itself from its experience is there in the background. And this dream undoubtedly is the lure for continued heavy investments in computer time and program-writing at dozens of universities in this country and abroad—all working on chess as a model supposedly of decision-making processes. Yet the results to date have been hit-and-miss, uncoordinated, and not very promising for other than curiosity value.

As David Levy has put it, programmers seem to have adopted a head-in-the-sand approach consisting of three stages: "(1) write a program that plays legal chess. . . . (2) play some games against the program. . . . (3) if tired of chess programming then give up. . . ." and go back to stage (2). The major centers for work in this field seem content to work independently. Basic suggestions made over twenty years ago (such as Shannon's—that an *experimental* procedure be established to assign values to the various aspects of a move) have fallen on deaf ears. Few chess masters are programmers, and vice versa.

It is pretty well accepted that current programs play at about Class B or Class C level (on the U.S. Chess Federation rating system beginning with masters, experts, Class A). The average player is amused by the fact that the M.I.T. program of some years back, known as MacHack, used to finish somewhere in the middle of the

315

crosstable in local tournaments. Or that the Russian program, running on a slower machine, handily beat a Stanford program in a four-game match. Or that there is an annual U.S. Computer Chess Championship, which was won for the first three years by the Northwestern University program known successively as "Chess 3.0," "Chess 3.5," and "Chess 4.0." It's improving!

There is obviously a great temptation to try to measure a player such as Bobby Fischer against some purely mathematical standard. No less an authority than Mikhail Botvinnik, who has taken the most professional look at the possibilities of chess programming from both sides of the fence, claims that a computer will be World Champion before the end of this century. How would a Fischer stack up against this monster?

One of the original intentions of this book was to attempt a comparison of Fischer and former World Champions by matching their play against a computer. After analyzing hundreds of games, however, it became obvious that even the best program was so unlikely to play up to a decent standard that such a comparison would be meaningless. However, a fascinating comparison did result from this attempt. By spending extra computer time on key positions, enlarging the "search" for moves, the percentage of moves made both by Fischer and by the computer became significant. And what emerged from this experiment was not a comparison of Fischer and, say, Lasker, but the thinking processes of Fischer and the program.

The computer "sees" moves to which many players (even, as we shall see, Larsen) have a blind spot. The computer has a raw, unbiased, more-bang-for-the-buck rationale for its choices, which tends to be both a limitation and a strength. Botvinnik's program in fact is totally threat-oriented, and the threats are purely materialistic in the final analysis. In his scheme, positional considerations are defined in terms of threat-potential. As we have seen throughout this book, if a general characterization of Fischer's style is possible it is that his play tends to be a string of tactical exercises held together by threats. It is a pity that Botvinnik's program is not known in the United States, and that so little exchange of information or work has occurred in this field.

The game I have chosen to illustrate the "thinking" processes of a chess program is one for which Botvinnik's notes are also available. (When the notes first appeared in *Chess Life*, they represented Botvinnik's first contribution to an American publication.)

Bled 1961

FISCHER   TAL

(Notes in italics by M. M. Botvinnik)

1 P-K4	P-QB4
2 Kt-KB3	Kt-QB3
3 P-Q4	PxP
4 KtxP	P-K3
5 Kt-QB3	Q-B2

This defense, in the style of L. Paulsen, has become popular again during the last few years. The meaning of this maneuver evidently is to provoke White to continue 6 KKt-Kt5, Q-Kt1; after the inevitable 7 . . . P-QR3 8 Kt-Q4 it becomes about the same position as after the immediate 5 . . . P-QR3, with the difference that the Black Queen's position on QKt1 has a better advantage.

      6 P-KKt3!   **. . .**

A very cunning and well-masked idea; it looks as if White intends to develop his KB to KKt2, but actually White has different plans.

      6 . . .   **Kt-B3**

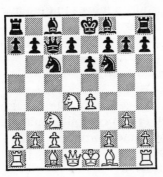

TAL

After 6 . . . Kt-B3

FISCHER

    The Northwestern chess program, on a Control Data Corporation 6600 computer, is the one we now begin using. At present it does not have a separate memory or set of instructions for the openings; hence we have "given" it the above position for White. It is curious that even with this limitation it replies 1 . . . Kt-KB3 to 1 P-Q4, the most common answer to the Queen Pawn opening in current master practice!

    For the following five moves (or "half-moves" as they are called in the half-world of programming—more on terminology later) for

White, that is, for the computer, an extended searching "width" was allowed. Thus the computer was told to examine eight possible continuations for White, then twelve possible answers by Black to *each* of these, then four White replies to *each* of these, and again four Black moves, then one White, one Black, and one White. A programmer would say that the "limits" of the particular setting for these moves were "8, 12, 4, 4, 1, 1, 1." When its work is done, the computer spits out not only its move, but also what it considered to be the best moves on both sides for the next seven half-moves. Thus in trying to make move 7 for White, it analyzed through Black's tenth move. It came up with: 7 B-KB4. The line it "expected" for both sides was 7 . . . P-K4 8 KKt-Kt5 Q-Q1 9 B-K3 B-Kt5 10 B-QB4 BxKt+. It's not a bad opening at all, but it seems to players who are conditioned by the current trends that it is a mixture of several opening systems. When Black plays his Queen to QB2, he intends to keep it on that diagonal (QKt1-KR7); and Black cannot afford to dispense with his black-squared Bishop even if it means doubling White's Pawns. We are already at the crux of the problem: How does one weigh the relative merits of doubling the opponent's Pawns as against the resulting weakness on certain squares? Can a numerical value adequately express this relationship, when it will take a dozen moves to demonstrate the problems of weak squares?

Botvinnik comments: *I am not very familiar with this variation and do not remember just where it appeared previously; however, it is evident that after 6 . . . Kt-KB3 Black's game is objectively lost. 6 . . . P-QR3 was a MUST.*

As the game progresses, we set up the actual position each time for the computer, whether the computer made the same move as Fischer or not. Here the game continued:

7 KKt-Kt5!	**Q-Kt1**
8 B-KB4	. . .

The computer spent fifteen minutes on the previous move and fourteen on this one. It not only found Fischer's move but also Tal's reply. Strangely, it recommended an immediate capture of the Knight on the following move as being best.

8 . . .	**Kt-K4**

To continue with 8 . . . P-K4 9 B-KKt5 would not have been satisfactory for Black.

9 B-K2!	. . .

The computer proposed the immediate BxKt. Capturing the

Knight is not the most natural move for most players here. In fact, when Fischer does take it on the next move, it seems startling enough for him to give it an exclamation point in his own notes to the game.

Botvinnik comments: *Accurate and powerful. White is defending the KB3 square, after which the threat of 10 Q-Q4 cannot be successfully defended.*

9 ...   **B-QB4**

It is difficult to call this move a weak one, because the "strong" 9 ... P-QR3 10 Q-Q4 P-Q3 11 O-O-O PxKt 12 BxKt would have left Black in a hopeless position. Black decides to control the Q5 square, but the trouble comes from the other side.

10 BxKt!   **...**

Now the computer backed away from this move and proposed 10 B-Kt5, again with the idea of doubling some Pawns. Why it did not now recommend BxKt, after eighteen minutes of thought and after "seeing" it on the previous move, is one of those mysteries which have kept a lot of chess players awake at night.

10 ...   **QxB**

11 P-B4   **Q-Kt1**

These two "half-moves" and White's follow-up were analyzed as best by the computer. It found the following move in one minute flat!

12 P-K5   **P-QR3**

Botvinnik says: *Obviously, to continue with 12 ... Kt-Kt1 13 Kt-K4 would not have been any better!*

13 PxKt   **...**

The computer is now set on a faster "width" of 8, 12, 4, 1, 1. It made this move in thirty seconds. Botvinnik agrees: *Leads to winning a Pawn and a better position. It would be weaker to play 13 Kt-Q4, Q-R2 or Kt-Kt1.*

13 ...   **PxKt**

14 PxP   **R-Kt1**

Twenty seconds! Now another quirk of the computer appears. Thinking on the fourteenth move of White, it decided that 14 ... R-Kt1 15 Kt-K4 B-Kt5+ were the best moves for both sides. On the next move, it decides that 15 ... B-K2 is Black's best, even though nothing has changed. The extra half-move of analysis that causes this vacillation is obviously vital to its decision-making.

15 Kt-K4   **B-K2**

16 Q-Q4   **...**

The computer has now played exactly as Fischer for the past six moves—which is not bad, especially in view of the fact that the last five moves took less than seven minutes to decide upon! Botvinnik: *The exchange of the Black Bishop for a Knight is now inevitable.*

| 16 ... | R-R5 |

In this difficult position M. Tal possibly did not play his best. 16 ... R-R4 would have been a loss of an important tempo. 16 ... Q-B2 (!) suggests itself, as the young R. Fischer would have still had a lot of work to do.

The computer expected 16 ... R-R5.

| 17 Kt-B6+ | BxKt |

Of course, not 17 ... K-Q1 18 KtxR RxQ 19 KtxB and P-Kt8(Q).

| 18 QxB | ... |

The Black King is in danger. The threat is B-R5. Also there are unpleasant threats of B-Q3 followed by BxKRP, and Q-R6 followed by QxP. It took a minute each for the computer to make these obvious continuations. It failed to see Black's reply:

| 18 ... | Q-B2 |

Getting ready to counterattack 19 B-R5 through 19 ... R-K5+ followed by P-Q4. But if 19 B-Q3 Black evidently had only one defense, 19 ... Q-B4. 18 ... R-K5 would not have been better because of Q-R6.

| 19 O-O-O! | ... |

Here the computer tried to prove it had a "fighting King" with 19 K-Q2. The importance of the initiative obviously escaped it. It's true that the King move holds all the Pawns, but at what a price! Castling looks risky, but it immediately brings the big guns to bear on the center, where the Black King must make his home. Botvinnik adds: *The White King is completely safe on the Queenside and Black has lost his last chance for counterplay. The temporary winning back of a Pawn is meaningless.*

| 19 ... | RxRP |
| 20 K-Kt1 | ... |

Again the machine missed the point, recommending 20 B-Q3!?

| 20 ... | R-R3 |

The trouble for Black is that if 20 ... Q-R4 21 P-Kt3! the Black Queen would be tied up defending the Rook and the threat of 22 B-R5 could not be met.

| 21 BxP | R-Kt3 |

Naturally enough, the nonhuman player found these. *Now the Rook is forced to abandon its vertical line because if 21 ... R-R2*

22 KR-K1 and it would be difficult to defend against the threat of RxP+. But 21 B-R5! would have been a more logical finishing stroke. (See page 33.)

	22 B-Q3	P-K4

Found in two minutes. The stage is now set for the big move. . . .

TAL

After 22 . . . P-K4

FISCHER

	23 PxP!	. . .

. . . which the machine misses! But its suggested move, 23 Q-Kt5, was not all that bad. After 23 . . . P-R3 24 Q-Kt4 P-Q3 25 P-B5 White at least has the Queens on the board and might succeed with a direct frontal attack. Fischer's move, of course, leaves no doubt. *It is not so much the effectiveness of the sacrifice that's important here, but the quick simplification of the game with the realization of the advantage. Naturally, 23 QxP+ would have led to the endgame with an extra Pawn, which would also be enough for victory. White soon gains a second Rook for his Queen and also wins all of Black's Pawns!*

23 . . .	RxQ
24 PxR	Q-B4
25 BxP	Q-KKt4
26 BxR	QxBP
27 KR-B1	QxP
28 BxP+	K-Q1

This entire, relatively forced sequence took the computer just about two minutes in all, with accuracy on both sides.

	29 B-K6	. . .

But it overlooks this little finesse. It doesn't "see" that the Bishop can be temporarily sacrificed because of the pin on the Queen file.

29 . . .	Q-R3
30 BxP	. . .

The machine again fails to see this combination.

30 ...	**BxB**
31 R-B7	...

At this point the resistance should have been abandoned. There were still sixteen needless moves made.

Although computers have a reputation for being poor in the endgame, it is likely that it would have won this one easily. The main fault of current programs is not that they fail to prosecute their advantage, but that they underestimate counterthreats by their opponents. For the record, the remaining moves were: 31 ... QxP 32 QRxB+ K-K1 33 QR-K7+ K-Q1 34 R-Q7+ K-B1 (the computer found no rhyme or reason for the choice of which Rook to check with or which square for the King to choose) 35 R-B7+ K-Q1 36 KR-Q7+ K-K1 37 R-Q1 P-Kt3 38 R-QKt7 Q-R4 39 P-KKt4 Q-R6 40 P-Kt5 Q-KB6 41 R-K1+ K-B1 42 R-Kt8+ K-Kt2 43 RxP Q-KKt6 44 R-Q1 Q-B2 45 KR-Q6 Q-B1 46 P-Kt3 K-R2 47 R-QR6 Resigns.

Botvinnik sums up: *What can one say about this game? M. Tal did not guess the artful and cunning scheme of his youthful partner in the opening and could not save the game. R. Fischer played with inventiveness and with great technical perfection. There is no doubt that during the next 15–20 years the chess world will witness the struggle of two exceptionally powerful talents—M. Tal and R. Fischer. From this rivalry the art of chess will only gain. In the perspective of this great competition, the present game is only a small episode. However, it already must be clear to Tal—don't put a finger into young Fischer's mouth!*

It should be apparent from this game that computers don't play good chess primarily because they have no good criterion for deciding *which* moves should be explored, and *how far*. There is a lot of talk about pruning (that is, somehow limiting the number of moves analyzed at various stages of the "search" so that the computer can "look ahead" further), and it is an important improvement. But positional moves are generally based on expectations that go far beyond the depth of moves current computers can handle. In short, it seems that the basic *modus operandi* of present chess-playing programs has a built-in, serious limitation.

The CDC 6600 computer on which the above game was analyzed handles about three million instructions per *second*. This facility compares favorably with that of the first all-electronic digital computer (ENIAC, or Electronic Numerical Integrator And Calculator), which exhibited a speed of five *thousand* additions a second, back in 1946. The first digital computer was entirely mechanical: it consisted of seventy-eight interconnected adding machines and desk calculators controlled by holes punched in a paper tape. Known as the Harvard Mark I, this 1944 precursor of our current hardware could turn out all of three operations a second. Since the capabilities of the computers in use when Claude Shannon first proposed a chess program in 1948 were so limited, it is surprising that he envisioned a searching method whereby a move was chosen on the basis of a look-ahead of at most two or three moves. It is the opinion of many programmers who are also good chessplayers, such as David Forthoffer of CDC, that Shannon in fact launched the computer-chess venture on the wrong course.

The first application of Shannon's prospectus was the program written in 1953 by A. M. Turing. Levy comments dryly, "It exhibited poor and aimless play." An interesting feature of his evaluation of a position was the total mobility of the pieces, which he defined inexplicably as the sum of the *square root* of the number of moves each piece could make in the position. Already we can see the purely mathematical approach breaking down: In most chess positions it is not the total *number* of squares controlled which counts, but *which* squares.

The two most important advances after Turing came in 1957 with the Bernstein program on an IBM 704 at M.I.T., and in 1967 with the Greenblatt program, "MacHack." As machine speeds and programming ingenuity have increased, computer chess has become a reasonable approximation of the average human effort. Its greatest strength at the moment is its absolute objectivity; its greatest weakness, as we have already suggested, is its inherent shortsightedness.

The following middle game and endgame illustrate both features.

FISCHER

After 37 B-B4

LARSEN

Match, Denver 1971

Larsen has built up a respectable position and now hopes to capitalize on the exposed position of the Black King. Fischer just played 36 ... R-R1, with the apparent intention of attacking the Rook Pawn. The position was given to the same Northwestern program as mentioned above, and in three minutes it came up with:

| 37 ... | R-R5! |

Most chessplayers are conditioned to move pieces which are under attack so obviously as is the Rook at Black's KB2. For some reason, they are also inclined to overlook the effect of pins. But if the computer has enough range, it will find the most hidden combinational possibility as long as it meets the program's numerical guidelines. Larsen not only overlooked Fischer's ingenious defense, but also missed his best reply:

| 38 R-QB1? | ... |

The computer correctly picked 38 R-Kt4! as the best defense. Larsen was no doubt blinded by his original idea of getting at the King, and did not want to exchange Rooks.

| 38 ... | BxP! |

White's Bishop is pinned. The computer found this in four minutes. Fischer saw it instantly.

| 39 BxR | RxP+ |
| 40 K-Kt2 | KxR |

A minute each for the computer on the last two moves, still aping Fischer.

| 41 B-Q5 | P-Kt3? |

Here Fischer correctly played 41 ... B-R3 and won the ending. From here on, the programmer made White's moves, and the computer gradually dissipated its advantage.

| 42 R-QKt1 | ... |

It's curious that the same idea it saw on move 37 for Black the computer misses here. Yet 42 R-QKt1 is, to the average player, the most obvious move on the board.

42 ...	B-B5
43 BxB	RxB
44 RxP	P-Q4
45 R-Kt2	P-B5
46 R-R2	K-Kt5?
47 P-R4	P-B6+

The computer correctly pushes its advanced Pawn, but does not "understand" that White's Pawn, which can only be stopped by the Rook, will be far more dangerous. White's Rook will have both a defensive role, horizontally, and an attacking role, behind its Pawn.

48	K-B2	R-K5
49	P-R5	P-Q5
50	P-R6	R-K1

COMPUTER

After 50 . . . R-K1

PROGRAMMER

51	R-R4!	R-K7+

Checking moves, which the computer likes to examine first in the middle game, tend to be unduly prized by its program in the endgame. Black appears to have mating possibilities.

52	K-B1	R-Q7

Saving a Pawn in this type of position is like protesting the water bill in the middle of a fire. 52 . . . R-QKt7 at least threatens K-Kt6, to which, however, R-R1 is always a satisfactory answer. Black could draw simply by moving his King to the Queenside on move 51, or here by returning the Rook to K1, QR1.

53	P-R7	R-Q8+
54	K-B2	R-Q7+
55	K-K1	R-K7+
56	K-B1	R-K1
57	P-R8(Q)	Resigns

The computer's short-range tactical ability will be of some significance when it can also draw on general chess theory. Here is the real challenge for programmers, especially if their ultimate goal is a simulation of human thought processes. What Plato said about kings ("Until philosophers become kings, and kings philosophers . . .") seems to be the nub of the matter. Until chess masters become programmers, or vice versa, it seems unlikely that a conceptual breakthrough will occur.

The terminology of the computer field puts many otherwise interested players off. The "alpha beta algorithm" is simply a procedure for stopping the search short when a sufficiently strong defect in a move is discovered. It's like saying, "We need not check out all the variations if after one of them our King gets mated." "Quiescent positions" are those in which all the exchanges have occurred on both sides. "Half-moves" are the moves by either side; 1 P-K4 P-K4 is a "move." (Suppose that a White Pawn is at QR2 and a White King at QR3; the Pawn can get to QR8 by six half-moves by White or by five half-moves by White and two by Black—placing two pieces *en prise*.) A programmer would say (as does Levy) that "the state of the art will only progress as a function of hardware speeds," whereas a player might say that "the computer will only get better by going faster." And there is a good deal of humor in the language. The Northwestern program was able to find Fischer's move 37 . . . R-R5! against Larsen, in the above line, by employing a "module" known as "Banana," or "Super beyond," the programmers' designation for a way of exploring moves that have a strong point not evident in the first level of analysis. Before a computer can hope to challenge a Fischer, some skillful programmer is going to have to come up with a "banana" of his own.

36 The Immortal Games

In the middle of the last century, Adolph Anderssen captured the imagination of the chess world with two spectacular mating combinations. They were quickly anthologized (in Lasker's chess magazine, they were definitively annotated) as "The Evergreen Game" and "The Immortal Game." They are noteworthy more for the prettiness of the final positions—Queen sacrifice, followed by unusual checkmates by minor pieces—than they are for depth of calculation or for strategic considerations. It is not surprising that Anderssen made his mark as a problem composer before he showed his strength as a player.

Since then there have been thousands of masterpieces, with Queen sacrifices, complex long-range calculations, and problem-like mating combinations. But in the judgment of players who lived during the careers of Lasker, Capablanca, and Alekhine—as well as in the eyes of admirers of Tal, Spassky, and Botvinnik, there are two games in this century which have a unique aura about them. One was played by a thirteen-year-old who could win but one other game in the tournament; the other was played by the U.S. Champion on his way to a 11–0 clean sweep of the field. These two circumstances no doubt added a romantic flair to the games. Yet they remain, many years later, as stunning as when they were first created over the board.

Fischer's two "immortal" games have two other ironies about them: They were played against brothers, with victory coming with the black pieces. No single combinational shot distinguishes them. They are simply overflowing with tactical energy and with delightful changes in orientation from piece play to mating threats. It is this last feature which places them on a level above magnificent achievements by any number of masters.

No book on Fischer would be complete without these two games. Because they have been so heavily annotated elsewhere (in Fischer's own books, best), I will discuss only those moves which have to do with the psychological impact of the games on players as they first see them.

Rosenwald III Tournament

New York 1956

	D. BYRNE	FISCHER
1	Kt-KB3	Kt-KB3
2	P-B4	P-KKt3
3	Kt-B3	B-Kt2
4	P-Q4	O-O
5	B-B4	P-Q4
6	Q-Kt3	PxP
7	QxBP	P-B3
8	P-K4	QKt-Q2
9	R-Q1	Kt-Kt3
10	Q-B5	B-Kt5
11	B-KKt5	. . .

Up to now, it all looks even enough. But Byrne now tries to apply a little extra pressure when his center is already overextended. Fischer's position is compact and he is fully developed. If only he can open up lines for the Queen, or get at White's support for the weak King Pawn! The answer almost suggests itself . . .

FISCHER

After 11 B-KKt5

D. BYRNE

11 ...	Kt-R5!
12 Q-R3	...

Yes, White would be forked by Knight and Queen after 12 KtxKt
KtxP 13 Q-B1 Q-R4+ 14 Kt-B3 BxKt, winning the Queen Bishop.
And the Black King Pawn cannot well be taken because after the
Queen exchange R-K1 would create all kinds of chances against
the weakened center. Black also had to calculate BxP and Q-Kt4,
in specific lines.

12 ...	KtxKt
13 PxKt	KtxP
14 BxP	...

If White doesn't have this, he has simply lost a Pawn. White
has opened the King file for the possible gain of the exchange.

14 ...	Q-Kt3
15 B-B4	...

Suddenly realizing he can't afford to win the exchange, since
he would lose another Pawn after 15 BxR BxB 16 Q-Kt3 KtxP! Now
White has his eye on KB7 and hopes to catch a piece if Black tries
to mix it with him.

15 ...	KtxQBP!

Fischer takes the plunge, realizing that he is hereby giving up
control of his QB4. The least of his calculations is 16 QxKt KR-K1,
pinning and winning the Bishop. Fischer had to see his Queen
sacrifice now or never, since the following is forced:

16 B-B5	KR-K1+
17 K-B1	...

Now Black has two pieces in take. Out of the blue Black trans-
forms the jousting over pieces and Pawns into an attack on the
White King!

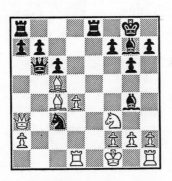

FISCHER

After 17 K-B1

D. BYRNE

17 . . .   B-K3!

One way or the other (18 BxB Q-Kt4+), Black grabs the white diagonal to the King, and immediately gains control of the game. Control is what is important here: Black has the option of taking a draw by perpetual check, or going after the win.

18 BxQ   BxB+

See pages 146–147 for a full discussion of the tactical possibilities inherent in the discovered checks after either 18 . . . BxB+ or 18 . . . Q-Kt4+.

19 K-Kt1	Kt-K7+
20 K-B1	KtxP+
21 K-Kt1	Kt-K7+
22 K-B1	Kt-B6+
23 K-Kt1	PxB

Now the reckoning. With the Knight protected, Black can afford to regain some material. It is ample, after the following further protective move:

24 Q-Kt4	R-R5
25 QxP	KtxR
26 P-KR3	RxP
27 K-R2	KtxP
28 R-K1	RxR
29 Q-Q8+	B-B1
30 KtxR	B-Q4
31 Kt-B3	Kt-K5
32 Q-Kt8	P-QKt4
33 P-R4	P-R4
34 Kt-K5	K-Kt2
35 K-Kt1	B-B4+
36 K-B1	. . .

Now Fischer has the pleasure of weaving a mating net. Perhaps an earlier resignation would have pleased him more.

36 . . .	Kt-Kt6+
37 K-K1	B-Kt5+
38 K-Q1	B-Kt6+
39 K-B1	Kt-K7+
40 K-Kt1	Kt-B6+
41 K-B1	R-B7 mate

The dramatic final point of his second "immortal" game also hinged on control of the white diagonals leading to the enemy King.

U.S. Championship

New York 1963–64

R. BYRNE	FISCHER
1 P-Q4	Kt-KB3
2 P-QB4	P-KKt3
3 P-KKt3	P-B3
4 B-Kt2	P-Q4
5 PxP	PxP
6 Kt-QB3	B-Kt2
7 P-K3	O-O
8 KKt-K2	Kt-B3
9 O-O	P-Kt3
10 P-Kt3	B-QR3
11 B-QR3	R-K1
12 Q-Q2	. . .

The position has a drawish symmetrical look. Black's last move is especially deceptive in that it appeared to be aimed merely at removing the Rook from potential attack by White's Queen Bishop. White's development is more strategic in that his King Bishop's diagonal is unblocked and his Queen Pawn is doubly protected. Fischer's development is tactical, and the next move is his logical follow-up:

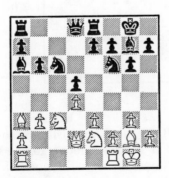

FISCHER

After 12 Q-Q2

R. BYRNE

12 . . .   P-K4!

This breakthrough is Panzer-like. The Black QP is apparently defenseless, but the latent threat against White's King Knight holds it for the moment.

| 13 PxP | KtxP |
| 14 KR-Q1 | ... |

Much sweat has gone into the analysis of QR-Q1, supposedly better than the text but unnatural-looking. To save his Brilliancy Prize in his own mind's eye, Fischer finally found a continuation in 14 ... Q-B1, with the idea of pinning the Bishop after 15 KtxP KtxKt 16 R-Q1, and then sacrificing the exchange to gain the long diagonal with his Queen Bishop. What is remarkable in all this is Fischer's willingness to go for broke at the first opportunity, casting first a Pawn and then the exchange before him.

| 14 ... | Kt-Q6! |
| 15 Q-B2 | KtxP! |

All of a sudden a symmetrical-looking position has turned into an alley fight. Byrne no doubt expected this sacrifice, but not the next one.

16 KxKt	Kt-Kt5+
17 K-Kt1	KtxKP
18 Q-Q2	...

FISCHER

After 18 Q-Q2

R. BYRNE

| 18 ... | KtxB! |

It's the King he's after. The King Bishop is the whole basis of White's game ... and it is easy enough to see that after 18 ... KtxR 19 RxKt Black's Queen Pawn would soon fall. Yet most players would grab the Rook on a purely mathematical count; and this is the difference between most players and Fischer.

19 KxKt	P-Q5!
20 KtxP	B-Kt2+
21 K-B1	Q-Q2!
Resigns!	

Fischer says he was bitterly disappointed that Byrne did not allow him to play out the full combination: 22 Q-KB2 Q-R6+ 23 K-Kt1 R-K8+! 24 RxR BxKt and "mate in a few." Byrne's comment was trenchant: "The culminating combination is of such depth that even at the very moment at which I resigned both grandmasters who were commenting on the play for the spectators in a separate room believed I had a won game!"

Fischer creates games like this because he pushes his opportunities to their very limits. And these are not the last.

VIII *Epilogue*

by ISAAC KASHDAN

Nine world champions preceded Bobby Fischer to the crown in the twentieth century. I have selected the following games as representative of the play in matches involving these titans of chess. Fortunately, chess is that rare game in which we can put past performances side by side with the efforts of our contemporaries, and judge the strength of the players by the quality of their games. Whether or not we can accurately gauge who was the greatest champion of all, it is nevertheless refreshing to play over again these historic games along with the masterpieces of Bobby Fischer.

After ratings and statistics and recent memories are all weighed, it is the games themselves that tell us how similar in technique, in creativity, and in fighting spirit Caissa's champions have been.

37 I Meet the Champions

The Fischer-Spassky match in 1972 stirred more interest in chess than any other event in the long history of this remarkable game. The events before as well as during the match made the front pages of every newspaper. Bobby and Boris were discussed as regularly as the other top figures in the worlds of sports and entertainment.

To most people they are still the only chess champions. Whatever opinion the average man has about chess is inevitably colored by the personalities of Fischer and Spassky. Chess, it seems, is mainly a game for ill-mannered kids and Russians. It is not essential to be weird to play chess, but it helps.

Yet we know there have been other chess champions. What were they like? Did they have traits in common? If we knew more about their predecessors, could we have predicted that a Fischer or a Spassky would rise to the top? Let me try to answer by discussing some of the champions I have met and come to know.

The first time I saw a world chess champion was in 1924, in my native New York. One of the greatest gatherings of chess masters ever assembled were in the double round-robin tournament that year. The reigning champion was José R. Capablanca of Cuba, in his prime at thirty-six. He had not lost a game in almost ten years, and was the outstanding favorite.

A major contender was Dr. Emanuel Lasker of Germany, who had held the title from 1894 until his defeat by Capablanca in 1921, just three years before. Lasker was now fifty-six. Also in the tournament was Alexander Alekhine, the thirty-two-year-old Russian who was soon to take over the championship. At the time Alekhine was the leader of a dashing group of men, mostly in their thirties, who claimed they had revolutionized the game. They had been beating the old guard, and had high hopes that one of them would come through in this magnificent tournament.

EMANUEL LASKER

It was Lasker who won the tournament, with Capablanca second and Alekhine third. Who was the best chess player of the three? Were they better than anyone who preceded them? Might there be still greater players in the future? Such comparisons are never easy, and some may consider them meaningless. I shall outline a few points worth considering.

Lasker held the world championship for twenty-seven years. Will Fischer beat that record? He would have to remain champion until the year 2000! That is a long time for supremacy in any field. Lasker had one advantage that no modern champion can claim. He could play when and with whom he pleased. To an extent he owned the championship title once he won it from Wilhelm Steinitz.

There were years when Lasker devoted himself to mathematics and philosophy, playing little or no chess. Challengers were always after him, but Lasker would accept only when he was ready. The long layoffs rarely bothered him. When he sat down to play, he was and remained the champion. In one respect he antedated Fischer. He believed that chess was a profession, and that the best players should be well paid for their efforts. He was roundly criticized for setting well-nigh impossible conditions, but he generally had his way. In time, he helped to improve standards for match and tournament play, to the advantage of all his successors.

Lasker did very little studying in chess. He was no expert on openings. He founded no school of chess, developed no system, and had few followers. Yet Lasker won. The more important a game was, the more likely it was that he would win. He would play the man as much as the position. He had an uncanny sense for what would trouble his opponent, and this was what he played. Lasker probably had more "lost" games than any champion before or since, but he saved most of them. The losses were always found in analysis, but over the board Lasker was in control.

JOSÉ R. CAPABLANCA

The most urgent of Lasker's challengers, once he arrived on the scene, was Capablanca. Here was a man as different from Lasker as could be imagined. Instead of the learned professor, as ready to expound on mathematics or philosophy as on chess, Capablanca was the man of the world, a suave diplomat who moved in the highest social circles.

Capablanca was the chess machine. In some types of games, he was perfection. He practically never made an error. In a ten-year stretch he did not lose a single game. He played much faster than his opponents, rarely remaining at the board for more than a few minutes. He was no student of the game, any more than Lasker, using any openings that were fashionable at the time. Once he had the kind of clearcut position he preferred, his accuracy would prevail. The slightest advantage in the ending was sufficient for Capablanca.

Capablanca had challenged Lasker to a match for the title in 1913, but the First World War intervened. Later Lasker kept stalling during the negotiations. He was twenty years older than the Cuban, and had suffered severe privations during the war. Finally the match was arranged in Cuba, for a purse of $20,000. This was much the largest amount ever offered for a chess event, and Lasker needed the money. Capablanca won by 4–0 and 10 draws. He was undoubtedly the better player at the time, but on a number of later occasions the older Lasker still came ahead.

After winning the championship Capablanca was supreme in the chess world. He was considered at least as far ahead of his contemporaries as Fischer is today. In 1925 Capablanca wrote that chess was getting too easy. He would never lose a game if he was satisfied to draw, and in a few years, he predicted, there would be a number of other masters who could not be defeated.

ALEXANDER ALEKHINE

Alekhine was the best of the group who had started before the First World War and matured shortly after. Breyer, Reti, Bogoljubow, and Nimzovitch were others. They believed there were depths to chess that had never been explored. It was not just a matter of winning. There were fantastic ideas, artistic elements that had to be brought to the surface. The hypermoderns, as they were called, were ready to devote their lives to the search.

Alekhine was the most fanatic. He had been well educated, with a degree in law, but nothing interested him but chess. He played over every game he could find and could quote thousands of them from memory. He studied the most complex variations in the openings, preparing traps which he would save for particular opponents. He was ready to try anything that would complicate the game. He was an attacking genius, finding combinations in what would seem to anyone else to be placid situations. Are we talking about Fischer or Tal? No, this was Alekhine, long before they were born!

Six years after he won the title, Capablanca accepted Alekhine's challenge. There was seemingly little risk. The match would go to the first winner of six games. Since Alekhine had never won a single game from Capablanca, it was incredible that he should win six. But it happened. Alekhine, with the black pieces in the Exchange Variation of the French Defense, won the very first game, to the astonishment of the chess world. It was the longest match in chess history, with Alekhine winning by 6–3 and 25 draws. Capablanca was as accurate as ever, except in the complex situations that Alekhine was able to create every so often.

For the rest of his life Capablanca tried for a return match, but Alekhine had the title and was not at all interested in risking it. He played two matches with Eufim Bogoljubow, a Russian who had immigrated to Germany. Alekhine won easily. In 1935 he played Dr. Max Euwe and lost, another astonishing upset for the chess world. Alekhine was clearly out of condition. Two years later Alekhine won a return match, which Euwe had agreed to. Euwe was a professor of mathematics who loved chess, but it was never his life's passion. He was a fine, gifted player, but perhaps was too much a gentleman and scholar for the rigors of championship combat. Today Euwe is president of the International Chess Federation and probably the most respected chess master of the age.

When World War II started in 1939, chess was practically suspended once more. Alekhine's career for some years was shadowed by controversy, with much discussion of title matches, but no activity. He died, still champion, in 1946.

THE RUSSIANS

The latest challenger had been Mikhail Botvinnik of the Soviet Union. For years the Russians had taken little part in international chess. Some of their best players had moved elsewhere, with Alekhine and Bogoljubow as prime examples. But they had gained strength by accessions during the war. There was Paul Keres of Estonia, Andrei Lilienthal of Hungary, and later, Mikhail Tal of Latvia. The greatest of the true Russians was Botvinnik. He was one of the few allowed to play in other countries, and he was successful in several major tournaments.

For the first time since the title had been established in the 1880s there was no World Champion. There was no precedent to act upon. Fortunately there was another new factor. The International Chess Federation, organized in 1924 and gaining in prestige, decided to take over. A tournament among the best players in the world was arranged, with the winner to be acknowledged as the new champion. It was also agreed that a championship match would be held every three years, with the procedure to be firmly supervised by the federation.

Without going into details, Botvinnik was the clear winner of the tournament and acclaimed as the greatest player in the world. That was in 1948, the start of Russian control of the title until Fischer came along. There were title matches every three years, with a Russian always the challenger. The Russians claimed that this was the way it had to be. It was not the individuals but the Soviet system that was superior. This had some basis in fact. The Soviets encouraged their grandmasters to a far greater extent than any other country. Anyone close to the championship was certain of financial support and the kind of status and prestige that could not be imagined in chess circles here.

In 1951 Botvinnik tied with David Bronstein, thus barely retaining the title. Bronstein had become the challenger by winning the first Interzonal Tournament, with twenty participants. It was Vassily Smyslov in 1954 and again the result was a tie, with Botvinnik still champion. Three years later Smyslov was again the challenger. This time he beat Botvinnik by 12½ to 9½ to become the World Champion. He did not last long. The rules called for a return match the following year, and for the first time Botvinnik won a championship match, regaining the title by 12½–10½.

A virtual repetition occurred in the next cycle. The successful challenger in 1960 was Tal, who beat out Fischer among others on the way up. Tal beat Botvinnik easily by 12½–8½, to become the youngest champion ever at twenty-three. Again there was a return match, with an astounding reversal. It was Botvinnik by 13–8.

Tal had played brilliantly in the first match, with the magic combinations that made him the most exciting player of the day. By the return match Tal had developed kidney trouble, from which he has suffered periodically.

Botvinnik had survived, but he was to lose the title for the third and last time to Tigran Petrosian. This was by 12½–9½ in 1963. The rules had been changed to do away with the automatic return match. Botvinnik was given no further opportunity. Petrosian held the title for six years. He defeated Boris Spassky by 12½–11½ in 1966, but lost to him, 12½–10½, in 1969. Three years later Fischer came along.

38 Championship Chess from Lasker to Spassky

5th MATCH GAME

Havana 1921

Queen's Gambit Declined

CAPABLANCA	LASKER
1 P-Q4	P-Q4
2 Kt-KB3	Kt-KB3
3 P-B4	P-K3
4 B-Kt5	QKt-Q2
5 P-K3	B-K2
6 Kt-B3	O-O
7 R-B1	P-QKt3

An old move that was already considered inferior at the time of the match. Better is 7 ... P-B3 8 B-Q3 PxP 9 BxP Kt-Q4, and Black will equalize after several exchanges. This maneuver for Black was popularized by Capablanca.

Lasker was not interested in simplifying in the opening, and may have deliberately played the more difficult variation.

8 PxP	PxP
9 Q-R4	P-B4

This sacrifices a Pawn, which Lasker preferred to the tame 9 ... B-Kt2 10 B-QR6 BxB 11 QxB, then White has considerably more space.

343

10	Q-B6	R-Kt1
11	KtxP	B-Kt2

Black has 11 . . . KtxKt 12 QxKt B-Kt2 13 BxB QxB 14 Q-Kt5 QxQ 15 KtxQ PxP 16 PxP Kt-B3, with a big edge in development changes.

12	KtxB+	QxKt
13	Q-R4	QR-B1

The threat of opening the file before White has castled looks strong, but it does not work out. Better is 13 . . . BxKt 14 PxB PxP 15 QxQP Kt-K4 16 B-K2 QR-Q1 17 Q-KB4 R-Q3, with good play.

14	Q-R3	. . .

Lasker may have missed this pin. If 14 B-QR6 PxP 15 RxR RxR 16 O-O? Kt-B4 wins, or if 14 BxKt KtxB 15 B-R6 PxP 16 RxR RxR 17 O-O PxP, with advantage. It is important that the Queen at K2 protects the Bishop.

14	. . .	Q-K3
15	BxKt	QxB
16	B-R6	. . .

Now there is a difference. If 16 . . . PxP 17 RxR RxR 18 O-O, and White regains the Pawn plus because the Black pieces are loose.

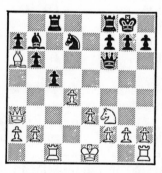

LASKER

After 16 B-R6

CAPABLANCA

16	. . .	BxKt

Lasker decides to give up the exchange for fighting chances. By doing so he maintains the initiative for a long time. He much prefers this to a dogged defense with a Pawn behind.

17	BxR	RxB
18	PxB	QxBP
19	R-KKt1	. . .

He could not castle because of 19 . . . R-B3.

19 ...	R-K1
20 Q-Q3	P-Kt3

This was an unnecessary precaution. Better was 20 . . . Q-R6, to win a second Pawn. If then 21 K-K2, Q-R4+, followed by QxRP.

21 K-B1	R-K5
22 Q-Q1	Q-R6+

Capablanca had offered a Pawn by 22 . . . RxKP 23 QxQ RxQ, because the ending would be much easier for him. Lasker rightly refuses the gift.

23 R-Kt2	Kt-B3

This threatens to win by R-Kt5. White must defend carefully.

24 K-Kt1	PxP
25 R-B4	...

This is the move Capablanca had relied on. It practically forces the exchange of Rooks. If 25 . . . R-Kt5 26 R-B8+ K-Kt2 27 RxR KtxR 28 QxP+ would win.

25 ...	PxP
26 RxR	KtxR

But not 26 . . . PxP+? 27 RxP KtxR 28 Q-Q8+ K-Kt2 29 Q-Q4+ wins the Knight.

27 Q-Q8+	K-Kt2
28 Q-Q4+	Kt-B3
29 PxP	Q-K3
30 R-KB2	P-KKt4
31 P-KR4	PxP

There is not much choice. If 31 . . . P-KR3 32 P-R5, and the pin on the Knight can never be relieved. Better, however, was 31 . . . K-Kt3 32 PxP Kt-K5 33 Q-Q3 Q-Kt5+ 34 R-Kt2 Q-R5 35 Q-Kt1 K-Kt2, followed by KtxP, with good prospects.

32 QxRP	Kt-Kt5
33 Q-Kt5+	K-B1
34 R-B5	P-KR4

Again Capablanca tempts Lasker to exchange Queens, but after 34 . . . QxP+ 35 QxQ KtxQ 36 R-B2, the Rook will quickly penetrate to the Queenside for a sure win.

35 Q-Q8+	K-Kt2
36 Q-Kt5+	K-B1
37 Q-Q8+	K-Kt2
38 Q-Kt5+	K-B1
39 P-Kt3	Q-Q3
40 Q-B4	Q-Q8+

41 Q-B1	Q-Q2
42 RxRP	. . .

White has nothing better. If 42 Q-B3, KtxP still follows. With both Kings open to checks, the game should be drawn.

42 . . .	KtxP
43 Q-B3	Q-Q5
44 Q-R8+	K-K2
45 Q-Kt7+	K-B1?

LASKER

After 45 . . . K-B1?

CAPABLANCA

This was the last move before the time control, and the fatal error. Lasker probably expected a repetition of moves, as happened earlier, and wanted to adjourn and analyze the position before deciding where his King belonged.

After 45 . . . K-B3, he was safe. There might follow 46 Q-B3+ K-Kt3 47 K-R1 Q-R8+ 48 K-R2 P-B4, or 46 Q-B6+ K-K2 47 Q-B7+ K-B3. If White in this position tries 48 R-R4?, with the idea QxR 49 Q-Q8+, he will lose. Black forces mate by 48 . . . Kt-Kt5+, the longest variation being 49 K-R1 Q-K5+ 50 K-Kt1 Q-K8+ 51 K-Kt2 Q-B7+ 52 K-R3 Q-B6+ 53 Q-Kt3 Kt-B7+ 54 K-R2 Q-R8 mate.

46 Q-Kt8+	Resigns

For now if 46 . . . K-Kt2 47 Q-R8+ wins the Queen, and if 46 . . . K-K2 47 Q-K5+ is just as decisive.

1st MATCH GAME

Buenos Aires 1927

French Defense

CAPABLANCA	ALEKHINE
1 P-K4	P-K3
2 P-Q4	P-Q4
3 Kt-QB3	B-Kt5
4 PxP	. . .

The Exchange Variation of the French Defense, one of the most drawish variations in the game. For a number of moves Capablanca plays lackadaisically, while Alekhine looks for chances.

4 . . .	PxP
5 B-Q3	Kt-QB3
6 Kt-K2	KKt-K2
7 O-O	B-KB4
8 BxB	KtxB
9 Q-Q3	Q-Q2
10 Kt-Q1	. . .

This loses time, and Black soon gains the initiative. The normal 10 B-B4 was in order.

10 . . .	O-O
11 Kt-K3	KtxKt
12 BxKt	KR-K1
13 Kt-B4	. . .

The Knight is poorly placed here. 13 B-B4 is still preferable, to be followed by P-QB3.

13 . . .	B-Q3
14 KR-K1	. . .

If 14 KtxP BxP+ 15 KxB QxKt, and Black has attacking chances, with his Rooks getting into action quickly. If then 16 P-QB4 Q-R4+ 17 K-Kt1 QR-Q1 18 P-Q5 R-Q3.

The text is hardly better, giving Alekhine a tactical opportunity. 14 P-QB3 was essential.

14 . . .	Kt-Kt5
15 Q-Kt3	. . .

The threats were more serious than Capablanca realized. His

best was 15 Q-Q2 Q-B4 16 KR-QB1. Black can then develop an
attack by 16 . . . P-KR4.

15 . . .		Q-B4	
16 QR-B1		. . .	

ALEKHINE

After 16 QR-B1

CAPABLANCA

This loses a Pawn, as Alekhine demonstrates in a neat combination. The unattractive alternative was 16 Kt-Q3 KtxKt 17 QxKt
QxQ 18 PxQ, with a much superior ending for Black.

16 . . .   KtxBP!

This is the first point. There is no gain by 16 . . . BxKt 17 QxKt,
or 16 . . . KtxRP 17 QxKt BxKt 18 BxB QxB 19 QxQP.

17 RxKt   QxKt!

And this is the major point that Alekhine had foreseen, and that
Capablanca may have overlooked. If instead 17 . . . BxKt 18 R-B5
would have regained the Pawn.

18 P-Kt3   Q-B4

This keeps the Pawn, since if 19 QxKtP QxR. Alekhine had
considered playing for attack by 18 . . . Q-B6 19 QxKtP P-KR4, but
the White Queen returns quickly via Kt5.

19 QR-K2   P-QKt3
20 Q-Kt5   P-KR4
21 P-KR4   R-K5
22 B-Q2   . . .

This is his best chance, giving up a second Pawn to get his pieces
into action. Black was threatening 22 . . . RxRP! 23 PxR Q-Kt5+,
with a forced mate. If 22 Q-Q3 Q-B6, followed by QR-K1, and
White would be completely tied up.

22 . . .   RxQP

He must soon return the Pawn. A good alternative was 22 . . . QR-K1 23 QxR+ RxQ 24 RxR+ K-R2, when the White Pawns and Bishop would prove weak.

23	B-B3	R-Q6
24	B-K5	R-Q1

Alekhine realizes that a Pawn must go, and plays to improve his position. If 24 . . . BxB 25 RxB Q-B6 26 RxRP, as occurs in the game.

25	BxB	RxB
26	R-K5	Q-B6
27	RxRP	QxR

And not 27 . . . R-K3? 28 Q-K8+! and White mates on the next move.

28	R-K8+	K-R2
29	QxR+	Q-Kt3
30	Q-Q1	R-K3

Alekhine sacrifices his extra Pawn for the King file and an entry to the White King. Combined with the advance of the passed QP, this is the most forceful way to win.

31	R-QR8	R-K4
32	RxP	P-QB4
33	R-Q7	Q-K3
34	Q-Q3+	P-Kt3
35	R-Q8	P-Q5
36	P-R4	. . .

ALEKHINE

After 36 P-R4

CAPABLANCA

There is little White can do. Black has achieved his ideal formation, and can now win in several ways.

36 . . .	R-K8+

This is the direct attack, which must succeed. Black can also win the Rook, in curious fashion, by 36 . . . Q-K2. If then 37 R-QB8 or

QR8, Q-Kt2, with the added threat of R-K8+ and mate. Or if 37 R-QKt8 Q-B2 38 R-KB8 K-Kt2 39 R-QR8 Q-Kt2, as before.

37	K-Kt2	Q-B3+
38	P-B3	R-K6
39	Q-Q1	Q-K3
40	P-KKt4	R-K7+
41	K-R3	Q-K6
42	Q-KR1	Q-B5

Now there is no answer to R-KB7.

43	P-KR5	R-KB7
	Resigns	

26th MATCH GAME

Holland 1935

Dutch Defense

EUWE	ALEKHINE
1 P-Q4	P-K3
2 P-QB4	P-KB4
3 P-KKt3	B-Kt5+
4 B-Q2	B-K2

Alekhine frequently played this maneuver, with the idea that White's Bishop is misplaced on Q2. It is probably no gain for either side.

5 B-Kt2	Kt-KB3
6 Kt-QB3	O-O
7 Kt-B3	. . .

This is the routine developing move. White might try to keep his Pawns more mobile by 7 Kt-R3 or 7 Q-Kt3.

7 . . .	Kt-K5

The point is that if 8 KtxKt PxKt, the White Knight does not have the square Q2. A good alternative is 7 . . . P-Q4, to build up the Stonewall formation.

8 O-O	P-QKt3

In a previous game of the match Alekhine played 8 . . . B-B3, which led to several exchanges after 9 KtxKt PxKt 10 Kt-K1 BxP.

9 Q-B2	B-Kt2
10 Kt-K5	KtxKt
11 BxKt	. . .

The simplest, leaving White with a strong center. If 11 BxB KtxP+ 12 K-Kt2 KtxQP 13 Q-Q3 QKt-B3 14 KtxKt KtxKt 15 BxR QxB, Black would have two Pawns as ample compensation for the exchange.

11 ...	BxB
12 KxB	Q-B1
13 P-Q5	P-Q3
14 Kt-Q3	P-K4
15 K-R1	...

So that if 15 ... P-B5 16 PxP PxP 17 R-KKt1. But 15 P-B4, as was played two moves later, would have been effective here.

15 ...	P-B3
16 Q-Kt3	...

Black was threatening 16 ... PxP 17 PxP Q-B5. White must secure the Queen Pawn.

16 ...	K-R1
17 P-B4	P-K5
18 Kt-Kt4	...

This is the first of seven consecutive moves with this Knight, which turns out to be the most active piece in the game. Black's reply is virtually forced, to avoid the Knight occupying Q5.

18 ...	P-B4
19 Kt-B2	Kt-Q2
20 Kt-K3	B-B3

ALEKHINE

After 20 ... B-B3

EUWE

This allows the sacrifice of a piece for three Pawns and a powerful advance in the center. Euwe gladly accepted the challenge. Alekhine had realized the danger, but believed he would have sufficient counterplay. 20 ... Kt-B3 was safer, but White could soon mount an attack by P-KR3 and P-Kt4.

21 KtxP	BxB
22 KtxQP	Q-Kt1
23 KtxP	B-B3
24 Kt-Q2	P-KKt4

This is the only chance to open lines and attack on the Kingside before the Pawns come storming through.

25 P-K4	PxP
26 PxP	B-Q5
27 P-K5	Q-K1
28 P-K6	R-KKt1

Now White must be on guard. If 29 PxKt, Q-K7 regains the Knight with advantage. Probably the best reply was 29 Q-KR3.

29 Kt-B3	Q-Kt3
30 R-KKt1	...

He must return some material, to challenge the file. If 30 Kt-Kt5, Kt-K4, followed by . . . P-KR3, will improve Black's chances.

30 ...	BxR
31 RxB	...

ALEKHINE

After 31 RxB

EUWE

31 ...	Q-B3

After defending well, Alekhine weakens. Best is 31 . . . Q-B4. If then 32 PxKt RxR+ 33 KxR QxBP or QxP(2) will at least draw. The Pawns are no longer dangerous, and the Rook will get into action. If 32 Kt-Kt5, P-KR3. There is no Q-R3+, as happens in the game.

32 Kt-Kt5	R-Kt2

If now 32 . . . P-KR3 33 PxKt PxKt 34 Q-R3+ K-Kt2 35 RxP+, and R-B5 wins the Queen. Another win after 32 . . . P-KR3 is by 33 Kt-B7+ K-R2 34 Q-Q3+ R-Kt3 35 Kt-K5 KtxKt 36 PxKt Q-Kt2 37 P-Q6 Q-Kt2+ 38 Q-Q5 QxQ+ 39 PxQ, and the remarkable Pawn mass cannot be stopped.

33	PxKt	RxP

This loses. He could still hold the game with 33 . . . QxBP 34 Q-QB3 Q-Q5 (the threat is QxR+) 35 QxQ PxQ 36 Kt-K6 RxP.

34	Q-K3	R-K2
35	Kt-K6	R-KB1
36	Q-K5	QxQ

The two connected passed Pawns prove too strong, but there is little to be done. If 36 . . . RxKt 37 PxR QxQ 38 PxQ R-K1 39 R-K1 RxP 40 K-Kt2 wins easily, as the King gets to Q5.

37	PxQ	R-B4
38	R-K1	. . .

38 R-Kt5 is also good, since if RxR 39 KtxR RxP? 40 Kt-B7+wins. The Pawns would soon march.

38	. . .	P-KR3

This makes it easier for White, as the Knight can move and free the Pawns. Black's best is 38 . . . K-Kt1 and then mark time. White can still break through by 39 K-Kt2 R-K1 40 K-Kt3 P-KR4 41 P-KR4 R-K2 42 K-Kt2 R-K1 43 R-K3 R-K2 44 R-Kt3+, followed by R-Kt5.

39	Kt-Q8	R-B7

Of course, if 39 . . . RxP 40 RxR RxR 41 Kt-B7+, as above.

40	P-K6	R-Q7
41	Kt-B6	R-K1
42	P-K7	P-Kt4

As good as any. It takes one more maneuver with the galloping Knight to clinch matters.

43	Kt-Q8	K-Kt2
44	Kt-Kt7	K-B3
45	R-K6+	K-Kt4
46	Kt-Q6	RxKP
47	Kt-K4+	Resigns

WORLD CHAMPIONSHIP TOURNAMENT

Holland 1948

Queen's Gambit Declined

BOTVINNIK	EUWE
1 P-Q4	P-Q4
2 Kt-KB3	Kt-KB3

3 P-B4	P-K3
4 Kt-B3	P-B3
5 P-K3	QKt-Q2
6 B-Q3	PxP
7 BxBP	P-QKt4

The Meran Variation, a fighting plan which leads to intricate play. It was very much in fashion at the time, and a particular favorite of Botvinnik, who found innovations for both sides.

8 B-Q3	P-QR3
9 P-K4	P-B4

This is the typical move, to challenge the center. White must play aggressively if he is to retain any advantage.

10 P-K5	PxP
11 KtxKtP	PxKt

Frequently played was 11 . . . KtxP 12 KtxKt PxKt, when White has good alternatives in 13 Q-B3, 13 Q-Kt3, or 13 O-O. Less effective is 13 BxP+ B-Q2 14 KtxB Q-R4+.

12 PxKt	Q-Kt3

This seems best. Not 12 . . . QxP? 13 B-Kt5 wins the Queen.

13 PxP	BxP
14 O-O	Kt-B4

Black's problem is that castling is risky, yet the King cannot remain indefinitely in the center. If 14 . . . O-O 15 Q-K2 Kt-B4 16 BxP+ KxB 17 Kt-Kt5+ K-Kt1 18 Q-R5, or 17 . . . K-Kt3 18 Q-Kt4, with a dangerous attack.

15 B-KB4	B-Kt2
16 R-K1	R-Q1

Here it was essential to simplify by 16 . . . KtxB 17 QxKt BxKt 18 QxB O-O. White would still have attacking chances, but Black's center Pawns would be a factor.

17 R-QB1	R-Q4

Now Black cannot try the exchanges and castle, because B-B7 would win. With his development complete, Botvinnik is ready to swap on his own terms, knowing that he will dominate the position.

18 B-K5	BxB
19 RxB	RxR
20 KtxR	KtxB
21 QxKt	P-B3

EUWE

After 21 . . . P-B3

BOTVINNIK

There is no longer a saving move. If 21 . . . O-O 22 Kt-Q7 wins, or 22 Q-Kt3+ K-R1 23 R-B7! If 21 . . . R-Kt1 22 QxRP RxP+ 23 K-B1, and there is no defense to QxP+. If 21 . . . K-K2 22 Q-R3+ P-Kt5 23 Q-KKt3, and White will soon break through.

22 Q-KKt3!   . . .

This is the only move to win, but ample for the purpose. If the Knight moves, Black could finally castle with safety.

22 . . .	PxKt
23 Q-Kt7	R-B1
24 R-B7	QxR

This is the only way to prolong resistance. If 24 . . . Q-Q3 25 RxB P-Q6 26 R-R7 Q-Q1 27 QxRP or QxKP, and mate soon follows.

25 QxQ	B-Q4
26 QxKP	P-Q6
27 Q-K3	B-B5
28 P-QKt3	R-B2

If 28 . . . B-Q4 29 QxQP, Black's game is hopeless. His one slight chance is to hold the QP.

29 P-B3   . . .

To get the King nearer. There is no rush about taking the Bishop.

29 . . .	R-Q2
30 Q-Q2	P-K4
31 PxB	PxP
32 K-B2	K-B2

32 . . . P-B6 looks dangerous, but White is now ready to continue 33 QxBP P-Q7 34 Q-B8+ K-K2 35 QxR+ KxQ 36 K-K2, winning.

33 K-K3	K-K3
34 Q-Kt4	R-QB2
35 K-Q2	R-B3
36 P-QR4	Resigns

The QRP can keep advancing. If ever . . . P-B6+, the reply is QxP.

9th MATCH GAME

Moscow 1954

French Defense

SMYSLOV	BOTVINNIK
1 P-K4	P-K3
2 P-Q4	P-Q4
3 Kt-QB3	B-Kt5
4 P-K5	P-QB4
5 P-QR3	B-R4

Botvinnik, who was the specialist on the French Defense, played this move several times in the match. More usual is 5 . . . BxKt+.

| 6 P-QKt4 | . . . |

This Pawn sacrifice, attributed to Alekhine, gives White a lasting initiative.

| 6 . . . | PxQP |

The alternative is 6 . . . PxKtP 7 Kt-Kt5 PxP+ 8 P-B3, when White has a strong attack.

| 7 Q-Kt4 | . . . |

In the first and third match games Smyslov played 7 Kt-Kt5, but gained no advantage after B-B2 8 P-KB4 Kt-K2.

| 7 . . . | Kt-K2 |

If 7 . . . K-B1 8 Kt-Kt5 B-Kt3 9 B-Q3, or 8 PxB PxKt 9 Kt-B3, with advantage to White in either case. An interesting possibility is 7 . . . Q-B2 8 QxKtP QxKt+ 9 K-Q1 QxR 10 QxR K-B1 11 PxB, again with a plus for White.

| 8 PxB | . . . |

Black has more counter after the immediate 8 QxKtP R-Kt1 9 QxRP B-B2 10 Kt-Kt5 P-R3 11 KtxP BxP 12 KKt-B3 Q-B2.

8 . . .	PxKt
9 QxKtP	R-Kt1
10 QxRP	Kt-Q2

This was to help defend the Kingside, but it does not turn out well. The alternative is 10 . . . QKt-B3, which was played by Mikhail Tal against Bobby Fischer in a remarkable game in the

Chess Olympics at Leipzig 1960. The continuation was 11 Kt-B3 Q-B2 12 B-QKt5 B-Q2 13 O-O O-O-O 14 B-Kt5 KtxKP 15 KtxKt BxB 16 KtxP BxR 17 KtxR RxB 18 KtxKP RxP+ 19 K-R1 Q-K4 20 RxB QxKt 21 KxR Q-Kt5+ Drawn. (See page 187.)

| | 11 Kt-B3 | Kt-B1 |

Better was 11 . . . Q-B2, and after 12 B-KB4 Kt-B1. As played the Bishop gets to the stronger KKt5 square.

	12 Q-Q3	QxP
	13 P-KR4	B-Q2
	14 B-Kt5	R-B1
	15 Kt-Q4	. . .

The Knight adds to White's power in the center. If now 15 . . . R-B5, which Botvinnik may have intended, 16 Q-K3 R-R5 (but not 16 . . . Kt-B4 17 KtxKt R-K5? 18 Kt-Q6 mate) 17 R-QKt1 RxP 18 Kt-Kt5, with a decided advantage for White.

| | 15 . . . | Kt-B4 |
| | 16 R-QKt1 | R-B5 |

This is still not good, but there is little that Black can undertake. If 16 . . . QxP 17 KtxKt PxKt 18 RxP, and White has all the better of it, in middle game or ending. If 16 . . . P-Kt3 17 Kt-Kt5, with the threat of QxKt! or 16 . . . KtxKt 17 QxKt P-Kt3 18 B-Q3, when the KRP will soon be decisive.

| | 17 KtxKt | PxKt |
| | 18 RxP | R-K5+ |

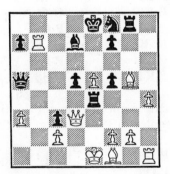

BOTVINNIK

After 18 . . . R-K5+

SMYSLOV

To this Smyslov has a brilliant refutation, which wins quickly. Botvinnik stated later that he had intended 18 . . . RxB 19 PxR R-K5+, which would also lose after 20 B-K2 Kt-Kt3 21 K-B1. If then 21 . . . Kt-B5 22 R-R8+ K-K2 23 Q-Kt5, or if 21 . . . B-B3 22 R-Kt8+ K-K2 23 Q-R6.

19 QxR!   . . .

This is clear enough, based on the virtual mating net the Black King is in.

19 . . .	QPxQ
20 R-Kt8+	B-B1
21 B-Kt5+	QxB

After 21 . . . Kt-Q2, it is of course mate in two after 22 RxB+.

| 22 RxQ | Kt-K3 |
| 23 B-B6 | . . . |

Now there is no stopping the passed pawn.

23 . . .	RxP
24 P-R5	B-R3
25 P-R6	Resigns

6th MATCH GAME

Moscow 1960

King's Indian Defense

BOTVINNIK	TAL
1 P-QB4	Kt-KB3
2 Kt-KB3	P-KKt3
3 P-KKt3	B-Kt2
4 B-Kt2	O-O
5 P-Q4	P-Q3
6 Kt-B3	QKt-Q2
7 O-O	P-K4
8 P-K4	P-B3

8 . . . R-K1 and . . . PxP is one way to get the Black pieces moving, but it cedes the center to White's Pawns. Tal prefers to wait before exchanging.

| 9 P-KR3 | Q-Kt3 |
| 10 P-Q5 | . . . |

The threat was 10 . . . PxP 11 KtxP KtxP if 10 R-K1 R-K1, with the same plan. A good try for White is 10 R-Kt1 PxP 11 KtxP KtxP? 12 KtxKt BxKt 13 P-QKt4 Kt-K4 14 P-B5 PxP 15 PxP Q-Q1 16 B-R6. Reshevsky defeated Lombardy in this variation in the U.S. Championship in 1959. Best for Black is 11 . . . Q-Kt5.

10 ...	PxP
11 BPxP	Kt-B4
12 Kt-K1	B-Q2
13 Kt-Q3	KtxKt
14 QxKt	KR-B1

In similar positions Black often tries for P-KB4. But if 14 . . .
Kt-R4 15 B-K3 Q-Q1 16 Q-K2 P-B4 17 PxP, and there is no good way
to recapture. 14 . . . Kt-K1 is playable, but as usual Tal takes the
more active stance.

15 R-Kt1	Kt-R4
16 B-K3	Q-Kt5
17 Q-K2	R-B5
18 KR-B1	QR-QB1
19 K-R2	P-B4

Tal knows that if 20 PxP, he must recapture with the Bishop,
which would normally be inferior. He must have already planned
the coming sacrifice.

| 20 PxP | BxP |
| 21 R-QR1 | ... |

If 21 P-R3 Q-Kt6 22 Kt-K4 R-B7 23 RxR RxR 24 Q-Q1 Kt-B5, with
complications similar to the game position.

| 21 ... | Kt-B5 |

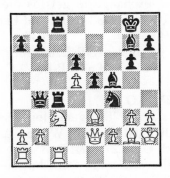

TAL

After 21 . . . Kt-B5

BOTVINNIK

Asked later whether giving up the Knight was sound, Tal replied:
"In my opinion the arguments which this move raised were completely pointless. It suffices to say that all the other continuations
were bad." He might have added: "That is the way I play chess.
I hope you like it."

Black obtains one Pawn for the Knight, plus opening the line for
his KB. This should not be enough, but the play is extremely diffi-

cult, and the slightest misstep will be fatal. Actually the retreat
21 . . . Kt-B3, to avoid the threatened P-Kt4, was safe enough.

	22 PxKt	PxP
	23 B-Q2	. . .

If 23 BxRP Q-R4 wins. Best for White is 23 P-R3 Q-Kt6 24 BxRP
B-K4 (if at once 24 . . . P-Kt3 25 Q-Q1, and the Bishop will escape).
There are then three main lines:

1. If 25 K-Kt1 P-Kt3 26 Q-Q1 QxKtP 27 R-R2 RxKt, and Black will
win.

2. If 25 P-B3 P-Kt3 26 Q-Q1 QxKtP 27 R-R2 RxKt 28 RxQ RxR
29 Q-Q2 BxR 30 QxB R(8)-B7 31 Q-Q4 R-K1 32 QxBP R(1)-K7
33 Q-Kt3, and a draw should result.

3. If 25 B-B3 P-Kt3 26 Q-Q1 QxKtP 27 R-R2 RxKt 28 RxQ RxR
29 Q-Q2 B-K5, or 29 Q-K2 R(1)-B6, White is well ahead in material, but the threats by Black are still formidable.

	23 . . .	QxP

This allows White a strong counter. Correct was 23 . . . B-K4
24 B-B3 QxP 25 Kt-Q1 QxQR 26 RxQ BxR, and though Black is
still the equivalent of a piece down, he has good compensation.

	24 QR-Kt1	. . .

He must give up the exchange to get his pieces active. If 24
Kt-Q1 Q-K4 25 QxQ BxQ 26 B-KB3 R-B7! and Black wins.

	24 . . .	P-B6

The best chance to get that needed line for the KB. If 24 . . .
BxR 25 RxB Q-B7 26 B-K4 RxB (if now P-B6 27 QxR!) 27 QxR QxB
28 Q-K6+ wins.

	25 RxQ	. . .

This was Botvinnik's error. The game looks safe with a piece
ahead, but Tal soon disillusions him. White was still for choice
after 25 BxP BxR 26 RxB Q-B7 27 B-K4 RxB. Now 28 QxR is wrong
because of B-K4+, followed by . . . QxB, but surprisingly White
has 28 KtxR! If then 28 . . . B-K4+ 29 K-Kt2 QxR 30 KtxP! BxKt
31 Q-K6+ K-Kt2 32 Q-Q7+ wins. Or if 28 . . . QxR 29 KtxP R-B1
30 Q-K6+ K-R1 31 Kt-B7+ RxKt 32 QxR, with advantage.

	25 . . .	PxQ
	26 R-Kt3	R-Q5

Tal is out to push through that Pawn at K7. It is worth at least a
piece.

	27 B-K1	. . .

Forced, for if 27 B-K3 RxKt 28 QRxR R-Q8 wins.

27 ...	B-K4+
28 K-Kt1	...

TAL

After 28 K-Kt1

BOTVINNIK

28 ...	B-B5

Now it is Tal who misses a tactical point. He had a quick win with 28 ... RxKt! 29 QRxR R-Q8 30 R-B4 B-Kt7. The move played is good enough, however.

29 KtxP	RxR
30 KtxR(4)	RxB+
31 B-B1	B-K5
32 Kt-K2	...

32 RxP will not do because of B-Q6.

32 ...	B-K4
33 P-B4	B-B3
34 RxP	BxP
35 R-QB7	...

Again White is thwarted. If 35 RxQRP RxK⁺ 36 BxR B-Q5+ wins. Now Tal, with a Pawn ahead and two powerful Bishops, has no further difficulty.

35 ...	BxP
36 RxQRP	B-B5
37 R-R8+	K-B2

Another little inaccuracy. Better is 37 ... K-Kt2 38 R-R7+ K-R3, or 38 R-K8 P-Q4. The difference is a few additional moves.

38 R-R7+	K-K3
39 R-R3	P-Q4
40 K-B2	B-R5+
41 K-Kt2	K-Q3
42 Kt-Kt3	BxKt
43 BxB	PxB

44 KxB	K-Q4
45 R-R7	P-B6
46 R-QB7	K-Q5
Resigns	

5th MATCH GAME

Moscow 1963

Gruenfeld Defense

PETROSIAN	BOTVINNIK
1 P-QB4	P-KKt3
2 P-Q4	Kt-KB3
3 Kt-QB3	P-Q4
4 Kt-B3	B-Kt2
5 P-K3	O-O
6 B-K2	. . .

This is straightforward development, with no great effort to obtain an advantage in the opening. More usual is 6 Q-Kt3.

| 6 . . . | PxP |

This gains a move, since White moves his KB a second time, but cedes control of the center. Alternatives are 6 . . . P-K3, or 6 . . . P-B4 7 PxBP Q-R4.

| 7 BxP | P-B4 |
| 8 P-Q5 | P-K3 |

The kind of simplification that Botvinnik usually avoids, but White is threatening to gain ground by P-K4.

| 9 PxP | . . . |

Now if 9 P-K4 PxP 10 PxP R-K1+, and Black is all right. If then 11 B-K2 QKt-Q2 12 O-O Kt-Kt3.

9 . . .	QxQ+
10 KxQ	BxP
11 BxB	PxB
12 K-K2	. . .

Chances are about equal. Black has an isolated Pawn, but his majority on the Queenside might start moving.

| 12 . . . | Kt-B3 |
| 13 R-Q1 | QR-Q1 |

Better is 13 . . . K-B2, to secure the KP. Black should plan on advancing his Queenside, rather than further exchanges.

14	RxR	RxR
15	Kt-KKt5	R-K1
16	KKt-K4	. . .

The Knight is firmly established on this key square, bearing on several weak points.

16	. . .	KtxKt
17	KtxKt	P-Kt3
18	R-Kt1	Kt-Kt5
19	B-Q2	. . .

BOTVINNIK

After 19 B-Q2

PETROSIAN

19	. . .	Kt-Q4

If 19 . . . KtxP 20 R-QR1 Kt-Kt5 21 BxKt PxB 22 RxP BxP 23 R-QKt7, and although material will be even, Black's Pawns will prove much weaker.

20	P-QR4	. . .

This and the next move effectively hold back the Black Pawns, which will later be subject to attack.

20	. . .	R-QB1
21	P-QKt3	B-B1
22	R-QB1	. . .

There was the possibility of 22 . . . P-B5 23 R-QB1 PxP! 24 RxR P-Kt7 25 R-B1 PxR(Q), with a sure draw.

22	. . .	B-K2

This is the correct square, to balance the White Knight. But there is a threat based on the unprotected position of the Black Rook, which could have been avoided by 22 . . . R-B2. Also good is 22 . . . P-QR3 23 P-QKt4 P-B5 24 P-Kt5 PxP 26 PxP B-K2, when the QR file would later be useful for Black.

23 P-QKt4	. . .

The point. The QBP will be a lasting weakness whether it remains on its present square or advances. The White King being nearer to the scene is a further advantage.

23 . . .	P-B5
24 P-Kt5	K-B2

After this tame move White's plan succeeds. The fighting chance was 24 . . . B-R6 25 R-B2 P-B6 26 BxP (if 26 KtxP or B-B1, Kt-Kt5 wins) B-Kt5 27 K-Q2 (but not 27 K-Q3 BxB 28 KtxB Kt-Kt5+) R-B5 28 BxB (White must be careful at every step—if 28 K-Q3, RxKt wins), RxKt 29 B-Q6 RxRP, and Black is better off than in the game.

25 B-B3	. . .

Now the Pawn is thoroughly blockaded, and White can concentrate on winning it.

25 . . .	B-R6
26 R-B2	. . .

But not 26 R-QR1? KtxB+ 27 KtxKt B-Kt7 28 Kt-K4 K-K2, and Black wins!

26 . . .	KtxB+

Necessary, as White threatened 27 Kt-Q2, followed by a Bishop move and RxP.

27 RxKt	B-Kt5
28 R-B2	K-K2
29 Kt-Q2	P-B6

The Rook ending is just as bad for Black. If 29 . . . BxKt 30 KxB K-Q3 31 K-B3 K-B4 32 R-Q2, threatening R-Q4, and if 32 . . . P-K4 33 P-K4 and R-Q5 mate.

30 Kt-K4	B-R4
31 K-Q3	R-Q1+
32 K-B4	R-Q8

If 32 . . . R-Q7, the Rook cannot be captured, but 33 K-Kt3 is a simple reply.

33 KtxP	R-KR8

Here Black should have exchanged the minor pieces, with longer resistance after 33 . . . BxKt 34 KxB R-KR8 35 P-R3 K-Q2.

34 Kt-K4	. . .

BOTVINNIK

After 34 Kt-K4

PETROSIAN

The Knight returns to its dominant position. The Pawn plus is now less important than the inroad of the White pieces, as Petrosian demonstrates by energetic play.

34 ...	RxP

No better is 34 ... R-R8 35 K-Q4 RxP+ 36 K-K5 R-Kt5 37 R-B7+ K-Q1 38 RxQRP RxP+ 39 KxP, with a clear win for White.

35 K-Q4	K-Q2
36 P-Kt3	...

The simplest. 36 P-Kt4 would allow counter chances by P-R4.

36 ...	B-Kt5
37 K-K5	R-R4+

The march of the White King cannot be halted. If 37 ... B-K2 38 R-Q2+.

38 K-B6	B-K2+
39 K-Kt7	P-K4

Black has no good moves. If 39 R-R8 40 K-B7 R-Q8 41 R-Q2+ ends any resistance.

40 R-B6	R-R8
41 K-B7	R-R8
42 R-K6	B-Q1

Again there is little choice. If 42 ... B-Kt5 43 Kt-B6+ K-B1 44 RxKP RxP 45 KtxP, or if 42 ... B-B4 43 RxP RxP 44 KtxB+ PxKt 45 RxP.

43 R-Q6+	K-B1
44 K-K8	B-B2
45 R-QB6	R-Q8

If 45 ... RxP 46 Kt-B3, followed by Kt-Q5, wins the Bishop.

46 Kt-Kt5	R-Q1+
47 K-B7	R-Q2+
48 K-Kt8	Resigns

The Kingside Pawns must now fall.

19th MATCH GAME

Moscow 1969

Sicilian Defense

SPASSKY	PETROSIAN
1 P-K4	P-QB4
2 Kt-KB3	P-Q3
3 P-Q4	PxP
4 KtxP	Kt-KB3
5 Kt-QB3	P-QR3
6 B-KKt5	QKt-Q2

The opening is the Najdorf Variation of the Sicilian. More usual here is 6 . . . P-K3 7 P-B4 B-K2 8 Q-B3 Q-B2 9 O-O-O, or 7 . . . Q-Kt3 8 Q-Q2.

7 B-QB4	Q-R4

If now 7 . . . P-K3 8 BxKP can be tried, with a dangerous attack for the piece.

8 Q-Q2	P-R3

It is questionable whether it is worth the loss of a move to exchange the Bishop for Knight. Here 8 . . . P-K3 is usual.

9 BxKt	KtxB
10 O-O-O	P-K3

Not having advanced the KP earlier, he might now have considered 10 . . . P-K4 11 KKt-K2 B-K3, to try to catch up on his development. White might then vary with 11 Kt-B5 BxKt 12 PxB R-B1 13 B-Kt3, with a strong game.

11 KR-K1	B-K2

Petrosian's problem is which way to castle, with problems on either wing. He opts for the Kingside, and runs into a powerful attack. The alternative was 11 . . . B-Q2 12 P-B4 O-O-O. If then 13 P-K5 P-Q4, or if 13 P-B5 P-Q4 14 PxQP PxBP. White need not rush the advance, and would retain a marked positional superiority.

12 P-B4	O-O
13 B-Kt3	R-K1
14 K-Kt1	. . .

This is not a loss of time, as it opens the possibility of Kt-Q5, and avoids any danger of check on the diagonal at a later stage.

14 ...	B-B1
15 P-Kt4	...

With the center under control and his pieces all active, White is ready for the onslaught. There will be many effective threats, whether or not the offered Pawn is taken.

15 ...	KtxKtP

White will succeed in opening lines against any defense. If 15 ... P-QKt4 16 P-Kt5 PxP 17 PxP Kt-R4 18 P-Kt6 PxP 19 Q-Kt5, with a winning attack. Perhaps best is 15 ... P-K4 16 PxP PxP 17 Kt-B5 BxKt 18 KtPxB QR-Q1 19 Q-Kt2, when White will also develop threats.

16 Q-Kt2	Kt-B3
17 R-Kt1	B-Q2
18 P-B5	K-R1

Getting off the White Bishop's diagonal. The threat was 19 PxP PxP 20 Kt-B5. If 18 ... P-K4 19 KKt-K2, when RxP and Q-Kt6 are menaced.

19 QR-KB1	Q-Q1

This abandons the K4 square and allows Spassky a brilliant breakthrough. There was not much better, however. If 19 ... P-K4 20 Kt-K6! PxKt 21 PxP BxP 22 RxKt wins. Longer resistance was possible after 19 ... PxP 20 KtxP BxKt 21 RxB Q-Q1 22 BxP R-K4.

20 PxP	PxP

Preferable is 20 ... BxP, to exchange at least one of White's attacking pieces. The game might continue 21 KtxB PxKt 22 Kt-K2, to be followed by Kt-B4. If then 22 ... P-K4 23 B-B7 wins the exchange, for if 23 R-K2 RxKt.

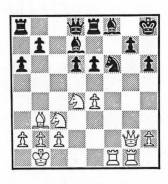

PETROSIAN

After 20 ... PxP

SPASSKY

21 P-K5!   . . .

With this and the following move the one passive White piece
enters the fray, with calamitous results for Black. Also good enough
is 21 Kt-B3, with P-K5 or Kt-KR4 to come.

21 . . .   PxP
22 Kt-K4!   Kt-R4

If 22 . . . KtxKt 23 RxB+ mates at once, and if 22 . . . PxKt 23
KtxKt P-KKt4 (the threat is 24 Q-Kt6, and of course if 23 . . . PxKt 24
Q-Kt8 mate) 24 Q-R3 R-K2 25 RxP B-Kt2 26 RxB! KxR 27 R-Kt1+!
KxKt 28 Q-R4+ K-K4 29 Q-Kt3+, and mate next move.

23 Q-Kt6   PxKt

This loses quickly. The most difficult variation is after 23 . . .
Kt-B5 24 RxKt PxR 25 Kt-KB3 Q-Kt3. 26 Kt-K5 should win, but not
26 Kt-B6 QxR+ 27 KtxQ PxKt, with ample material for the Queen.
White's best is the surprising 26 R-Kt5! The threat is then 27 Kt-B6.
Black does not have 26 . . . Q-Kt4, with the idea of . . . Q-KB4, as
would have been possible after 26 R-Kt2 or Kt4. If 26 . . . PxR 27
QKtxP forces mate, or 26 . . . Q-Q1 27 Kt-K5, with much more
effect. In this variation, if earlier 25 . . . Q-R4 26 Kt-B6 Q-KB4 27
QxRP+! with mate to follow.

24 Kt-Kt5   Resigns

If 24 . . . PxKt 25 QxKt+ K-Kt1 26 Q-B7+ K-R1 27 R-B3, and it is
over. 24 . . . QxKt would only delay matters.

Index

(*Wherever possible, full names are listed even though only surnames appear in the text. English equivalents for Russian and other names vary from source to source; here we have followed British usage with a few exceptions, such as "Kholmov," which might not be located easily under "Holmov". For simplicity we have restricted "events" to the location and date by year, rather than the full title. For example, "New York 1966–1967" is shown rather than "U.S. Championship, 1966." A few titles have been used where confusion might otherwise result. Other matter is included by analogy: after all, to many chessplayers, the "Sicilian Defense" is an event.*)